Mary McGrigor grew up in a medieval Scottish castle which resulted in her great love of history. Married to a soldier at age twenty, until her husband, Sir Charles McGrigor, left the army to buy a sheep farm in Argyll where she has lived for over sixty years. Beginning with local histories, she then branched out into historical biographies. Much involved in farming, she also bred and broke in Highland ponies and rode over the hills above Loch Awe. With a family of four children, she now has twelve grandchildren and two great-granddaughters.

To my wonderful family.

Mary McGrigor

THE REBEL'S REDEEMERS

THE LIFE AND TIMES OF GENERAL JOHN CAMPBELL, LATER 4TH DUKE OF ARGYLL AND OF DUNCAN FORBES OF CULLODEN, LORD PRESIDENT OF THE SESSION.

AUSTIN MACAULEY PUBLISHERS™

LONDON • CAMBRIDGE • NEW YORK • SHARJAH

A CIP catalogue record for this title is available from the British Library.

ISBN 9781528923156 (Paperback)
ISBN 9781528964050 (ePub e-book)

www.austinmacauley.com

First Published (2020)
Austin Macauley Publishers Ltd
25 Canada Square
Canary Wharf
London
E14 5LQ

My deepest thanks to my granddaughter Aretha Campbell for all her help with this book.

Preface

On Tuesday 1 July 1685, the High Street of Edinburgh was crammed with spectators. Men, women and children jostled each other, fighting for a clear view of the Earl of Argyll being led to his place of execution. All eyes were fixed on the door of the Council House, where the Earl, taken from his place of imprisonment in Edinburgh Castle, awaited what was known to be his inevitable fate.

Couriers had ridden hard from London, stopping only to change horses and for snatches of food and rest, carrying the specific written orders of King James VII of Scotland and II of England that Archibald Campbell, 9th Earl of Argyll, must die.

The charge was one of treachery, surprisingly not for the part that he had so recently played in collaboration with the Duke of Monmouth, a natural son of Charles II, to overthrow the latter's Roman Catholic brother King James, but for refusing to comply with the Test Act of 1681.

This was the stature imposed in the reign of Charles II when the King had sent his brother, then Duke of York, as Royal Commissioner to Scotland. York, who, aware of the aversion of a strongly Presbyterian country to a Roman Catholic King, had engineered the statute to ensure his own succession. Argyll had refused to accept it, except on his own specific terms, declaring that he took it 'as far as it is consistent with itself and the Protestant religion'. [1]

Imprisoned for words construed as treason, he had managed to escape from Edinburgh Castle disguised as the page of his stepdaughter, Lady Sophia Lindsay. Reaching Holland, where he had a small estate, he had planned with Monmouth to invade Scotland while the latter was to land on the south coast of England. The attempt had ended disastrously. Both leaders had been arrested and inevitably condemned to death. Argyll was to die by the 'maiden', an early form of guillotine, then used in Scotland.

Almost as he left the Council House to walk to his place of death, he made an impassioned plea to the authorities to show mercy to his son, John. This second son, while accompanying him on his sea-borne invasion from Holland, had done so merely as a spectator. 'Some weakness in his hands making him incapable of using a weapon'. [2]

Shortly after this, at about two o'clock in the afternoon, Argyll walked to the place of execution. Heads were craned to see him. A small man, dwarfed by the Dean of Edinburgh and the Episcopalian minister on either side, he nonetheless held himself erect. Privileged as a peer to wear a hat, his hands remained untied. From the scaffold he addressed the multitude, his voice ringing loud and clear. "I pray God may provide for the security of the Church, and that Antichrist, nor the gates of hell may ever prevail against it." Then led to the place where the executioner stood ready, he took hold of the instrument of death, calling it 'the sweetest maiden ever I kissed'.

Asking the executioner to wait until he gave a sign he prayed, "Lord Jesus, receive me into thy glory." He raised his hand. The knife descended. And Argyll was dead.

Chapter 1
Restoration of Clan Campbell

Despite the cruelty and injustice of Argyll's death, the year 1685 proved to be of portent both to his family and to the cause for which he gave his life. Almost as the 'maiden' crashed down on the scaffold his grandson, a little red-haired boy of five years old, called John (eldest son of Argyll's heir, Lord Lorne then an exile in Holland) fell out of a third floor window of his aunt, the Countess of Moray's house at Donibristle in Fife, and survived unhurt. Those who rushed to rescue him considered this miraculous, a sign, that the house of Argyll would soon be somehow restored.

Later, in the same year, an event of equal significance, although unrecognised at the time, occurred when, on 10 November, at Bunchrew, three miles northwest of Inverness, Duncan, younger son of Duncan Forbes the 3rd Laird of Culloden and his wife, the former Mary Innes, was born.

Little is known of the early life of young Duncan other than that he was an exceptionally brilliant pupil at Inverness Grammar School where he made particular prowess in Latin and that afterwards he studied in Marischal College at Aberdeen University. Subsequently, as a younger son, without future inheritance of land, he went abroad to the University of Leyden to qualify in his chosen profession of the law.

Archibald, 9th Earl of Argyll left behind a family in dire financial straits. His estates were forfeited leaving his widow and children so poor that the Earl of Lothian married his daughter Jean out of pity to save her from starving.

Argyll's sons, John and Charles, were both sentenced to death. Charles was spared execution; it is said at the instigation of some ladies of the court who, believing him to be already married to his stepsister Lady Sophia Lindsay, who later in fact became his wife, pled his cause on her behalf. The Earl's second son John, together with his first cousin Charles, son of Lord Neil Campbell of Ardmaddy, his late father's brother, took a gamble. The two of them, disguised in woman's clothes, surrendered themselves to Lord Dumbarton, commander of the government forces in Scotland, stationed in his castle on the Clyde. Both, as they expected, were sentenced to death. Then, perhaps in John's case because of obvious deformity, the verdict for both of them was reduced to banishment and the forfeiture of all their rights and property.

The disability of John of Mamore has not been fully described; the probability that he suffered from infantile arthritis being merely a wild guess. Penniless and without employment he seems to have managed somehow to return to Holland, where his family had a small estate. His whereabouts are unrecorded until, four years later. In 1689, his banishment ended as the King himself fled the country when his eldest Protestant daughter, Princess Mary and her husband the Stadtholder of the Netherlands, more commonly known as William of Orange, arrived triumphantly, in London.

John's older brother, Archibald Campbell, the deceased Earl's eldest son, now 10th Earl of Argyll, returned from Holland. Restored to his titles and estates, he was one of the three Commissioners, sent by the Scottish parliament, to offer the crown of Scotland to William and Mary, the invitation being formally delivered on 11 May 1689.

Argyll's younger brothers, John and Charles, redeemed from banishment, also came back to Scotland where the strength of Clan Campbell, enforced by royal favour, was once again secured.

Three years later, in 1692, John Campbell of Mamore married Elizabeth Elphinstone, eldest daughter of John, 8th Lord Elphinstone. Their first child, a son and heir, was born in the following year.

John of Mamore, as the second son of his late father, did not inherit great wealth. The land of Mamore, from which his title pertained, is a steep, rock-bound area above the north shore of Loch Leven. The small town of Kinloch, now developed by an aluminium company, stands at the head of the loch.

A house, long vanished, below the present whitewashed building of Mamore Lodge, on the slope of the mountain called Am Bodach (the old man) rising to over 3,000 feet, is believed to have been the Campbell's home in Lochaber. The 9th Earl of Argyll, John's father, acquired feudal leases largely by underwriting the debts incurred by Royalists during the Civil War between King Charles I and his Parliament.

It is likely, however, that if they lived there at all it was only during the summer months. Archibald, John's eldest brother, was achieving ever-increasing favour with King William, who created him Duke of Argyll in 1701. Subsequently, John of Mamore was appointed Surveyor of the King's Works and a Groom of the Bedchamber, both influential if not enormously lucrative positions. Also, in accordance with the rising power of his family, he entered the political scene, firstly as Member of Parliament for Argyll, in the Scottish Parliament of 1700, then, in the newly formed British Parliament which followed the Treaty of Union in 1707, as representative for Dumbarton in two separate sessions.

Logically, in view of these appointments, and taking into consideration the difficulty of travelling to and fro the Highlands of Scotland prior to the building of military roads, it would seem that John of Mamore must have lived largely in the region of his constituency. The old castle of Rosneath, on the Gaerloch, in Dunbartonshire, was a much-loved family home. The likelihood of his living either there, or in the vicinity of the increasingly important city of Glasgow, is strengthened by the fact that three of his six daughters married Lowland lairds. A younger daughter, Primrose, became the wife of Simon Fraser, 11th Lord Lovat, with whom, if the novelist Neil Munro is to believed, she had the most miserable life.

Of his seven sons, three of whom died young, very few details of their early lives have come to light. John of Mamore himself had been educated by a private tutor. Details of this man's employment, including the salary he was paid, are found in the meticulous descriptions of his stepmother's housekeeping in the old castle of Inveraray.[3]

Despite his family connections John of Mamore's eldest son, who, like himself was named John, could not look forward to a sinecure guaranteed by favour of the crown. Aware of the necessity to forge his own career, he was destined to become a soldier from an early age. He is not known to have attended a university. Nonetheless, he was well educated and afterwards wrote a good hand. Commissioned as an Ensign in the 3rd Regiment of Foot Guards on 3 October 1710, he became Brigade Major only five months later and then Lieutenant-Colonel of his regiment, by this time serving in Spain.

This rapid rise in rank, although due in part to his own ability, was certainly largely influenced by his cousin and namesake, John Campbell, now the 2nd Duke of Argyll.

Argyll, at the age of thirty-five, had already achieved distinction both as soldier and politician. Born in 1680 he himself had been appointed to the colonelcy of his father's Argyllshire Regiment when he was only fourteen. A brave man, inclined to be impetuous, possessed both of strong opinions and quick temper, the sobriquet of 'Red John' given to him by his clan to whom he was an inspirational leader, came from the colour of his hair. Subsequently, having succeeded his father to the dukedom, in 1703, when he was just twenty-three, he had been created a Privy Councillor and a Knight of the Thistle before, as an Extraordinary Lord of Session, becoming an honorary member of the highest court in Scotland in 1705. This was the year when, as High Commissioner to the Scots Parliament in Edinburgh, he had instigated the proposal of the Treaty of Union, the dissolution of which he was to vote for so decisively, in a mere ten years' time.

With the Whig government in predominance his future had seemed secure, but in that year, following an election, the Tories had swept to power. The new Secretary of State, Henry St John, created Viscount Bolingbroke by Queen Anne, had much sympathy with the Jacobites whose cause was supported by France. Suspected of being in secret negotiation with Prince James Edward, the Catholic son of the deposed James VII and II, Bolingbroke had many enemies, none more outspoken against him than John Duke of Argyll.

Chapter 2
The War of the Spanish Succession

Bolingbroke seized the chance to get rid of Argyll by sending him to fight in Spain. People talked behind their hands, believing, that because of the desperate situation in that country, Argyll was being sent to his ruin. Nonetheless, despite the common misgiving, a large allowance to support the war was voted for in parliament and Argyll was appointed Ambassador Extraordinary and Plenipotentiary to King Charles III of Spain, and Commander-in-Chief of the British Forces in the kingdom.

The Duke, in accepting these commissions, was thought to be attempting an impossible task, which his enemies, much to their satisfaction, believed would encompass his destruction. The conflict, which had made Marlborough famous, seemed to be running on interminably causing financial crisis as well as the lives of many men. The reasons for it were complex; the solution even harder to foresee.

It was now eleven years since 1698 when William III and Louis XIV of France, although formerly at enmity, had joined forces in an attempt to adjust the European balance of power. To this purpose they had signed a treaty accepting the right of the young Joseph Ferdinand, son of the Elector of Bavaria, as successor to the ailing Charles II of Spain. King Charles, although annoyed at the interference, had made Joseph Ferdinand his heir. But the boy had then died leaving King Louis and the Habsburg Emperor of Austria, Leopold I, (both with mothers and wives who were Habsburg Spanish princesses) to vie for the Spanish throne.

In England the government of William III, alarmed by the aggrandisement of Louis XIV, together with Holland, had agreed to support the Austrian Emperor. So also had Frederick I, who (married to the sister of the Elector of Hanover later George I) was the first of the newly established Hohenzollern monarchy in Prussia. Alone amongst the German states Bavaria had taken the side of France as had Spain, in accordance with the late King's will. Portugal and Savoy, however, although initially allies of France, had changed sides in 1703 when Prince Eugene of Savoy seized much of northern Italy.

A joint French and Bavarian army had then invaded Austria but John Churchill, made Duke of Marlborough by Queen Anne, marching from the Netherlands to the Danube, had joined Prince Eugene to win the great victory of Blenheim in August 1704.

More successes had followed as a British and Dutch fleet captured Gibraltar to win control of the Mediterranean. Then, in the Spanish Netherlands, at the battle of Ramillies, John, Duke of Argyll, in command of a brigade, had saved the life of Marlborough, who, always antagonistic, was to prove a dangerous enemy in time to come. Later, Argyll had served with distinction at the battles of Oudenarde and at Malplaquet, where, showing death defying bravery, he led his men against the

French as musket balls tore through his clothes, hat and wig. [5] Further honours had then ensued including the Order of the Garter in 1710.

Argyll was by now a national hero, known to his clansmen as *Iain Ruadh nan Cath*, 'Red John of the Battles', as he is remembered to this day. Following Malplaquet where both sides lost men on an unprecedented scale, negotiations for peace, already put forward by the old and exhausted Louis XIV, were thwarted by the Whig government in England.

On 4 April 1711, the Duke, of Argyll, having sailed to The Hague, continued overland to Barcelona to take up his command. Reaching the port in Catalonia, where the British army, were encamped, he found his cousin, John Campbell of Mamore, who (gazetted 3 March 1711) was serving as Brigade Major in the 3rd Regiment of Foot Guards.

This is the first that is known of the young John Campbell, of whose early life so few traces remain. If born, as is believed in 1693, he must by the time of his meeting in Spain with his cousin the general, have been eighteen years old. Whether he himself had only just arrived, or whether he had actually taken part in the campaign of the previous year of 1710, when the combined British and Austrian armies had retreated back to Barcelona from Madrid, is uncertain. Certainly, however, he must have alerted his now famous cousin as to all that had happened during those fateful months of the previous summer and autumn.

It was the victories of Almenar, fought on the heights of Catalonia on 27 July and at Saragossa, capital of the Kingdom of Aragon, which had allowed the army of the Grand Alliance, supporting Archduke Charles of Austria to occupy Madrid for the second time. But thanks to the loss of men both in battles and from disease, the city had proved untenable. On 9 November, the Allied armies had retreated, heading back for Barcelona. The Archduke had advanced with 2,000 cavalry, followed by General Guido Starhemberg with the main body of men. Lastly, had come the British commanded by General James Stanhope.

In the meanwhile, the Bourbon army rapidly prepared by the French general the Duc de Vendôme was advancing from Talavera at a quite phenomenal speed. Swimming across the flooded river Henares at the head of his cavalry, Vendôme had quickly overtaken Stanhope who by that time had reached Brihuega to find only the left wing of the allied army, the rest being some miles away.

The allies were completely unprepared. The British contingent firing their guns until all their powder was used, had fought on desperately, setting fire to buildings in a frantic attempt to stop the enemy's advance. But it was useless. Faced with overwhelming odds, Stanhope had seen that nothing could prevent a massacre and to save his men's lives had surrendered being offered honourable terms.

So the British soldiers had become prisoners, but not for long as it had proved. Starhemberg, alerted by a message, was marching to relieve Stanhope when he found himself facing Vendôme and the French general had again been triumphant in the vicious battle of Villaviciosa fought on 10 December and largely won by Spanish dragoons.

By the time of General Campbell, the Duke of Argyll's arrival, the British soldiers, taken prisoner, had been exchanged but most by then, thanks to disease and hunger, were in a pitiable state. Always sympathetic to suffering, as later events were to prove, Major John Campbell described how, in a country so ravaged by years of war, both food and fodder for horses were almost impossible to find. Also, apart from these natural causes the battles of the previous year had decimated the army's ranks.

The Duke then realised the perfidy of Bolingbroke in giving him an almost impossible command. Couriers sent home to ask for reinforcements and supplies met with an impasse. The government, trying to negotiate a peace treaty, was unwilling to support its own army to continue the war with France.

Faced with this ultimatum Argyll, to raise credit to feed and clothe his troops, sold his own gold plate, for which he was only remunerated on his return to England in 1713.[6]

Knowing the difficulties facing his foes, the French commander, the Duc de Vendôme, boasted that 'he would dislodge the Allies out of all their posts in Catalonia before Christmas'[7]. Nonetheless the British dug themselves into Pratz de Roy, their position since the start of the campaign. The Duke de Vendôme then attacked the Castle of Cardona where the garrison was relieved by Count Starhemberg who drove off the French with the loss of two thousand men and no less than four thousand battering cannons, together with all his ammunition, in what ended as a total rout.[8]

Following this victory King Charles of Spain travelled through Italy to Frankfurt to be crowned with great solemnity as Holy Roman Emperor. In the following year the Duke of Argyll, with part of his forces, sailed for Port Mahon and took the island of Minorca for Britain. It was then that Minorca, once a haunt of Barbary pirates who kidnapped and sold the inhabitants as slaves, became, under British occupation, renowned as a naval base centred in the harbour Port Mahon.[3]

Despite this triumph the knives were out for him in Westminster. Jane Wharton, one of the Queen's Maids of Honour (later to be his second wife) wrote to him warning of a plot to poison him while he was in Spain. Told of this, Argyll took special precautions, both to ensure that the people in his kitchen were trustworthy and to make sure that anyone who dined with him was above suspicion. Whether or not they would be poisoners, if they actually existed, were in this way frightened off, the Duke survived unscathed. Made Governor of Minorca, he left a garrison to defend the island, before returning to Britain to support the rights of a Protestant successor on the likely death of Queen Anne.

Argyll returned to London to launch a diatribe against the proposed treaty with France in the House of Lords. He declared that having just ridden through France, on his way back and forth to Minorca, he had seen the misery of that country where he had "rode forty miles together without meeting a man fit to carry arms…what necessity was there to conclude a peace, so precipitately, with a Prince, whose dominion was so exhausted with men, money and provisions?"[9]

Shouting above the uproar of men on the government benches, he then shocked them into silence by declaring that 'he firmly believed the succession of the Electoral House of Hanover to be in danger from the present ministers, whom he durst charge with mal-administration both within these walls and without'.[10] He knew, he said, and could prove that the Treasurer had yearly remitted four thousand pounds to the Highland chiefs of Scotland who are known to be devoted to the Pretender, in order to keep them under discipline and ready for any attempt. Raising his voice above the protests he stated that the current policy of cutting down the army and removing officers known to be loyal to the House of Hanover, was a clear indication of the designs in hand, "It was a disgrace to the nation," he thundered. "To see men who had never looked an enemy in the face, advanced to the places of several brave officers, who, after they had often exposed their lives for their country, were now starving in prison for debt, contracted for want of pay."[11]

The result of this outburst was predictable. The Duke, with a temper to match his hair, had known before letting fly that he risked his own career. Sure enough, at a Council on 17 March 1713, he was deprived of all the employment which he held under the crown. Worse was to come when, a few days later, the command of the fourth troop of guards was bestowed on the young Lord Dundonald, and Argyll's government of Minorca was given to the Earl of Peterborough and of Edinburgh Castle to the Earl of Orkney. Likewise, the Earl of Stair, so notorious for his order for the Massacre of Glencoe, was also put out of office. Thus, with the fall of his two main protagonists, the succession of the Protestant Elector of Hanover seemed threatened at its birth.

Chapter 3
A Conflict of Generals

John Campbell of Mamore, despite Argyll's fall from power, survived on his own merit to be promoted to Captain-Lieutenant and then Lieutenant-Colonel of the 3rd Foot Guards in 1712. As such he commanded his regiment at Dunkirk, in the mopping-up operation which finally brought the long drawn out War of the Spanish Succession to an end.

Following the Treaty of Utrecht, in 1713, he too returned to Britain to follow his father's footsteps by beginning a political career. Still only twenty, he became Member of Parliament; for Bute, in 1713, and for Elgin from 1715-22.

Also returned from the Netherlands was Duncan Forbes of Culloden, a student in the quiet city of Leyden even as Marlborough's cannons had roared against the French. A native of the northeast of Scotland, he had come to the public notice in 1705, when, still only twenty, and at the college of law in Edinburgh, he had risked a dagger in his back to champion the cause of the unfortunate Captain Green, who together with his crew, was hanged on the sands of Leith.

This incident, a blatant cause of injustice, illustrates the profound mistrust and antagonism of the Scottish people towards the English at that time. A ship called *The Speedy Return*, belonging to 'The Company of Scotland' was captured by pirates near the island of Madagascar off the east coast of Africa. However, rumour then ran wild that she had been seized by the East India Company, rivals of the Scottish concern. Subsequently, an English ship called the *Worcester,* anchored in the Firth of Forth, was taken in forfeiture for the Scottish vessel which was believed to have disappeared. Her captain, a man named Green and his crew, arrested, tried and condemned on the most spurious evidence for the seizing of *The Speedy Return,* were sacrificed by the Scottish Privy Council to appease the mob. Despite his enormous influence, the Duke of Argyll, although the most powerful man in Scotland, failed to overturn the verdict and Forbes, in his own words, described how he himself,

"With the danger of my life attending the innocent but unfortunate men to the scaffold, where they died with the most affecting protestations of their innocence. I did not stop there for I carried the head of Captain Green to the grave; and in a few months after, letters came from the captain for whose murder, and from the very ship for whose capture, the unfortunate persons suffered, informing their friends that they were all safe." [12]

In 1713 Forbes's elder brother John (always known as 'Bumper John' because of his predilection for claret) who had been a member of the last Scottish Parliament, became M.P. for Nairnshire. As such he was one of Argyll's party, known as the Argathelians and was able to bring the rising young advocate to the notice of the

Duke himself. Shortly, Argyll was to appoint him steward of his estates in Scotland, a position for which Forbes refused to take any remuneration, although he could have asked for at least £600 a year.[13]

Meanwhile, in Edinburgh, Duncan, with his ear to the ground, was able to keep his brother informed of the rumours of a Jacobite Rising. He told him of an anonymous letter warning of the positive coming of the Pretender, "though, the French should give him no assistance…therefore, how soon this comes to hand you are to advise it with the Justices, that Forces be immediately ordered for this Country…the Highlanders have had very frequent meetings and have been rendezvousing their men this last week."[14]

Thanks largely to his loyalty and ability being recognised by the Duke of Argyll, Duncan Forbes became a Sheriff-Depute of Edinburgh and Justice of the Peace at the end of 1714.[15] The threat of a Rising still persisted but by the New Year Forbes was of the opinion that King George was gaining in popularity throughout the greater part of his realm. His optimism was short lived, as far as the people of the Highlands were concerned. When the King was proclaimed in Inverness and the Clerk ended the reading cried, "God save the King." The magistrates and their adherents, shouted, "God damn them and their King." Then later, when the Whigs were lighting candles in their windows, burning bonfires and ringing bells in honour of the new reign, the magistrates and their cronies, including the custom house officers, drank King James's health and confusion to King George and all his adherents.[16]

The Treaty of Union, passed by a large majority in the Scottish Parliament in 1707, had become increasingly unpopular in Scotland during the reign of Queen Anne. The euphoria with which the act had been welcomed had largely diminished, as the advantages to Scotland, promised by politicians, failed to materialise. Despite the fact that Scottish traders presently had access to the English markets, from which during the wars with Holland in the previous century they had been banned, the terms of the Union were detested by many people both north and south of the border. Old grievances rankled anew. In particular the tragic failure of the Darien Scheme, a plan to establish a trading post on the isthmus between North and South America now called Panama, which had ruined many subscribers and killed most of the unfortunate settlers, was now blamed on the rivalry of the East India Company, funded by English concerns.

Then there was fresh fury as it was learned that the War of the Spanish Succession, which kept so many soldiers abroad, had proved so enormously expensive. The Government, faced with near bankruptcy, introduced the Malt Tax, based on the yield per acre, which was of course greatly higher in England than on poor Scottish soil. The people of Scotland were furious, feeling themselves betrayed. The terms of the Treaty of Union had exempted them from paying a malt tax during the war, which was still in progress when it was signed. Moreover, although, by another clause officially exempted from contributing towards the cost of the conflict, they were now being asked to pay for it on a totally unjustifiable scale.

Scottish Members of Parliament urged that a motion to dissolve the Union be moved in the House of Lords. The protest was led by the Earl of Findlater, who, when Lord Seafield, had been one of the instigators of the Treaty. Having instanced the quashing of the Scottish Privy Council, the Treason Act, the barring of the peerage of Great Britain against Scottish nobles and the threatened malt tax as reasons to justify disruption, he now put forward the argument for its termination on the grounds that it was exacerbating friction between the two countries concerned. John, Duke of Argyll, had voted for the Union in 1707, principally because he saw it as a means of ensuring a Protestant succession to the throne. Now with this secured, he believed the advantages to be outweighed by the limitations, and, together with his brother Lord Ilay, he voted for its abolition.

The election resulted in a stalemate. Fifty-four peers voted for continuation; the same number against. However, for the former there were only thirteen proxies; for the latter seventeen. Therefore, the motion for sustaining the Union was carried by a mere four votes.

The increasing hatred of the Union gave welcome propaganda to the Jacobites. Now, twenty-six years after the deposition of James VII and II by his son in law, William of Orange, there were many who longed for the return of James Edward, better known to posterity as the 'Old Pretender' or the 'Old Chevalier', the son of James VII and II by his second wife, the Catholic Mary of Modena.

The Tory, Viscount Bolingbroke, who as Secretary of State for foreign affairs had signed the highly unpopular Treaty of Utrecht, and the Earl of Oxford, were in secret contact with the exiled Prince James Edward, known by his supporters, the Jacobites, as James VIII. They put it about that Queen Anne herself wanted her half-brother, rather than her distant German cousin, to inherit her throne although Bishop Burnett, who had the temerity to question the now obviously ailing Queen, received her promise of denial. Nonetheless, the Jacobite agents publicly proclaimed that she had made a secret will in which she promised to promote the succession of her half-brother on condition that he left her 'in peaceable enjoyment of the crown, during her own life'.[17]

Whatever the truth of this assertion, the last parliament of her reign, which assembled on 16 February 1714 focused upon the crisis caused by her impending death. The Queen was petitioned to demand that James Edward leave Bar-le-Duc, in Lorraine, his refuge since the Treaty of Utrecht. Further to this, in the event of him landing in Britain, the sum of £5,000 (later increased to £100,000) was the price put upon his head.

As the Queen's life was seen to be drawing to an end, her chief ministers held a council in Kensington Palace reputedly to discuss any possible way of proclaiming James Edward as the King. Whatever the truth of their intentions, the plans of Bolingbroke and his fellow conspirators were foiled when the staunchly Whig Dukes of Argyll and Somerset, stormed into the assembly claiming their rights as Privy Councillors to attend. Subsequently, when the Queen died two days later, on 1 August, the Tories, discountenanced and afraid of the opposition, did not support the Roman Catholic claimant, but assumed that a Hanoverian dynasty would very quickly collapse. Therefore the German Elector of Hanover, grandson of Princess Elizabeth, a daughter of King James VI of Scotland and 1st of England (the 'Winter Queen of Bohemia') became, at the invitation of the now combined Government, King of the British Isles.

King George with his two German mistresses and his few words of English was indeed on the throne. But the fact that James Edward Stuart, was waiting for a chance to invade the British Isles was common knowledge. Bolingbroke, threatened with impeachment, by the Commons of the new Whig government, fled to Paris in April 1714 to become James Edward's Secretary of State. A rising was indeed planned, but shortly before his departure from Bar-le-Duc, James received a message from his supporters in Britain that nothing was ready. The attack must be postponed.

John Erskine, 6th Earl of Mar, a Secretary of State for Scotland during the reign of King William, now hastened to London to swear loyalty to the new monarch. Expecting a royal welcome, after his long journey from Scotland, he was mortified when, at a levée, George I, perhaps confused of his identity, deliberately turned his back on him. Furious at an insult, made all the more humiliating for its having occurred in such a public place, Mar returned to Scotland now committed to the Jacobite cause.

As was usual in those days, he made the journey by sea. Boarding a collier in the Thames, he landed at Elie, in Fife. He then rode north to his own land at Braemar, in Aberdeenshire, where he began consultation and correspondence with the chiefs of many Highland clans. [18] On 27 August he held his now famous deer-hunt, or *tinchal,* attended by an estimated 800 men. Ten days later, on 6 September, he raised the royal standard at Braemar.

The flag, a blue banner with the royal arms on one side, and a thistle with the motto 'No Union' on the reverse unfurled in a strong wind. The spectators cheered wildly, throwing their bonnets high. Then cries of joy turned to groans of disbelief as the golden ball on top of the standard blew off and crashed to the ground. To the Highlanders, superstitious almost to a man, this was an omen of disaster, which must bedevil the campaign.

Yet despite this inauspicious beginning Mar, a man of aesthetic taste, who was more attuned to architecture and garden design than to conducting a war, was proclaimed the General of the Scottish army of the exiled King James VIII. Aware of his own lack of experience in Highland warfare, he promised his supporters that he would find a general to lead the western clans.

The Rising, so long deferred, was imminent. On 3 September John Forbes, the Laird of Culloden, 'Bumper John', the Member of Parliament for Nairnshire, wrote to his wife from London telling her that,

"The Highlanders are actually encamped within ten or twelve miles of Perth. My Lord Mar is said to be the Principal man."

The Jacobites in nearby Inverness were certainly prepared to fight. On 13 September, Mackintosh of Borlum came into the town with about 400 of his best men and proclaimed the exiled Stewart king as James VIII and III.

Triumphant, the rebel force then marched about four miles to the East to lay siege to the house of Culloden. The old house with its two square towers surrounded by a barmkin wall had been built in the castellated style in the early fifteen hundreds. Bought by an earlier John Forbes, who having made a fortune in the fur trade had become Provost of Inverness, in 1625, the estate of largely good farmland, planted with stands of fine trees, contained the castle, a mill and the fishings of Culloden. Now as the Jacobite forces approached the castle walls, Bumper John's brave wife Jean, with two hundred of their tenants, repelled the attack.

With her was her brother-in-law, Duncan Forbes, a member of the Faculty of Advocates. Famously it was Duncan who defied the Jacobite Earl of Seaforth's order to surrender, this being the first notable action of the man who was destined to become the champion of the government in the north. In November 1715 the siege was finally raised when the laird John, arrived in company with Simon Fraser, Lord

Lovat (at that time an avowed Hanoverian) who, with his men of Stratherick, sent the Jacobites scurrying down to join the Earl of Mar in Perth.

Meanwhile, the Hanoverian Government, by now greatly alarmed, found a leader for their army in Scotland in the person of the already accredited soldier, John Campbell, Duke of Argyll, who was made Commander-in-Chief of the forces in Scotland and once again Governor of Edinburgh Castle.

On 8 October 1715, in London, Argyll had an audience with King George I, who, despite his lack of English, received him with much greater cordiality than he had shown to Mar. On the 14th Argyll, with his brother Lord Ilay and the Campbell Earl of Loudoun, reached Stirling. From there he dispatched Lord Ilay to Inveraray where the 'fencible men', [the militia,] were immediately summoned to arms.[19]

Because he had recognised his ability, when under his command in Spain, Argyll summoned the young John Campbell of Mamore, who, had just become Member of Parliament for Elgin, to be his ADC. The granting of a commission in the army to a Member of Parliament was not then unusual. Attendance by representatives of given areas, although no doubt pleasing to their constituents, was by no means compulsory. Thus Lieutenant-Colonel, John Campbell, the younger of Mamore, was freed from his parliamentary duties on the orders of *Ruadh nan Cath*.

Chapter 4
Drawn Swords of Civil War

Scotland, in the first part of the 18th century was still largely a feudal state. In the Highlands the great landlords included the MacKenzie Earls of Seaforth, the Earl of Seafield, the Dukes of Gordon and the Gordon Earls of Huntly. In Perthshire the Murray Marquess of Atholl held supremacy, although the great Campbell chief, the Earl of Breadalbane, held a huge sweep of land from Loch Tay to Argyll. More powerful still the Duke of Argyll had a greater area, stretching from north of Fort William to the south point of Kintyre and most of the islands of the Inner Hebrides, under his control. The Marquess of Atholl, could call out 6,000 men to arms. Argyll, in a time of emergency, even more.[20]

John Earl of Mar, predominant in the centre and east of Scotland, in keeping with his promise to the exiled king, chose a local laird, General Alexander Gordon of Auchintoul, to lead the Jacobites against the Hanoverian King. He had picked a man who was a fair match for Red John of the Battles for all the latter's expertise.

Gordon had led an extraordinary life even by the standards of the time. Born in Aberdeenshire in 1670, a younger son of the fervent Catholic Lord Auchintoul, aged only fourteen, he, together with an even younger brother, had been taken off to Paris by Louis Innes, Principal of the Scots College, where, since the Reformation, so many sons of the Scottish nobility had been educated in the Roman Catholic Faith.

On leaving the Scots College, Alexander had first been a cadet in one of the companies raised by King James VII, 'to assist in the wars he then had in Catalonia' [21] Following this, in 1695, he had joined the Russian army of Peter the Great. The Czar had found him a man after his own heart. Told that at a wedding, he had physically beaten six men who had disparaged the honour of Scotland, he had summoned him personally to his presence and immediately made him a major. Thereafter, he had risen to be a Major-General until aware of the Czar's fickle nature towards even the greatest of his favourites, he had managed to escape, together with his wife, a daughter of General Patrick Gordon, another mercenary soldier, who had also found fame and fortune, in the army of the Czar.

Reaching Scotland in 1711, to find that his elder brother had died without an heir, Alexander Gordon had settled in the family home of Auchintoul. Now, six years later, he was once again in arms.

The Highland chiefs, summoned by Mar to his standard, were slow to appear. Only MacDonald of Glengarry responded promptly. He is known to have been at the Braes of Glenorchy about 20 September. There he was joined by Colin Campbell of Glendaruel, deputising for John, Earl of Breadalbane, who notorious for his double-dealing was now declaring himself too old and inflicted with gout to take the field.

Argyll had set up his headquarters at Stirling, in knowledge of which, Mar conceived a plan to lure him away to defend his own country by attacking Inveraray.

On 4 October 1715, from his camp at Perth, the Earl of Mar wrote to Lieutenant-General Gordon 'who had got charge of the expedition which had for its object to seize Inveraray House and Town, and plant a garrison there'.

"Sir, I had the favour of yours by the 30th September last night, and am very glad you expect to be joined soon by those who ought to have been with you long ago."

"I have ordered as you desired, Glengyll, Rob Roy, Ballhaldie, and the M'Griggars (sic) with them, to join you, and to follow the orders you give them."

"Your Chief, his Highlandmen were last night in Strathardle and co."

"After you have done me the work at Inveraray which upon resistance, I think you had better do by Bloccard [sic] than Storm, you may proceed Westward conform to former Orders; but by reason of my not marching from hence so soon as I had intended, you would not march so far that way, but that you can join us upon occasion nearer than Monteth, [sic] if there be need for it and co. My service to Glengarry and Glendaruel & co. (signed) Mar."[22]

Argyll refused to be drawn. Instead of moving himself he sent his brother, Lord Ilay, to defend the town where their ancestor, the first Earl of Argyll, had built a castle at the foot of the River Aray near the head of the sea inlet of Loch Fyne, in the late fourteen hundreds.

Meanwhile, Gregor Macgregor of Glengyle, nephew of Rob Roy, seized the chance to raid the land round Loch Lomond belonging to the Duke of Montrose. Argyll had already called out his brother to defend Inveraray. Now he summoned his uncle, John of Mamore, father of his young A.D.C.

The fact of his being so readily available suggests that the elder John of Mamore may have been living in his constituency. Now a man in his sixties, no mention made of the deformity of his hands which had so incapacitated him during his father's campaign, he struck a commanding figure as he rode at the head of 'a fine train of the gentlemen of the shire' this being Dumbarton, for which he was Member of Parliament. Preceding the mounted men were foot soldiers, a body of men from Dumbarton, who marched up the northwest shore of the loch until, in darkness, they arrived at Luss.

Here 'they were joined by Sir Humphrey Colquhoun of Luss and James Grant of Pluscarden, his son-in-law, followed by about forty or fifty stately fellows in their short hose and belted plaids, armed each of them with a well fixed gun on his shoulder, a strong handsome target, with a sharp pointed steel of above half an ell in length screwed into the naval of it, on his left arm; a sturdy claymore by his side, and a pistol or two with a durk and knife on his belt'.[23]

While this was happening another party of men consisting of a hundred sailors and about a hundred and twenty members of the Paisley Volunteers were sailing up Loch Lomond. Their little fleet consisted of three long boats and four pinnaces, brought from the Men of War then lying in the Clyde, which had been towed up the river Leven by horses.

The combined force totally defeated the MacGregors who were 'cowed and frighted away to the rest of the rebels, encamped at Strathphillan, about 16 miles away from the head of the loch, where being all joined as above, they continued until the 18th October about which time they were also joined by Stuart of Appin with

250 men, Sir John Mclean with 400, McDougal of Lorn with about 50, and a part of Breadalbane's men, making up by the modestest computation 2400 men'.[24]

The Earl of Mar's letter to General Gordon, ordering him to take Inveraray 'by Bloccard rather than Storm', had been written on 4 October. Further to this, on the 8th, he had ordered the two battalions of Breadalbane's men to join Gordon at Strathfillan where four days later they arrived. They brought up the strength of the General's army, termed 'the rebels' by Peter Rae, to nearly 2,500 men. On the 17th October Gordon reached Inveraray. He took up a position on what was called 'The Black Camp' to the northeast of the town beside the river Aray.[25]

The little town of Inveraray was defended by a force of Campbells only 1,000 strong. However, Gordon lacked heavy artillery with which to bombard the old castle, which thanks to its strong walls withstood all attempts at attack. The siege lasted a week until the General, realising that persistence was useless, obeyed Mar's summons to return to Perth. [26]

Reaching Auchterarder on 11th November Gordon found that the Jacobite army, which had just marched from Perth, had been strengthened by the arrival of both infantry and cavalry of Highland clans from both the west and the north. Mar now commanded a force approximately 9,000 strong.

Meanwhile in Stirling, the army of the Duke of Argyll, greatly outnumbered, consisted of only 4,000 largely untrained men. On 18th October, came word that no less than 6,000 seasoned Dutch troops, sailing from Holland, had been authorised to reinforce his army. It was, doubtful, however, whether they could reach him before he was forced to fight.[27] Nonetheless, as he was himself aware, he had one great advantage over his adversary; that of experience in warfare. Argyll was a strategist. Mar, as he well knew, was not.

Mar had already made half-hearted attempts to attack Argyll both from the north and the south. Now, he ordered Gordon with 3,000 men and some cavalry, to occupy the little town of Dunblane. Argyll, through his spies, aware of Mar's advance, knew that his own army was not strong enough to hold the Forth, which in increasingly cold weather, was beginning to freeze.[28] Without hesitation, he then decided to bring the Jacobite army to battle before it could cross the river.

His strategy decided; he stationed his men on the high ground above Dunblane to the north of the Forth. Mar was left with no alternative but to fight him on the lower stretch of Sheriffmuir, where Argyll could best deploy his small body of cavalry.

Although it was only November, winter had set in early that year. While the officers, young John of Mamore among them, did at least have the shelter of tents, the men, in the fashion of their ancestors, lay wrapped in their plaids, edging towards the campfires, but by morning frozen like corpses to the unrelenting ground.

As day broke on 13th November 1715, 'Red John of the Battles', with several senior officers and his ADC the young John of Mamore beside him, rode up to a viewpoint where they reined in to take a reconnaissance through the frost filled mists of the dawn. Standing there in the freezing wind, which seemed to tear into the very cloth of their red coats and made even the horses shiver, they heard the distant sound of bagpipes approaching across the moor.

Noting the direction from which they came, Argyll realised that he was about to be outflanked over ground, which, although normally a quagmire, was now, after nights of freezing, hard enough to bear the weight of men. Quickly he gave orders to extend the front line, but the movement was still unaccomplished before the centre of the Highland army attacked his left flank.

'The Flower of the rebel Army' as a contemporary historian wrote, was headed by its clan chiefs 'who led them on to the attack with uncommon bravery. They began the action by a general discharge of their fire-arms and received the first fire of the royal troops without shrinking... but the Captain of Clanranald who led them on in chief, was kill'd which was like to have struck a damp upon the rebels, as they had a great respect for that gentleman which was little short of adoration'.

Young Clanranald had left his newly built castle of Ormaclett, on South Uist to lead his clan into battle. An easy target on horseback, he was killed by a musket ball. His men wavered as he fell, but MacDonald of Glengarry, darting from the lines, ran forward waving his bonnet shouting revenge. The Highlanders wavered, then 'followed him like furies, close up to the muzzles of the muskets, pushed by the bayonets with their targets [targes] and with their broad swords spread nothing but death and terror wherever they came'.[29]

Argyll saw the left flank of his force overpowered. The Hanoverian soldiers had not yet been specially trained to resist the impetus of a Highland charge. Terrified they ran and the Jacobites seeing them sensed victory. But almost in the moment of triumph, Argyll, from the higher ground, led his cavalry upon them, driving them towards the River Allen, with murderous swords. Yet even as he pursued them his mind was torn with compunction at the killing of enemies who, like himself, were Highland men. "Oh spare the poor blue bonnets," he cried as he saw them being driven into the river to drown, words which his descendant, Jack Campbell, would remember when placed in a similar command.

A climax of the battle came when Rob Roy MacGregor of Glengyle, who had arrived late on the field, refused to allow his men to charge thus giving rise to speculation that MacGregor, although proclaiming himself a Jacobite, was secretly in league with Argyll.

With the left wing of the enemy defeated, the Duke placed his men within enclosures, bound by mud walls, near the river to wait what he believed to be the inevitable counter attack by a force far larger than his own. The sky darkened, he and his young A.D.C. astride their chargers, gripped the pommels of their swords, while foot-soldiers took aim down the barrels of their muskets laid over the rude turf walls.

It is claimed that Mar, whose forces outnumbered Argyll's by three to one, must, had he advanced, have won the day. But with typical indecision, he dithered and then withdrew while Argyll, who could scarcely believe what had happened, returned his exhausted army towards Dunblane.

Behind the armies, dead and wounded men lay amidst ice-fringed pools, trampled by soldiers and horses, into a mess of mire and blood. As the ground sparkled with hoar frost, brilliant under the moon, only foxes and human scavengers crept out to strip dead bodies of anything that could be put to use.

Early in December the promised reinforcements from Holland arrived to strengthen the Government army. On the 22nd of the month the Old Pretender, as James VIII and III is better remembered, finally arrived at Peterhead. He held a brief court at Scone but by this time the reinforced Hanoverian army was driving the Jacobites before them to the north. On 4th February, 1716 realising that his cause was lost, the Pretender boarded a ship at Montrose and sailed away from Scotland to a life of exile abroad.

Chapter 5
Retribution

The Duke of Argyll, believing then that all immediate danger of rebellion was at an end, put his army in winter quarters from where, in the event of an emergency, the men could quickly be recalled to arms.

Having done so, he handed over command to General Cadogan, a soldier with whom, for his political beliefs, he was soon to be at odds.

Argyll then went to Edinburgh, where, by the magistrates of the city, he was magnificently entertained. Setting out for London on 1st March, he reached the capital on the 6th to be warmly received by George I. A few months later, however, in what amounted to a national scandal, he was dismissed from all his offices at the instigation of the sovereign whose succession he had so strongly upheld.

Rumour then ran wild amongst the populace as to why, after such a successful campaign to vanquish the King's enemies in Scotland, Argyll had been treated in this way. It was generally supposed that certain members of the government believed that he had not pursued the campaign in Scotland with as much vindictiveness as they had wished. 'That he had not made the campaign bloody enough; that his Grace had it in his power to cut them all to pieces, instead of allowing them to disperse in the manner they did' But, says his biographer and contemporary Robert Campbell, 'There must have been some other reason than those commonly reported, that could move his Majesty to withdraw his countenance from a subject who had delivered so well of his family'.[30]

One such cause, as reported by the same author, was the trial of some of the leaders of the rebellion, which instead of taking place in Edinburgh, was transferred south of the Border to Carlisle. This was in direct contradiction of the terms of the Treaty of Union which clearly dictated that 'the jurisdiction of the Court of Justiciary is expressly reserved, and 'tis stipulated that no Subject of Scotland shall be tried by any other Court, or out of the Kingdom, for crimes committed within that part of the Island'.[31]

Foremost amongst those who protested against this travesty of the law was the young Scottish advocate Duncan Forbes of Culloden.

A member of the Faculty of Advocates since 1709, Forbes, while still a junior, had made a name for himself by publicly declaring that the medal, given to the Faculty by the Duchess of Gordon depicting the head of the Pretender, was an insult to Queen Anne. Turning on a member who asked, "Why not receive it?" He retorted, "It will be time enough to receive the medal when the Pretender is hanged!"

Forbes had been made Justice of the Peace and Sheriff-Depute of Edinburgh in 1714. Now, on 19th March 1716, at the age of only thirty, he was appointed Depute Lord Advocate. A staunch Whig, who had supported the government throughout the

Rising, he had been more effective than anyone in preventing many of the Highland clans, including Lord Lovat and his Frasers, from joining the Jacobite army. Now he pleaded for leniency towards the rebels, protesting, in particular, against the forfeiture of their estates. In May, when elected by the Presbytery of Inverness, he became one of the two commissioners for the General Assembly at which he won much commendation both from Argyll and his brother Lord Ilay for his adroit handling of the delegates.

Appalled by what he considered to be a breach of trust by the Government in ignoring the terms of the Act of Union, with regard to the treatment of Scottish prisoners, Forbes wrote to Robert Walpole, recently made Paymaster General, informing him, bluntly that while he had hitherto considered him to be an honest man, he would only adhere to this view if Walpole acknowledged his views. The letter (probably written in August) although undated and signed merely YZ, is clearly in Forbes's handwriting.

'It is by no means prudent to disoblige Scotland by open injuries which may create general dissatisfactions, not to be ended but with the ruin of that part of the United Kingdom...measures unnecessarily disobliging to the King's friends, exasperating the disaffected, and in a particular manner ruinous to Scotland'. As a Scotsman he declared he was 'resolved to assert no fact, and to give the character of no person that I will not answer at the peril of my head, if by clearing it I may do my King and Country service'.

While admitting that the "Pretender's followers deserved death and such punishment as the Law decreed," he nonetheless insisted that, "Humanity and prudence forbade it." Instead a more suitable course would have been,

'To have punished only as many as was necessary for terror, and the weakening of the strength of the rebels for the future; and to extend mercy to as many as it could conveniently be indulged to with the security of the Government'. [32]

Forbes went on to point out, that in the event of the present policy of forfeiture and imprisonment of rebels in England being pursued, the government would find it necessary to raise a standing army to enforce it. The forfeitures alone would hardly defray the expenses of the Committee of Enquiry that was currently being established. What was the point, he argued, for losing the affections of the people for the sake of the small sum which the forfeitures might raise, estimated at £20,000 at the most, when that event will bring only £100,000 charge for maintaining an army to keep the nation orderly.[33]

While agreeing that the guilty should be punished, he thought that, 'It should go no farther than is necessary for the security of the Government and for the terror of others who might attempt the like afterwards'. Having suggested that an indemnity by Act of Parliament might be granted to all who might surrender by a certain day and all but the worst offenders be allowed their freedom on bail, he then railed against what he described as 'the band of self-seekers, who are most odious to the people' who were at that time ruling the country. Foremost amongst the men Forbes so detested was General Cadogan, 'who lately made such a dishonourable treaty with the rebel Glengarry. And yet Argyll himself to whom so much is due as the bulwark against Popery and tyranny, is disgraced!'[34]

Red John of the Battles, outspoken like Forbes against what he took to be contravention of the law and now at loggerheads with General Cadogan, was amongst those who petitioned the ministry for clemency to the Earl of Derwentwater and Viscount Kenmure, condemned for their part in the Rising, and sentenced to death. It was thought that their appeal would be ignored but the Earl of Nottingham, President of the Council, ordered it to be given to his Majesty. Nottingham paid the price of kindness. The King, in a fury, barked out his refusal to the petition and the President, "pressing it both in the House and the Council Board, was taken so ill that he and his family were turned out of all their places. Some were of the opinion, that this was some part of the heinous crime his Grace of Argyll was charged with."[35]

The real reason, however, for Argyll's loss of face with George I was his affinity to the Prince of Wales, who, in defiance of his father's wishes, appointed him on his staff. Matters reached boiling point in the summer of 1717 when, as the King announced his intention of returning to his native Hanover for a visit, Argyll had the temerity to suggest that the Prince should become sole regent in his absence. The King, hardly on speaking terms with his son, then listened to Argyll's enemies, who, headed by the Duke of Marlborough, contrived his fall from office. Argyll was out of favour, yet such was his power in Scotland, that not even the King of England dared to attempt the restriction of his power in the north of the realm.

Chapter 6
'Smiling Mary, Soft and Fair as Dawn'

Despite, what in fact proved to be a temporary fall from grace, John Duke of Argyll remained in ever-increasing favour with George, Prince of Wales and his wife, the charming and intelligent Caroline of Brandenburg Ansbach. Argyll was much about the court. His first wife died in January 1717, leaving no children and he wasted no time in remarrying, anxious as he was for a son. His second wife, whom he married in June 1717, only five months after becoming a widower, was Jane Warburton, a young lady from Cheshire, who, having been a Maid of Honour to Queen Anne, was now acting in the same capacity to Caroline Princess of Wales. Intent on increasing his influence through members of own his family, Argyll successfully introduced his young cousin, John Campbell of Mamore, who had recently fought at his side as his ADC to the Prince and Princess of Wales.

John, still in his early twenties, had inherited the good looks of his family. A portrait of him as a young man shows him sitting cross-legged, wearing breeches below a velvet coat. His hair is long and un-powdered; his face open and unlined. His hands, resting on a book, indicate a studious frame of mind. Hardly, is it surprising that he caught the eye, not only of the Princess, but also of the Maids of Honour of her court. Amongst them was the Honourable Mary Bellenden, a young lady two years younger than himself.

Mary was the daughter of John, 2nd Lord Bellenden of Broughton in Midlothian, who, born John Kerr, son of the 2nd Earl of Roxburgh, had inherited his title through his mother. Bellenden, as a young man, in the reign of Charles II, had held the office of Hereditable Usher and Doorkeeper of the Scottish Exchequer. Later, as a Jacobite, in 1689, having shot a soldier who had declared for William and Mary, he had been held prisoner in Edinburgh Castle for some time.

Despite her father's politics, his daughter had been singled out for her high birth and her beauty to be a lady-in-waiting to the Princess of Wales. The poet Gray called her 'smiling Mary, soft and fair as dawn' while Horace Walpole, another admirer, wrote that 'her face and person were charming, lively she was, almost to étourderie, and so agreeable that I never heard her mentioned afterwards by one of her contemporaries, who did not prefer her as the most perfect creature they ever knew'.[36]

Whereas the court of the old King George 1 was tedious, composed largely of the elder Whig politicians, that of his son and daughter-law, both of whom he quite openly disliked, was full of life and entertainment. Horace Walpole (the younger son of Robert) a gossip columnist of his day, described some of the goings on.

'The most promising young lords and gentlemen of that party [Whig] and the prettiest and liveliest of the young ladies, formed the new court of the Prince and

Princess of Wales. The apartment of the bedchamber-women in waiting became the fashionable evening rendezvous of the most distinguished wits and beauties, Lord Chesterfield, then Lord Stanhope, Lord Scarborough, Carr Lord Hervey, elder brother of the more known John Lord Hervey…General (at that time only Colonel) Charles Churchill, and others not necessary to rehearse, were constant attendants. Miss Lepelle, afterwards Lady Hervey, my mother Lady Walpole, Mrs Selwyn, mother of the famous George, and herself of much vivacity and pretty Mrs Howard, and above all for universal admiration, Miss Bellenden, one of the maids of honour'.[37]

The court was not without its scandals, as Walpole gleefully reports.

'The pretty Mrs Howard gave him plenty of use for his pen. Born Henrietta Hobart, she was the daughter of a baronet, who, although of an ancient line, was too impoverished to give her more than a token dowry when she married a Mr Howard, who, although the younger brother of the Earl of Suffolk whom he was eventually to succeed, was also the reverse of opulent'.[38]

When it was known that Queen Anne was dying, the young couple, seizing the chance of advancement, went off to Hanover to ingratiate themselves with the future king. With little or no money, they somehow had to make a splash so when Mr Howard gave a dinner to the Hanoverian ministers his wife had to pay for it by cutting off her beautiful hair. These being the days when full-bodied wigs were fashionable, she most likely sold her tresses for twenty, or even thirty, guineas, a sacrifice they both thought well worthwhile.

The result was not immediately obvious. Princess Sophia Dorothea, wife of the Elector of Hanover [later George 1] took greatly to Henrietta, but Sophia Dorothea was in disgrace. Her doomed love for Count Konigsmark, which had ended with his being strangled and buried beneath her dressing-room floor, had been discovered. Her husband, on his succession, refused to bring her to England. It seemed as though the ambitious scheme of the Howards was about to fall apart.

In England the King ignored them. His son, the Prince of Wales, was equally disinterested. Nonetheless, it would seem on account of her looks, Henrietta Howard was appointed one of the bedchamber-women to the Princess of Wales.

In 1705, while still in Hanover, the Margravine Charlotte Caroline of Brandenburg Ansbach, had married the Elector's son. Arriving in England in 1714, she received a warm welcome largely because it was known that she had refused to make the most brilliant match in Europe by turning down the Archduke Charles, the Holy Roman Emperor, and King of Spain, on account of his being a Roman Catholic.

George, Prince of Wales, and his wife had both been born in 1683 but here the similarity ended for she had a vastly superior intellect to her husband who, although very courageous, had little intellectual power. Handsome, rather than beautiful – the dreaded scourge of smallpox had left her virtually unscarred – Caroline, as she was always known, also possessed the rare combination of being both clever and kind. She was loved by the ladies of her retinue, who were all convulsed with fear and grief when she nearly died from loss of blood and septicaemia after a miscarriage in 1716. Despite this she managed to produce a living son in the following year and it was at the christening of this infant that her husband quarrelled furiously with his father George I.

Mary Bellenden began her life as a Maid of Honour in the household of the Prince and Princess of Wales. Initially they lived in the Queen's Apartments at

Hampton Court, done up for them, with the least possible expense (even the old curtains were dyed and re-hung) by George I on his accession in 1714. However, it was actually in St James's Palace in Whitehall that she witnessed the extraordinary scene which took place at the christening of the little Prince George, second son of the Princess, who was born there on 3rd November 1717.

Mrs Howard, by this time Lady Suffolk, then in waiting as a woman of the bedchamber, later told Horace Walpole exactly what happened. Although by then an old woman, her memory of those amazing events remained extraordinarily clear. She herself, together with the rest of the Princess's ladies, stood on one side of the great canopied bed within which lay the mother and her newborn child. On the other side were the godmother and godfathers. The Prince, in an effort to conciliate his father, had asked him to be one of the latter. He wanted his uncle, the Duke of York, Bishop of Osnaburg, to be the other but his father, in blunt defiance of his wishes, had insisted that the Duke of Newcastle, a man whom he knew the Prince detested, become the second sponsor in York's place.

The christening ceremony proceeded in an atmosphere of mute hostility, the Prince, like a dog held back by a leash, fuming silently until it was done. He just managed to control his fury before, as the Bishop ended the service, he was round the foot of the bed confronting Newcastle, waving his hand and his forefinger in a menacing attitude in front of his face. As Newcastle, astounded, stepped backwards, the Prince in his broken English spat out the words. "You are a rascal, but I will find you," meaning, so his hearers understood, 'I shall find a time to be revenged'.[39]

The immediate result of this outburst was fury on the part of King George. The next morning, Lady Suffolk, on going to the Princess's apartments, was shocked and terrified to find the yeomen in the guard-chamber pointing their halberds at her breast. They told her she could go no further. She protested vehemently that it was her duty to attend the Princess. "No matter," they said, they had been ordered to tell her that she could not enter the Princess's rooms.

This, it transpired, was part of the King's punishment for the behaviour of his wayward son. George I was so furious at the Prince's rudeness in his presence that he had determined to humiliate him in every possible way. The Prince's insult to the Duke of Newcastle was, in his father's eyes, nothing less than a challenge to a duel. To prevent such a public scandal he had him put under arrest. The order was soon rescinded but, on the same evening, the Prince and Princess were ordered to leave the palace.

Left homeless they moved across Piccadilly to the house of her chamberlain, the Earl of Grantham, in Albermarle Street.[40]

Apparently, the commotion of the abrupt move of an entire household, including a newly born child, left Mary Bellenden unperturbed. A ballad written upon the quarrel between George I and his son over the choice of godfathers for the little Prince George, includes the lines,

'But Bellenden we needs must praise, who as down the stairs she jumps,
Sings over the hills and far away, despising doleful dumps'.[41]

Subsequently, the Prince and Princess of Wales moved to Leicester House, a mansion set behind a forecourt, built by Robert Sidney, 2nd Earl of Leicester, in 1635, in the northeast corner of Leicester Square. Once there they established their own court, which, while lacking the magnificence of that of the Palace of St James's, was nonetheless more entertaining than that of the old king. Horse racing and musical evenings on the river at Richmond were two of the entertainments of the summer months.

In 1720, the rift with King George I at least partially healed, they moved back into the city. The Prince of Wales held his levées in the morning with only gentlemen in attendance. Here were other diversions, like the machine which produced colour printing and a new type of military device shown to Sir John Evelyn, the great horticulturist of his day.[42] The royal family dined, as then was fashionable, at about two to three in the afternoon. Then, three times a week there were drawing rooms, at which anyone of importance in London was expected to attend, failure to do so being considered as showing disrespect. The numbers varied according to the time of year. The King went annually to Hanover, the Prince of Wales to Richmond Palace and the aristocracy to their country estates so that it was usually late autumn, before the large family coaches rumbled slowly back to town.

In addition to the normal drawing rooms, there were celebrations for Christmas and Twelfth Night, the accession and coronation days, and for the birthdays of all the royal family, princes and princesses alike. Sometimes the rooms were so crowded that it was almost impossible to move. Women in their heavily embroidered gowns, the skirts spread over panniers adding to the weight, sometimes fainted in the crush while men, equally resplendent in coats worn over waistcoats, embossed with gold and silver thread, and wearing the now fashionable wigs, likewise gasped for air in the over-heated rooms. Nonetheless, except on the excuse of illness, it was imperative for anyone intent on preserving their social standing, or with political ambition, to attend the court.

Fortunately, for the Prince of Wales, and as it turned out for England, his wife held him in her thrall. Nonetheless, though devoted to her as he certainly was, like many men of all ages, he could not resist a pretty face. Unfortunately, for Mary Bellenden her beauty caught his eye. 'The Prince frequented the waiting-room and [43] felt a stronger inclination for her than he ever entertained but for his Princess', wrote Walpole, describing the plight in which the poor girl found herself through no fault of her own. She was in fact horrified and in fact terrified of the amorous advances of the German prince. Walpole, putting it tactfully, assured his readers that,

'Miss Bellenden by no means felt a reciprocal passion. The Prince's gallantry was by no means delicate, and his avarice disgusted her. One evening, sitting by her, he took out his purse and counted his money. He repeated the numeration; the giddy Miss Bellenden lost her patience and cried out, "Sir, I cannot bear it if you count your money any more, I will go out of the room."'[44]

Mary Bellenden was not to be bribed. Already deeply in love with the courtier, John Campbell, she shrank away in horror from the fumbling hands of his employer, as Walpole graphically describes.

'The chink of the gold did not tempt her any more than the person of his Royal Highness. In fact her heart was engaged; and so the Prince, finding his love fruitless, suspected. He was even so generous as to promise her, "that if she would discover the object of her Choice, and would engage not to marry without his privity, he would consent to the match, and would be kind to her husband." She gave him the promise he exacted, but without acknowledging the person, and then, lest his Highness should throw any obstacle in the way, married without his knowledge, Colonel Campbell, one of the grooms of his bedchamber, and who long afterwards would succeed to the title of Argyll at the death of Duke Archibald'.[45]

34

Chapter 7
Connivance and Corruption on a Grand Scale

The bare facts of the secret marriage thus so pithily described, can only hint at the terror which drove Mary Bellenden to seek protection from the man she loved. Petrified of the Prince, whose rages displayed the strong streak of cruelty that she knew too well, she dreaded the repercussions which must inevitably occur. Both she and her husband expected instant dismissal from the court. Disgraced, they would have found themselves near penniless, as neither possessed large estates. John Campbell, as he well knew, risked his whole future in marrying the girl whom the Prince doggedly pursued, however, his advances were repulsed. The young colonel stood to lose everything, his status as Groom of the Bedchamber, his political career as Member of Parliament for Elgin, his prospects of commanding another regiment should the King take the part of his son.

Fortunately, King George although now partly reconciled to his heir, was nonetheless dependent in Scotland on the Duke of Argyll. The affront of the Campbell's marriage was for this reason tactfully overlooked and the newly married couple spared the dishonour of banishment from court.

In 1719 the Peerage Bill was introduced to the House of Lords by the Earls of Sunderland and Stanhope, who aimed to make the Whig predominance in Parliament unassailable. The number of English peers was to be increased by not more than six, while the sixteen elected Scottish peers were to be replaced by twenty-five hereditary members. The Bill, hotly contested in the House of Commons, was defeated by the opposition led by Walpole in a great and surprising victory.

Walpole disliked and distrusted Argyll but, recognising his enormous power, realised that he had to have him on his side. From this time onwards the Duke and his brother, the lawyer Lord Ilay, became the first lord's deputies in Scotland, controllers in everything but name.

In the north of Scotland and the Isles Argyll became ever more reliant on the administration of Duncan Forbes of Culloden, the man who factored his estates. In March 1718, Forbes became Burgess and Guild Brother of Glasgow city where, in a forthcoming uprising, he was soon to be the hero of the hour. In the following year, early in May, Forbes received a message from Lord Lovat, with whom, at this time, he was in close communication believing him, as it turned out mistakenly, to be utterly loyal to the crown. Lovat, for his part, with an eye to the main chance, made blatant use of Forbes's growing power. Addressing him as his 'Dear General' and signing himself 'Your slave' he was openly sycophantic in trying achieve his own aims of accruing both wealth and land. Now he warned of the approach of an enemy fleet which proved to be that of the force of Spanish and Irish, commanded by George Keith, the Earl Marischal, under the auspices of Cardinal Alberoni and the

Duke of Ormonde, which on 10th June 1717 was finally defeated by General Wightman in Glensheil.

Forbes at this time was much involved in appeals from the Court of Session of the House of Lords. Most concerned Jacobites, trying to regain or to avoid forfeiture on their estates. A vacancy in the Court of Session was causing him great alarm. Writing to his brother, on 19th December, he told him,

'We are frightened out of our wits here that Peter Haldane will be made Lord of Session in place of Fountainhill who has demitted'. [46]

Forbes had good reason for his fear. Haldane was dreaded by the Jacobites because of his extreme cruelty towards them when, as one of the Commissioners of Inquiry into their forfeiture after the Rising of 1715, he had condemned so many of their number. Forbes, as one of the councillors, representing the Dean and Faculty of Advocates, protested against his appointment, which, on the grounds that remonstrance should be allowed against unsuitable persons, was not sustained by the House of Lords.

The year of 1720 is remembered historically for a financial crisis resembling that of some of Lloyd's Insurance Companies and of spectacular bank failures in recent times. In the prime instance, the First Lord of the Treasury, the Earl of Sunderland, had initially agreed to the offer of the South Sea Company, to underwrite the government debt of £9,000,000, in return for the monopoly of trade in the South Seas. The joint-stock company, inaugurated in 1711, during the War of the Spanish Succession, aimed mainly to operate in Spanish South America. However, following the Treaty of Utrecht, the profits, which at first had seemed so lucrative, began rapidly to fall. Sunderland, nonetheless, convinced of the ultimate soundness of the project, then influenced Parliament to let the company incorporate in its own capital no less than £30,000,000 of the national debt, for the privilege of which it would pay an extra £7,000,000. Thus assured, the value of its shares rose dramatically, on the stock exchange. Politicians in high office headed the list of people rushing to invest on the surmise that a business, thought sound enough for government investment, must be a safe speculation. When in late August 1721, the news broke that the company had crashed and 'The South Sea Bubble' had broken, there was fury verging on rebellion.

The government, rightly blamed for the financial disaster, which brought ruination to families throughout the land, was in danger of collapse. It is claimed that had James Edward, the Old Pretender, at that moment 'landed at the Tower, he might have rode to St James's with very few hands held up against him' [47] This did not happen for the simple reason that the Jacobites, both in Britain and on the Continent, were taken by surprise by the suddenness of the 'South Seas' disaster.

In the interim the situation was saved by the adroit handling of the parliament by Sir Robert Walpole, who, by missing the deadline to buy shares himself, had conveniently escaped from the taint of bribery and corruption accorded to most of his colleagues. Dubbed the 'Skreen-Master General' he laboured to save members of the government, including Sunderland, from the retribution, which, certainly most of them deserved.

In doing so he won the commendation and gratitude of the Hanoverian supporters and of King George himself. Thus, through clever manipulation of the crisis, in which he had only by luck escaped involvement, the Norfolk squire, 'The

Great Man' as he came to be known, was exalted to the position of First Minister of the government.

Short and very heavy – he weighed over twenty stone – his character revealed itself in his hawk like nose and jutting lower lip. Aggressive by nature, and coarse as a Billingsgate fishmonger, he nonetheless possessed both humour and charm which he used to manipulate his ends. Power was his passion. Unmoved by the social advantage of a peerage, he refused ennoblement to remain in the House of Commons where he ruled like a colossus for a span of over twenty years.

The financial catastrophe of the South Sea Bubble had a spin-off in Scotland. The York Building Company had been established in 1675 when Charles II had granted letters patent to allow the erection of water works upon parts of the grounds of York House on the south side of the Strand. Water pumped from the Thames, was led through the streets in wooden pipes to supply St James's and Piccadilly.

The company had been incorporated by an Act of Parliament in 1691, the significance of which had been realised in 1715 when, following the Jacobite Rising of that year, a number of forfeited estates were offered for sale by the government. So little interest was shown, however, that another Act had been passed to allow prospective purchasers to grant annuities on their properties. The York Building Company, then conveniently for sale, had been snapped up by a group of speculators as a vehicle to exploit this opportunity. A subscription opened in the Mercer's Hall in London for raising a joint stock, had produced a capital sum of £1,259,575.

The Company had then proceeded to buy the forfeited estates and by 1720, all those surveyed by government officials had been acquired. Then, with the addition of further purchases, the York Building Company became briefly the largest landowner in Scotland.

Following the collapse of the South Sea Company, however, the York Buildings stock fell so rapidly that only the income of its Scottish estates, amounting to £13,700 annually, saved it from bankruptcy.

It was then that an entrepreneur called Aaron Hill, currently manager of the Drury Lane Theatre, saw his chance. Poet, dramatist, traveller, and dabbler in political economy, this man, whose previous enterprises of trying to make olive oil from beech nuts and of settling a colony in Carolina, had failed abysmally, now made his way to Speyside. Fired with a new enthusiasm he wrote to Colonel Horsey, Governor of the York Building Company, to tell him that the purchase of Scots pine woods of Abernethy Forest, must prove a profitable venture, the trees being ideally suited as masts for the Royal Navy.

Horsey took the bait and in January 1728 the York Building Company purchased 60,000 pine trees for £7,000 or 2s and 4p a tree, from Sir James Grant of Grant. The deal having been signed, some of the best trees were cut and sent as specimens to London, but the Master Mast-Maker at Deptford reported that, although of excellent quality, not one of the tree trunks sent to him was suitable as a mast for a ship. This was a major set-back but Colonel Horsey, undeterred, bought '120 working horses, wagons, wooden houses, saw-mills, iron mills', and 'every kind of implement and apparatus of the best and most expensive kind'[48]

Aaron Hill entertained by the Duchess of Gordon and given the freedom of their towns by the magistrates of Inverness and Aberdeen, ingenious as ever, invented a method by which large trees bound together were rowed down the river Spey. He also built roads into the forests, which, as the Minister of Abernethy, the Reverend

John Grant admitted, were 'of great benefit to the populace'. But Grant then unleashed his fury at the perfidy that was taking place, describing the associates of the York Buildings Company as 'the most profuse and profligate set that ever were heard of in this corner'. They were, so he declared, demoralising the local people by opening hogsheads of brandy. Five people, greatly intoxicated, had died in a single night, on top of which in the end [they] went off in debt to the proprietors and the country'.[49]

The Minister's tirade was justified. In the course of four years the York Building Company's timber venture lost nearly £28,000, in those days a very large sum. Details of over a hundred lawsuits, brought against the Company in Scotland, filling eleven volumes, remain in Register House. In 1725, when the commissioners of the forfeited estates finally closed their accounts, it was found that legal and other expenses had taken most of the profits to the point where only £1,000 was left to justify the fury and resentment caused by the sequestration of Jacobite estates.

In Scotland the rising young advocate, Duncan Forbes of Culloden, had already told Walpole, most bluntly that the government had made a mistake in trying to punish misguided individuals, instead of clamping down on probable further disorders. The Clan Act, ordering disarmament, had in fact done little to subdue the Highlanders. But, more effectively, the building of military roads by General Wade did facilitate the movement of soldiers throughout hitherto largely inaccessible regions, while the installation of garrisons, at strategic points, made it possible to effect, at least to some degree, the control of, what to most people in England, was a savage and foreign land.

Chapter 8
Glasgow Set Aflame

In England the Tory members of the House of Commons, landlords almost to a man, protested furiously against the land tax which the Whig dominated government had imposed. In 1714 the Malt Tax Act had been passed but, for the space of ten years, it had never become operative in Scotland. However, in 1724, Walpole's government, to placate the landlords, decided to impose a tax of three pence a bushel (half of what was paid in England) on Scottish malt. This caused mayhem in Scotland where the malt tax had specifically been excluded by the terms of the Treaty of Union. The Tories, who included many Jacobites, seized on the chance of disruption by inciting open rebellion. Mobs rioted in Glasgow. The country was close to civil war. Such was the public outcry that The Lord Advocate, the pug-nosed and aggressive Robert Dundas, a leader of the right-wing party the Squadrone, who had spoken against the Malt tax, was summarily dismissed.

This was the moment when Duncan Forbes of Culloden stepped forward to take control, as he made the vital decision to adopt a political career. Already the Member for the Inverness District of Burghs (Inverness, Fortrose, Nairn and Forres) he was now both re-elected to Parliament and – on 29 May – appointed King's Advocate for Scotland in Succession to Robert Dundas. The post carried a salary of between £500 and £600 a year, but, in accepting it, Forbes chose to forgo the fortune, which, had he continued as a barrister, he would almost certainly have accrued.

The choice of Forbes as King's Advocate was in fact a triumph for the Whigs. Dundas had been one of the Squadrone, the right-wing party, believed to be in sympathy with the Jacobites, which included General Cadogan with whom the Duke of Argyll, leader of the Argathelians, had long been at loggerheads. Now Forbes, already a public figure, recognised by the hawk-nose, significant of his stubborn and incorruptible character, was to demonstrate both ability and authority in bringing the perilous situation in Glasgow, under his authority.

Amongst those who had voted for the bill imposing the Malt Tax was the member for the Glasgow Burghs, Daniel Campbell of Shawfield, 'known as Great Daniel' for his wealth and bulk. Shawfield was a self-made man. The younger son of Walter Campbell, Captain of the Castle of Skipness, near Tarbert in Argyll, he had gone to America as a young man to make a fortune as a merchant and ship-owner, despite the fact, that in the sixteen nineties, Scotland was excluded from Atlantic trade. Returning to Glasgow he had become a tobacco merchant while enriching himself further in the innocuous slave trade.

Although of such prominence in the city of Glasgow he antagonised even the councillors by supporting the already unpopular government in what was seen to be a breach of faith. On 24th June a furious crowd attacked and set fire to the elegant mansion he had built with his great wealth. Fortunately, having been warned, he had managed to remove almost everything of value. Nonetheless, the civic authorities took fright. Two companies of the garrison of Dumbarton were called out, but even as they entered the city the mob stole the keys of the guardroom, whereupon Charles Miller, the Provost, unwilling to cause provocation by breaking them down, told the captain, a man named Bushell to billet his men in the town.

There followed a brief respite before mayhem broke out anew as the rioters found Shawfield's cellar and drank themselves silly with wine. Next morning the Provost ordered the doors of the guardroom to be forced and the troops installed. He then ordered the arrest of some of the rioters, but hardly had he done so before a woman beating a drum led the mob to renewed attack. The prisoners were freed and the men in the guardroom pelted with stones and bricks. Captain Bushell, in fear of his life and those of his men, then ordered them to open fire. A few people were killed and wounded in an action which rapidly became a scrum.

The Provost, panicking in a situation now out of control, verging it seemed on a wholesale massacre, ordered Captain Bushell to march his men back to Dumbarton 'where he might be safe'. [50] The captain did as he was ordered and with the rioters screaming and hurling missiles behind him, reached Dumbarton Castle that night.

At once there was public outcry. Such defiance of the law was intolerable. Glasgow's civic dignitaries and those in higher authority must be made to answer for what was held to be their fault. Most shocking of all was the fact that no one accepted responsibility. The Privy Council in Scotland no longer existed and the Secretary of State, the Duke of Roxburgh, himself at odds with Walpole, refused to interfere.

Forbes, as the Lord Advocate, set the wheels in motion. Thanks to two spies, who he had sent into the city, he knew by now that the rebellion against the malt tax was a carefully arranged conspiracy. Messengers sent to the northern towns had carried the word that the Royal burgh, in the south of Scotland, had agreed to ban the excise-men. Armed with this knowledge, Forbes attended the Convention of Royal Burghs, in Edinburgh where, under his direction, a resolution condemning the recent disturbance was passed and sent throughout the country.

Following this proclamation, on 9th July 1725, Forbes and General Wade with a strong contingent of the army, headed from Edinburgh for Glasgow. There they were joined by Captain Bushell with his two troops from Dumbarton, who hastened back to the city from which, only two weeks earlier, they had made such an ignominious retreat. With this strong detachment of the army, Wade and Forbes succeeded in dispelling the rebels and taking command of the city.

So quiet was the situation that, on the Sunday afternoon, they both went to church and greatly annoyed the minister by talking – and he claimed swearing – during his sermon which greatly upset the decorum of the service!

In London the Lords Justices instructed Forbes as Lord Advocate to bring the criminals to justice. Accordingly, Forbes presided over an enquiry, or precognition as it is called in Scotland, preliminary to the trials. Having interviewed over a hundred witnesses, he found himself exhausted and frustrated, complaining that to attempt a trial for high treason would be fruitless and a waste of time. It would, so he declared, 'be impossible to assemble a grand jury that would find bills against the rioters'.[51] Some of them were in fact tried and sentenced to be whipped by the common hangman, before being sent to the plantations in America.

The magistrates of the city of Glasgow were compelled to compensate Campbell of Shawfield for the damage to his house and property with the then large sum of £9,000. With this money he would shortly buy the whole of the island of Islay, off the coast of Kintyre, where, ironically, the main form of income was whisky distilled, both legally and illegally, from malt, a substance derived from barley, which, first soaked in water to germinate and then dried in a kiln, was the subject of the much detested tax.

Meanwhile Lord Ilay, as Justice General, had come to Scotland himself. It soon became obvious to him that the recent disturbances had resulted from the lack of any strong leadership in the various departments of government. Subsequently, with the aid of Duncan Forbes, now in his early forties dubbed 'King Duncan' in the north, together with Andrew Fletcher of Milton, just made a Lord in the Court of Session as Lord Milton, Lord Ilay, with the blessing of Walpole, took over the administration of the country.

Forbes, although sharing responsibility with Ilay, was soon in disagreement with him over the prosecution of the Glasgow magistrates 'whose guilt he does not think so plain as I do'.[52] The magistrates, in fact, were never brought to trial. This difference of opinion, however, proved to be the first instance of the antagonism which developed between Forbes and Ilay, fuelled by Ilay's jealousy of the former's rising power. Forbes in this instance, although angered, was to some extent mollified by a letter from Walpole expressing his gratitude for his 'vigilance and ability in struggling with the greatest difficulties that a man could possibly be engaged in'.[53]

Chapter 9
Problems of the Prince's Court

As the Duke of Argyll attained even greater ascendancy, the wife of his cousin, John Campbell of Mamore, was forced to endure humiliation as she waited on the Princess of Wales.

The Prince, spoilt and disagreeable whenever he failed to get his own way, furiously resentful of the way she had spurned his advances and married without his knowledge, took it out on Mary in every conceivable way. Horace Walpole, youngest son of the now first minister, and a great gossip of his day, describes the petty cruelties he inflicted by way of revenge.

'The Prince never forgave the breach of her word, and whenever she went to the drawing-room, as from her husband's situation she was sometimes obliged to do, although trembling at what she knew she was to undergo, the Prince always stepped up to her, and whispered some very harsh reproach in her ear. Mrs Howard was the intimate friend of Miss Bellenden; had been the confidante of the Prince's passion and, on Mrs Campbell's eclipse, succeeded to her friend's post of favourite, but not to her resistance'.[54]

Mrs Howard remained a close friend of Mary Bellenden who, far from being jealous of her association with the Prince, was only too thankful to be rid of his attentions to herself. There remained, however, the problem of the husband of whom Henrietta was frankly terrified.

She believed that she was safe enough in the house in Arlington Street, then closely guarded because of its occupation by the Prince of Wales and his household. However, she was petrified, when, at the beginning of summer, the royal family moved to the summer palace of Richmond, where the Prince loved hunting deer in the park, and which was thought to be healthier in the hot weather than the insalubrious city of London with its open, festering drains.

Because of the strict rules of etiquette, which governed the court, Henrietta Howard, as a mere woman of the bedchamber, could not travel in the coach of the Princess, protected as it would be by armed outriders and postilions. Convinced that her husband would try to abduct her during the journey, she confided her fears to her great friend Mary Bellenden, who either through her husband, John Campbell, or through the former Jane Warburton, the Maid of Honour (who had warned the Duke of someone trying to poison him in Spain) now Duchess of Argyll, arranged for the Duke and the Earl of Ilay to come to her aid.

Accordingly, at eight o'clock in the morning, on the day on which the Royal family were to travel, the Duke and his brother, acting the part of heroes rescuing a damsel in distress, called for Henrietta in one of their carriages. Slipping out of the house, heavily cloaked, she jumped in beside the two elderly gentlemen, who, distinguished by their long Campbell noses, reclined against the upholstery in their powdered wigs. Once she was aboard, the horses leapt into the traces, the great equipage lurched forward, firstly through the London streets, then out into the country, before she arrived in safety in Richmond and the house of the Prince of Wales.

The story did not end there as Horace Walpole describing the on-going drama, gleefully reports. During the summer a negotiation was commenced with the obstreperous husband, and he sold his own noisy honour and the possession of his wife for a pension of twelve hundred a year.[55]

On 3rd June 1727, King George I set out on his yearly visit to Hanover, which he still regarded as home, He planned to stop at Herrenhausen, in Osnabruck, the place of his birth, to meet his brother and sister, now the Queen of Prussia, and her son Prince Frederick, of whom he was particularly fond. Some way short of the city, while jolting along in his carriage, he had a stroke. Unconscious he was taken to Osnabruck where, on 11th June, he died.

His son, with whom he had quarrelled so violently before being reconciled, now succeeded him as George II. As monarch he moved into St James's Palace, the king's main residence since the Palace of Whitehall had burned down in 1698. Built on the site of a leper hospital by Henry VIII and dedicated to St James the Less, the building around four courtyards, including the gatehouse and the Chapel Royal, was constructed of red-brick in the Tudor style. The birthplace of both Charles I and of his son, the palace, used as a barracks by Oliver Cromwell, had been restored and embellished by Charles II. George I had used it as his official residence but thanks to his stringent economy, it had again become shabby and dilapidated. Curtains were torn and faded and paper peeled from the walls. Redecoration started but even when Baron Bielefeld visited in 1741, he complained that the official residence of the British monarch was no better than 'a lodging-house; crazy, smoky and dirty, sufficient of itself to inspire melancholy ideas'.[56]

Conversely, in view of the King's frugality, the office of gentlemen of the Privy Chamber was increased to the number of twenty. However, this being a post which carried no salary or perquisites other than certain legal immunities and social position, it was a good way of rewarding loyalty without entailing expense.[57]

The court of the new king, more lively than that of the old, was soon beset with scandal; the marital problems of Mrs Howard again became the talk of the town. The crisis came when her husband stormed into the quadrangle of the Palace yelling at the top of his voice, that he wanted his wife back. Hastily the guards pushed him out. However, totally nonplussed, he then wrote a letter to her ordering her to return to him. The Archbishop of Canterbury, persuaded to act as an intermediary, on his instructions, handed his missive to the Queen, 'who had the malicious pleasure of delivering the letter to her rival'.[58]

In striking contrast to the Howards, the Campbells, marriage, proved to be one of the happiest recorded in an age when infidelity was accepted with hardly an eyebrow raised. In 1720, the year of his marriage, John Campbell was gazetted Lieutenant-Colonel of Colonel James Ottway's Regiment of Foot, but army officers in times of peace had long periods of leave.

Thus John Campbell, with the help of his uncle, Lord Ilay (to whom it actually belonged) began to build Combe Bank, at Sunridge, near Sevenoaks in Kent, as a new home for his bride, The Palladium house, dating from 1720, was designed by the rising young Welsh architect Roger Morris, who, although already in vogue, was only twenty-five at the time. Later he was to become famous for the building and reconstruction of many great houses including Blair Castle and Inveraray in Scotland, while in England, Goodwood House in Sussex and Mereworth Castle in Kent are two of his most notable creations.

Combe Bank, surrounded at the time of its construction by 28 acres of parkland, is currently a school. In the early 1720s it was conveniently near to London for the young Mrs Campbell to accept the office of Keeper of the Palace of Somerset House in the Strand. This was the great mansion, built between 1547 and 1551 by Edward Seymour, Duke of Somerset, uncle and Lord Protector of the son of Henry VIII and Edward's sister, Jane Seymour, whose son reigned briefly as Edward VI. Fronting on to the Thames the house constructed round a courtyard, built in red brick in the Tudor style, stood between the river and the Strand astride the important route between the Tower of London and the Palace of Whitehall and the Houses of Parliament in Westminster. Occupied by Queen Elizabeth as a princess, it had then become the residence of successive queens until Katherine of Braganza, widow of Charles II, had returned to Portugal in 1693. Altered first by Inigo Jones, and then by Christopher Wren, the palace had been filled with music and laughter at the fashionable masked balls. By 1718, however, Vanburgh was to lament that Somerset House 'was no longer able to keep out the weather'. Running repairs were made but, by the time of Mary Campbell's appointment, the Palace was used mostly to house court officials, ambassadors and visiting royalty and as offices and storerooms.

Nonetheless, helped financially by this royal appointment, the newly married couple, contrived to live in some style in their own gracious new home. Their first child, a daughter called Caroline, probably in honour of the Princess of Wales, was born on 12th January 1721. A son called Archibald came in the following year. Sadly, he was to die of smallpox, then such a universal scourge.

The death of the little boy, so greatly mourned by his parents, seems to have strengthened the Princess of Wales's determination to have her own children vaccinated by the method introduced into Britain by Lady Mary Wortley Montagu who had seen it practiced in Turkey. Matter from the pustules of a smallpox sufferer was inserted under the skin of people, who by suffering the disease in mild form, gained immunity to this terrible pestilence.

In Britain the experiment of inoculation against smallpox had been tried and proved successful on a number of condemned prisoners who volunteered as guinea pigs in exchange for having their sentences repealed. Princess Caroline, who had suffered herself from smallpox, had already organised and paid for the orphans of the Parish Church of St James's in Westminster to be inoculated, despite the protests of churchmen and some, mostly Tory members, of the laity who declared that such interference with nature was contravening the will of God.

Such was the clamour of their opposition that Princess Caroline had to ask the permission of her father-in-law, King George I to have two of her own daughters, the Princesses Amelia and Caroline, inoculated in 1722, the year in which the one year old Archibald Campbell died so tragically of this horrible, and hitherto frequently, fatal disease.[59]

Happily, despite the sadness of Archibald's death, his parents continued to have four more sons. Firstly, John, destined to be the 5th Duke of Argyll, born in 1723, secondly Frederick, thirdly Henry, and lastly William. Thus, while the marriages of

John Campbell of Mamore's cousins, the Duke of Argyll and Lord Islay, failed to produce an heir [the former, by his second marriage to Jane Warburton was to have five daughters and the latter, whose wife died childless, only one illegitimate son] the dynasty of the dukedom of Argyll appeared to be secure.

Unlike his father, the second King George loved ceremony. He reinstated the function of the levée, when he and Queen Caroline dressed before their attendants as they had done when Prince and Princess of Wales.[60] They also dined in public. The Countess of Bristol complained that although 'a glorious sight' it was exhausting for the Lady in Waiting, who 'takes the cover off the dishes, carves for both their Majesties, the Prince and three Princesses, besides giving the Queen drink and tasting upon the knee'. [61]

Appearances were of the utmost importance and the wedding of his eldest daughter, Anne, the Princess Royal, to William IV of Holland, gave the King a chance to show off. A covered gallery was built at St James's to hold four thousand people. The chapel was sumptuously decorated and the King himself outshone the bridegroom in a suit of cloth of gold.

Passionately interested in the army he also loved military parades. A camp in Hyde Park, in 1722, was described as 'the finest sight in the world'. [62] Nonetheless, despite the King's enthusiasm for soldiering, the standing army was very unpopular, not only with the tax payers but with the general populace. The billeting of troops in local hostelries, before regular barracks were built, being particularly resented. Soldiers with nothing to do tended to be obstreperous, and when they could find it, were much given to drink. Sailors, on the other hand, although equally partial to their rum, were generally regarded as heroes, defending Britain from her enemies on the high and dangerous seas.

George II, however, adored his army, believing it to be his strongest support. He could rightly defy his critics when in Scotland the threat of an armed rising against the malt tax purported worse to come.

Chapter 10
Violence in Scotland's Capital

In 1733, with a general election in the offing, Walpole was forced by the opposition in parliament to make an ignominious withdrawal of his much-vaunted Excise Bill. Only in Scotland, where the Duke of Argyll and Lord Ilay, leaders of the Presbyterian faction, still held supreme power, did the Whig administration hold firm. The Representation Act which disqualified Scots judges from the House of Commons was aimed directly at Lord Grange, who, suspected of Jacobite sympathies, was amongst the men of influence, on both sides of the Border, conniving at the downfall of Walpole.

Nonetheless, in Scotland, Walpole's predominance had already been threatened by an event, which, although initially of small importance, carried an underlying threat. [63]

The trouble began in 1735 when a Revenue Officer seized a ship belonging to pirates off the coast of Fife, at that time a hotbed of smuggling. He then sold the cargo, which proved to be of some considerable worth. The pirates retaliated by robbing the Revenue Officer of what they, and most of the population of Edinburgh, considered to be theirs by right. However, the Revenue Officer, or Collector, as he was more commonly called, then somehow contrived to have the pirates arrested and thrown into the Tolbooth, [the common jail] where, after a summary trial, both were condemned to death.

The populace howled in fury once the sentence was known. Yet despite the public outcry the civic authorities insisted on the customary procedure by which, on the Sunday previous to their execution, criminals were taken to hear a sermon in a church nearby the jail. Arriving early, they were placed in the special seats reserved for felons but on looking round were surprised to find themselves in the custody of only a few old guards.

At sight of this, one of the pirates, surnamed Robinson, took a flying leap over the back of the seat, while the other, called Wilson, grabbed two of the guards with his hands and another with his teeth, and held them until his companion had escaped from the church into the protection of the mob of people outside. Wilson left behind then sat down quietly to await his fate.

Once the public learned what had happened Wilson became such a hero that the magistrates of Edinburgh resolved to take all possible precautions to prevent a riot on the day that he was due to be hanged. The officer, whose turn it was to do duty as Captain of the City Guard, was considered too incompetent to take charge. Therefore, a Captain John Porteous, a man of known courage and resolve, was told to take his place. Issued with charges of powder and shot, Porteous distributed them amongst his men, ordering them to load their pieces when they went on duty that day.

The execution itself was carried out with small disturbance until, as the corpse was cut down, all hell broke loose. Stones were hurled; the hangman and several of the guards were injured until others, in self-defence, fired into the crowd.

Meanwhile Captain Porteous, having seen the body lowered to the ground, marched off his men up the West Bow, a narrow winding passage from which there was little or no escape. Pressing behind them came the mob, screaming curses and pelting them with rocks. The guards, terrified, halted, swung round and fired. Several men fell dead. Others wounded crawled away. The march then continued to the Guard House where, with due military ceremony, the soldiers handed in their arms.

Afterwards, Captain Porteous, his own gun cold in his hand, went to join the magistrates in a tavern called the *Spread Eagle* Inn. There, to his astonishment, he found himself charged with murder on the grounds that he had not only given his men the orders to fire but had discharged his own piece. He stoutly denied both accusations, telling the magistrates that, of the three charges they had given him, two were in his cartouche box and the third in his still loaded gun. He then actually produced the weapon in proof that it had not been fired. Despite this the magistrates, with Porteous, proceeded to the Council Chamber pursued by a large and riotous mob yelling for justice to be done.

Once within the barred doors of the Chamber, with the crowd still clamouring outside, they held a hasty precognition [a Coroner's Inquest] which resulted in the unfortunate Captain being dragged off to the Tolbooth to await his trial. Sentenced to death for murder he was then, at Queen Caroline's special instigation, granted a reprieve so that new evidence could be found. The Queen had shown mercy. The mob still howled for revenge.

On the evening of the day on which, previous to the Queen's interference, his execution had been fixed to take place, a number of people entered the West Bow closing it behind them. Seizing a drum, they paraded through the Grass Market and the Cowgate to the East Bow of the city, which they also secured. They then marched up the main street and attacked the guardhouse where the few guards who were on duty, together with their officer, hastily surrendered on promise of their lives. The mobsters, having loaded themselves with all the available weapons proceeded to the prison where they tried to burst open the door. Failing to break it down they set fire to it and succeeded in burning a hole through which the Turnkey, in a state of terror, threw them the keys. Storming into the building they swarmed up the stairs to the cell where Porteous was held. Grabbing him, they pulled him down by the heels before dragging him to the place of execution where, in the absence of a gallows, having tortured him, they hanged him over a dyer's pole.

As this was happening some of the magistrates were actually drinking in an inn nearby. Alarmed by the commotion as the wretched Porteous was barbarously put to death, they ran out to try to save him but retreated back into the building under a vicious shower of stones. [64]

As dawn broke the people of Edinburgh found themselves held hostage by the insurgents. The guards were helpless: the city gates barred and held so that no word could be sent to the regular forces, known to be stationed nearby. The situation was only saved when the leaders of the riot took advantage of the commotion to simply vanish from sight. Order was thus restored but confidence in the civic authorities, believed to be minions of Argyll, was so badly shaken that the Tories seized the chance to exploit the incident in an attempt to undermine his power.

In England the members of both Houses of Parliament were incensed when given the details of the savagery which had occurred. Many suspected, in fact mistakenly, that Porteous could only have been murdered with the connivance of the civic authorities. Subsequently an inquiry into the disturbance was held in the House of Lords. George Drummond, Lord Provost of Edinburgh, and the four bailiffs, were summoned to be examined at the Bar. Their testimony completed, a Bill of Pains and penalties was then inaugurated by which the Provost was banned from taking any form of public office, and the city guards were dismissed. In addition, it was decreed that the Nether Bow Port should be demolished to allow easier access of troops should a further emergency arise.

Foremost amongst the protestors against this arbitrary action was Duncan Forbes of Culloden, who voiced his fury as he voted against the measure, denouncing it as 'an unwarranted outrage on the national feeling'. The long-nosed loose-limbed Scot, famous for his consumption of claret and the whisky distilled on his family estate, as the chief law officer of the Crown in Scotland, had to collect evidence, and examine witnesses. Known to be incorruptible, as the man who had struggled to save the unfortunate Jacobite prisoners after the Rising of 1715, he now refused to forsake his principles for the sake of coercion with the Government. The Bill of Pains and Penalties, aimed at punishing the civic authorities of Edinburgh, although strongly opposed by the Duke of Argyll, passed its first reading in the House of Lords. Forbes, summoned by the Lords to appear as a witness, declared,

"My Lords, we acted in that affair, as our consciences directed us; and there is no power on earth that dare call our actions in question."[65]

Sent down to the Commons, after many adjournments, it was then rejected, not only by all the Scottish members, but by some of the English as well. Forbes risked his own career by speaking in opposition, knowing himself to be the likely successor to Sir Hew Dalrymple, in the office of Lord President. Nonetheless he declaimed with vehemence,

"It would sound very ill that a British House of Commons in which there are but 45 representatives for Scotland should receive such a bill; Edinburgh is now a city of Great Britain, nay, the second city. And I appeal to the gentlemen who represent the cities and boroughs of England to know in what manner they would treat a bill inflicting such pains and penalties upon any of the cities which they represent. They are in honour obliged to protect the Commons of Scotland as much as the Commons of England; because the Scots trusted to their honour when they united with them upon the terms they did, they are in prudence obliged to protect the burgh of Scotland as much as the privileges of any burgh of England; because no encroachment can be made, no injury done to one but what may be made a precedent for doing the same to the other...If they accept of this bill, if they give it a reading, I shall soon expect to see a bill brought them from the other House for turning some of their members out of doors."[66]

The Bill, much amended, was finally passed on 21st June 1737. Thanks to Forbes's powers of persuasion most of the more offensive items were withdraw, although the Provost was prohibited from holding any further office as a magistrate. Also, a fine of £2,000, imposed on the city of Edinburgh was given to the widow of Porteous while efforts were to continue to bring her husband's murders to justice.

Chapter 11
Pursuer of Smugglers
and Reformer of Feudal Law

Despite his defiance of authority within the Parliament, Duncan Forbes, once in office as the Lord President, set about trying to increase the country's revenue by curbing the smuggling, over which, thanks to the inefficiency of his predecessor, Robert Dundas, there was little or no control. Five years after becoming Lord Advocate, in August 1730, he had written to John Scrope, Secretary to the Treasury, telling him that,

'The imminent distress, from the condition of our Revenue, has now for some time possessed my attention; the Customs from the defects of the law, from the corruption of officers, and from the perverseness of juries, are fallen to nothing; and never can by any art be raised, till those complaints are removed, which must be the work of some time, though our disease seems to demand a more speedy remedy'.[67]

Taking brandy as an example he told him that in view of the fact that the spirit, to which he himself was partial and which was drunk to excess throughout Scotland, cost two shillings a gallon. The smugglers, while making a rare profit themselves, were costing the country a fortune. The Excise in fact was so badly affected by the excessive use of [contraband] foreign spirits that,

'The price of grain is beat down to nothing by it, which is a very sensible loss to the men of estates, whose rents are almost universally paid in grain; as well as to the farmers'.[68]

By this he implied that people in Scotland by buying imported wines, however, illegally, were ruining the trade of ale brewed from homegrown barley. Reaching Edinburgh in the summer of 1731 Forbes discovering,

'The great remissness of the boards of Customs and Excise in putting the laws against the uncustomed brandy…[I] called both boards together and rattled them up as well as I could'.[69]

So successful was his 'rattling' that no less than 1,100 gallons of brandy were seized in St Andrews alone. Forbes, however, was very careful not to broadcast his triumph for fear of stepping on Lord Ilay's toes. Aware by now of his jealousy, he tried what appears to have been successful diplomacy, in allowing him to take the credit for himself.

Equally repugnant to Forbes was the ever-increasing use of tea. In a Memorial sent to London at the request of the Marquess of Tweedale, by then Secretary of State for Scotland, in October 1742, Forbes, having listed other grievances, declared that the prime cause of all the mischief was the excessive use of tea by one and all.

'Even the labouring people and the very lowest classes, like the fish carriers of Musselborough and the blue gown beggars, drink it at breakfast in place of the native-brewed ale, and the women of the same class consume the drug at their afternoon's entertainment to the exclusion of the twopenny'.[70]

Most of the tea was shipped in from Ostend and Gottenburg in such large quantities that the price fell to between 2s 6d to 4s a pound. With a pound of tea to last them a month Forbes declared that the women had taken to the drug because of its cheapness, and in imitation of their 'betters'.

Because of the current passion for tea the people of the main towns, including Glasgow and Edinburgh, which had the right of levying a duty of two pence on the pint of beer and ale for the raising of their chief fund to fund expenses, were now finding that their income was shrinking even lower than that of the excise. While admitting that this was partly due to the 'importation of brandy and other foreign spirits' the main cause for the drain on public funds was 'that most mischievous drug'.

In view of this Forbes suggested that a tax of 4s. In the pound should be imposed on all imported tea. He insisted that this measure would not affect the East India Company, because the smuggled tea came in from Gottenburg and Holland. In conclusion he said he felt assured that the [71] measures he suggested would meet with the approval of all concerned with the land 'for grain is the source of all rents in most parts of Scotland. Moreover the Royal Burghs with their present Parliamenary grant of two pence a pint on ale will assuredly be favourably disposed'.

Forbes did not receive universal approval of his suggestions as to how to restrict the widespread importation of contraband tea. He did, however, receive wide acclaim for his scheme to prevent both tea and brandy being sold in small quantities illegally.

Sir Andrew Mitchell, under Secretary to Tweedale, and a friend of Forbes, wrote to him from Whitehall on 24th July 1744.

'I must congratulate your Lordship for the reform you have made of the manners and opinions of our countrymen which the legislature could not have done and as it is probable that smuggling and perjury will be no more, I am rejoiced that you have the honour of driving them from our native land'.[72]

Hopeful, rather than strictly accurate, as Mitchell seems to have been, he nonetheless voiced the recognition of himself and his fellow politicians at the success, even if limited, of what Forbes was aiming to achieve.

The Memorial is also notable for Forbes's reference to the linen trade which he had done so much to foster. As early as 1726, as Lord Advocate, he had promoted a bill which became law in the following year. By this it was decreed that the money due for the development of the Fisheries and Manufactures (agreed by the Treaty of Union in 1707) should be utilised. He himself then became one of the twenty-one trustees who were appointed to distribute the allotted revenues, £6,000 to the Herring Fisheries, £2,650 to the Linen Industry and £700 to the Spinning Manufactory of course tarred wool. By 1743, although the catches of fish had barely increased, the manufacture of linen had become a flourishing business. So successful was it, that flax spun in Scotland, mainly by women on the farms, was now in great demand. Large quantities of linen yarn went to Manchester and to Ireland. Forbes wrote,

'As what I have said gives a very promising view of this manufacture, I must not conceal that it is the only thing that promises any good in this poor country'.[73]

His words are proved by statistics. The quantity of linen on which duty was paid to the Government, rated at £103,212 9s 3d in 1728 had risen to £293,864 12s 11d by 1748. The Secretary of State, Tweedale, writing to Forbes in May 1745, applauded his efforts to increase the trade by saying:

'It gives me great satisfaction to find that in your opinion the Linen Manufacture continues to prosper and will soon make a more remarkable progress'.

The impact on history made by Forbes's successful curbs on smuggling, overshadows that of his reform of the feudal methods of farming in the West Highlands and the Isles. In August 1737, as factor of the Duke of Argyll, he left Edinburgh on an expedition to the west. Arriving in Tiree, he camped in a leaking tent in pouring rain. His son, a young man of about twenty-seven, got a bad chill but Forbes cured him by bleeding him and giving him some of the rhubarb pills, which were such a panacea at the time.

Despite the worry of his son John's illness Forbes was soon to discover much amiss in Tiree. Immediately obvious was the fact that the island, which in the time of St Columba had been hailed as the granary of the Isles, now produced only one tenth of the amount of corn of previous years. This was because the land was so throttled with weeds that the corn could not be scythed, and was torn up by the roots, and worse even that, the straw was actually burnt!

The people were close to starving. Soon they would be driven by poverty to leave the island, which he believed, with proper management, could return to its former fertility.

Forbes, with his perceptive mind, was all too aware of the reason why this situation had occurred. For generations the land had been let to tacksmen, who subdivided it amongst their sub-tenants at will. The tacksmen held their position as officers in their landlord's – in this case Argyll's fiery tail. The strength of a great chief lay in the number of men who, in times of emergency, he could call to arms. Now, since the Disarming Act, which had followed the Rising of 1715, the swords and guns which had not been handed in, were hidden below the thatch. Forbes saw all too clearly, that the system, relied upon for centuries, was becoming redundant. The birth rate, moreover, was increasing and produce, rather than men-at-arms, was essential to survival in places hitherto a source for fighting men.

It is highly significant that the new leases drawn up by Forbes in 1739 omit all commitments to military service. Instead, as in a case on Mull, the tenants were committed to 'repairing harbours, mending roads and making or repairing the mill lead for the good of the community of the island'.[75]

Needless to say, he met aggression. The favourable terms of leasing for nineteen years offered to the tenants in Mull were rejected with fury. A Minister, the Rev. Maclean, offering far less than his farm was worth, found himself outbid and was raving mad. Nonetheless Forbes persisted in his policy and brought in a professional farmer from East Lothian thanks to whom, some of the local people at least, learned to make proper use of their land.

The tacksmen faced with increasing rents, had in many cases to emigrate or retire. This was the start of the great exodus to Canada and North America which was to accelerate over the coming years. Abolishment of Hereditary Jurisdiction, which Forbes himself was to legislate, would speed the end of the old regime. Change was under way, but before its effects could become evident the Highlands and the Isles were to be devastated by a rebellion hitherto unknown in strength.

Chapter 12
A Gentleman-in-Waiting
at the Court of King George II

Lieutenant-Colonel John Campbell, being much about the court, was witness to the extraordinary power of Queen Caroline, who, although always subservient to her husband, was, in a term of common parlance, 'the power behind the throne'. Small of stature but of commanding presence, she was not only clever – she mastered the English language, including some of the coarser profanities! Within only a few months – but eminently sensible – she was possessed of a sharp discerning mind.

Horace Walpole, a man much in her thrall, wrote in her praise.

'Her countenance was full of majesty or mildness as she pleased, and her penetrating eyes expressed whatever she had a mind they should. Her voice too was captivating, and her hands beautifully small, plump and graceful. Her understanding was uncommonly strong, and so was her resolution. From their earliest connection she was determined to govern the King, and deserved to do so, for her submission to his will was unbounded, her sense much superior, and his honour and interest always took place of her own; so that her love of power that was predominant, was dearly bought and rarely ill employed…Though his affection and confidence in her were implicit, he lived in dread of being supposed to be governed by her, and that silly parade was extended even to the most private moments of business with my father. Whenever he entered, the Queen rose, curtsied, and retired or offered to retire. Sometimes the King condescended to bid her stay-on both occasions unaware that she and Sir Robert had previously settled the business to be discussed. Sometimes the King would quash the proposal in question, and yield after talking it over with her – but then he boasted to Sir Robert that he himself had better considered it'.[76]

In addition to his childish pride King George was exceptionally mean.

'One of the Queen's delights was the improvement of the garden at Richmond and the King believed she paid for [it] all with her own money nor would he ever look at her intended plans, saying he did not care how she flung away her own revenue. He little suspected the aids Sir Robert furnished to her from the treasury. When she died, she was indebted twenty thousand pounds to the King'.[77]

Queen Caroline had much to contend with in addition to her husband's paucity. Her greatest sorrow was the enmity between her eldest son Frederick, the Prince of Wales and his father. History was repeating itself. King George had been at violent odds with his own father. Now he was battling with his son. Prince Frederick, by all accounts was tiresome. The flattery of the Tory opposition went straight to his head to the point where, soon after his arrival in England, he was suspected of being party to an act of open treachery. Irresponsible and extravagant he was quickly short of money, whereupon Sarah, the old Duchess of Marlborough, astute as ever to the aspirations of her family, suggested that her favourite granddaughter, Lady Diana Spenser, with a fortune of a hundred thousand pounds, should marry him.

The plans had to be kept secret due to the fact that, Lady Diana, a beautiful girl, who later became the Duchess of Bedford, was not of Royal birth, an essential qualification for marriages into the British Royal family at the time. The redoubtable Duchess of Marlborough, however, arranged for the ceremony to take place at her house in Windsor Great Park. The date was fixed. She nearly got away with it. But somehow the news reached the ears of Walpole who quickly, with the force of the King behind him, declared that any such match would be illegal. The scandal was suppressed, and Prince Frederick went on to marry the Princess Augusta of Saxe-Gotha, who, although a youngest daughter, was at least of Royal descent.

Another furore in the family ensued when Frederick nearly killed his wife by moving her, in the middle of the night, while she was actually in labour, from Hampton Court to the unprepared and unaired Palace of St James's.

Queen Caroline, told of this outrage, yet nonetheless hoping to achieve some reconciliation with her son, bundled herself into a carriage at seven o'clock in the morning. On her arrival, the Prince, far from making the apology which she expected, refused to speak to her. However, on conducting her out of the palace in tight-lipped silence, he noticed a crowd of people, who drawn by the excitement of a Royal birth, had gathered round the gate. Courting publicity, he knelt ostentatiously down in the dirt and kissed her hand upon which, as Walpole dryly commented, "Her indignation must have shrunk into contempt."[78]

Happily, George II did find some compatibility with his younger son, William, Duke of Cumberland, who, born in 1721, was only six years old when Colonel Campbell became a Gentleman in Waiting to the King. Prince William, a stocky little boy with a stubborn streak to his nature, shared his father's love of soldiers from an early age.

Walpole tells the story of how, when ticked off by his mother for some misdemeanour, he was sent up to his room. Returning, shuffling his feet and with a sulky expression on his face, she asked him what he had been doing.

"Reading."

"Reading what?"

"The Bible."

"And what did you read there?"

"About Jesus and Mary."

"And what about them?"

"Why, that Jesus said to Mary. Woman! What hast thou to do with me?"[79]

Little could Colonel Campbell guess then at the close association he was later to have with this truculent, but none the less determined, little boy.

The daughters of George II and Queen Caroline could also be intractable when they chose. The eldest, Princess Anne, the Princess Royal, imperious and ambitious, was sent over to Holland, married to the Prince of Orange. Bored with his rather unpretentious court, she seized the chance of her mother's death and her own supposed ill health to return to England. On the King, her father, however, getting wind of it, he packed her off, firstly to Bath and then back to Holland, without letting her spend even two nights in London as she so dearly desired.

Princess Amelia, or Emily, the second daughter, who, as Walpole says "was well inclined to meddle",[80] was courted by the Dukes of Newcastle and Grafton, neither of whom she married. Trained by her mother to be an intermediary with the ministers, she became her father's hostess following Queen Caroline's death. Eventually, after her father died, at odds with his grandson, her nephew who succeeded him as George III and loathing his mother, who now, as the Princess-dowager, intrigued with the heads of government more effectively than had she herself, Amelia made the excuse of her deafness to leave the court.

Princess Caroline, again according to Walpole 'one of the most excellent of women', was the mainstay of both her parents who relied on her for her good judgment. "Send for Caroline," was the universal cry when any kind of dispute amongst the family occurred "and then we shall know the truth." [81]

Sadly this youngest daughter who, greatly afflicted by her mother's death, then became crippled by arthritis, retired to a secluded life before she predeceased the father whom also she greatly loved. [82]

Chapter 13
Return to Active Service
a Palliative for Grief

Little is known about the private life of Colonel John Campbell of Mamore during his early years at court. Devoted to his wife and family, there was no cause for scandal for tattlers like Horace Walpole to report. By 1735 Mary Campbell had borne six children, firstly a daughter Caroline, born a year after her marriage in 1721, and then five sons all of whom, with the exception of Archibald who died of smallpox, survived. This in itself was an achievement at a time when so many children perished in infancy due largely to lack of hygiene and of medical knowledge of even the most basic kind. The great-grandson of the French King Louis XIV, when his mother was fatally ill with measles, was fed on a tincture of violets until a woman of the bedchamber had the sense and courage to whip him away to a wet-nurse so that he subsequently survived.

The health of the Campbell children depended, to a large extent, on the environment of Combe Bank in Kent. In those days Sevenoaks, the nearest small town, was considered to be remote. Safe in the country the children could run wild in the wooded park which surrounded the Palladian house with its graceful portico and pillars and its large, high ceilinged rooms, in which, in the summer time, the sun seemed to shine all day.

By 1735 the elder children of the family were fast growing up. Caroline, at fourteen, had much of her mother's beauty and the same graceful way of moving which caught the beholder's eye. John, at twelve was a strong lad and already interested in the army, which he aimed to make his career. The younger boys, Henry, Frederick and William, were also growing fast. It seems probable that Mary, for the seventh time pregnant, wished for another girl.

Tragically she died in childbirth for what reason we do not know. Obstetrics were then so primitive that septicaemia may well have been the cause. Her husband and children were heartbroken, distressed beyond any words. Mary, the beautiful, graceful, funny and above all loving wife and mother had, without any real warning, been snatched away from them by death.

John Campbell, with five motherless children to care for, felt himself trapped in a void created by the loss of his wife. Left in a situation where most men of his age and rank would have taken mistresses, he longed only for some sort of physical action to distract his mind from grief. While still the Member of Parliament for Dunbartonshire, he was also on the army list. An appeal to the King to allow him to return to active service seems, at first, to have been tactically refused.

Two years later, however, King George himself became a widower. As the Queen was dying she told him he should marry again, upon which his sobs began to rise and his tears to fall with double vehemence…wiping his eyes and sobbing between every word, with much ado he got out this answer "Non – j'aurai – des – maitresses." [83]

John Campbell's desire for action is more than understandable when we read of the stultifying dullness of the court of George II following his wife's death.

'The King's last years passed as regularly as clockwork. At nine at night he had cards in the apartment of his daughters, the Princesses Amelia and Caroline, with Lady Yarmouth, two or three of the Queen's ladies and as many of the most favoured officers of his own household. Every Saturday in summer he carried the courtiers without his daughters, to dine at Richmond: they went up in coaches and six in the middle of the day, with the heavy horse-guards kicking up the dust before them – dined, walked an hour in the garden, returned in the same dusty parade, and his Majesty fancied himself the most gallant and lively prince in Europe'.[84]

St James's Palace robbed of the presence of Queen Caroline, seemed dull and sombre as a morgue. The King avoiding the company of all except his daughters and his younger sons, crept about through the rooms and corridors, and rose early to light his own fire. Soon, perhaps recognising the sorrow they shared, he agreed to allow Colonel Campbell, to forgo his duties as gentleman of the bedchamber, and once again to take the field.

Whereas his years at court are undocumented, those when on active service are found in the notes of Sir Duncan Campbell of Barcaldine who kept the military records of his clan. In 1737 John Campbell of Mamore, was made Colonel of the 39th Foot before taking command of the 21st Foot, which later became better known as the Royal Scots Fusiliers, in the following year.

In those days a colonel actually owned his regiment being responsible for arming, clothing and feeding his men. He did not of necessity command it in battle although this was the time when remuneration from grateful governments, both British and foreign, together with plunder, the acknowledged perquisite of a conquering army, hopefully reimbursed some of the expenses which a commanding officer must inevitably incur.

In Scotland the Lord President of the Court of Session, Duncan Forbes of Culloden, had repeatedly urged the forming of Highland regiments, which, under the command of colonels known to be loyal to the King, would be officered by chiefs and cadets of Scottish families. He argued that this would ensure that soldiers raised in the Highlands would not only fight abroad but would maintain such order in their own country that it would be absolutely impossible to raise a rebellion in the Highlands. Lord Ilay then supported the suggestion so strongly that Walpole, convinced of the common-sense of Forbes's proposal, prevailed on the King to implement the motion which would make it law. Already, in 1730, six companies of the Black Watch, raised locally to prevent the cattle stealing so rampant in the Highlands, had been formed. In 1739, these independent territorials became the famous 'Forty-second' (later the 'Forty-third') regiment of the line.

The man most strongly affected by Queen Caroline's death, apart from her grieving spouse, was Sir Robert Walpole, now Britain's first Prime Minister in everything but name. Walpole, who, as the leader of the Whigs had at first taken office in 1720, by 1737, had remained there for an unprecedented seventeen years.

Throughout that time, he had had relied much on the support of the monarch thanks to Queen Caroline's unchallenged supremacy over her husband. Now, when no longer possessed of her influence, his enemies in the Tory party, many of them Jacobites at heart, were searching for cracks in the armour of the man who, for nearly two decades, had remained in the seat of power.

Four years earlier, in 1733, with a general election in the offing, Walpole had been forced by the opposition in parliament to make an ignominious withdrawal of his much-vaunted Excise Bill. Only in Scotland, where the Duke of Argyll and his brother Lord Ilay, as leaders of the Presbyterian faction, still held supreme power, did the Whig administration hold firm. The Representation Act which disqualified Scots judges from the House of Commons, was aimed directly at Lord Grange, who, suspected of Jacobite sympathies, was amongst the men of influence, on both sides of the Border, who connived at the downfall of Walpole.

The Duke of Argyll, however, who clearly considered this proposed legislation to be aimed at the reduction of his own authority, retaliated with a long speech to the Lords. In conclusion he forecast further unrest in the event of the Bill becoming law.

'I have now, my Lords, given my opinion with respect to the present Bill, so far as I have had an opportunity to know anything of its tendency, or the evidence upon which it is founded; and, I think, if we consent to the passing it into a law, at least in the shape it is now in, we do what is both imprudent and unjust'.[85]

Significantly, the riots in Edinburgh had accelerated the already growing hostility between Sir Robert Walpole and Argyll. This was further intensified in 1739, when Walpole, with great reluctance, declared war on Spain.

The conflict, to be known as the 'War of Jenkin's Ear' stemmed from the agreement included in the Treaty of Seville, signed in 1729, by which the British consented not to trade with the Spanish Colonies. The Spanish were allowed to board British ships, sailing in their territorial waters to search for contraband cargoes. However, two years after the agreement had been reached, one Robert Jenkins, captain of the merchant ship *Rebecca,* claimed that in a scuffle a Spanish coastguard had sliced off his ear. Seven years later, when war fever was rampant, Jenkins was brought into the House of Commons bearing his pickled ear.

The clamour for conflict increased until on 23rd October 1739, Walpole, much against his better judgment, was virtually forced by both his supporters and opponents, to declare war on Spain. In 1742, however, Britain's soldiers and resources had to be deflected to Europe where the War of the Austrian Succession, a conflict on a hitherto unprecedented scale, against Prussia and France, had begun.

Two years previously, in October 1740, the Emperor Charles V of Austria had died without a son. His daughter, Maria Theresa, Queen of Hungary, however, was recognised by all the European countries, with the exception of Bavaria, as heir to all his domains. Nonetheless, within the space of a year, Frederick II of Prussia, had conquered the Austrian army and annexed the whole of Silesia. The French then invaded Bohemia and captured Prague while the Bavarians encroached upon Vienna, capital of the Habsburg Empire.

Suddenly, the situation changed. The Hungarians rose as a man to defend their young Queen. Prague was recaptured, The Bavarians driven back from Vienna. Charles Albert, the new Holy Roman Emperor, was forced to resign his claim to Austria and to grant his dominions to the Queen of Hungary pending the signing of the Peace of Berlin.

Meanwhile, Frederick II of Prussia, having achieved possession of both Silesia and Saxony, had withdrawn from the conflict. Thus by 1743 the whole situation in

Europe had changed. Maria Theresa, exalted by her success, now herself aimed to conquer territories, which included Alsace and Lorraine. The war, which had begun three years earlier with the dissolution of the Austrian Empire of her father Charles V, had developed into a coalition to destroy the might of France.

In England Sir Robert Walpole, who had strongly opposed the war with Spain, now even more fervently argued against fighting France, believing, as it proved correctly, that this would provoke the Jacobite Rising he had struggled so long to suppress.

Ironically, it was in Scotland, that the man who had been his former supporter, as the leader of the Hanoverian cause, now denounced him for showing incompetence in defending the realm. On 15th April 1740, in a debate on the state of the nation, the Duke of Argyll delivered an impassioned speech to the House of Lords. He began by censuring the blockade of the Spanish fleet by the British navy, calling it 'a very useless, ill-judged piece of service'. It would, so he claimed, have been better if the Spanish fleet had sailed so that our men-of-war could have pursued them to America and destroyed them, if not in the Atlantic, in the Caribbean Sea. Now he was told that the Spaniards had escaped so that 'we have for two years, at a vast expense, been endeavouring to do what we find turns out to no manner of account, while there were many services which the fleet might have performed that must have put an end to the war in our favour before this time'.

Having then decried the management of the army, which he claimed belied common sense, he affirmed that he saw no reason why the 'future management of this war [should not] be put upon a more sure and advantageous footing for the nation, than it has hitherto been'.[86]

Although this proved to be the last speech he made in parliament, the Duke then proceeded to use all his influence to persuade the electorate in Scotland to vote against Walpole. On 18th June 1741, Bubb Dodington, one of the opposition who had been involved in managing the election in England, wrote triumphantly to Argyll,

'The elections are over; and our success in them has, I must confess, exceeded my most sanguine expectations...Cornwall gave the first foundation for any reasonable hopes, and Scotland has brought the work to such a degree of perfection, that it would be, now, as criminal to despair of success, as it would have been before, presumptuous to have expected it'.[87]

Walpole, with the majority of the new parliament against him, struggled on for a few months. But, in February 1742, the great minister, who was First Lord of the Treasury for twenty-two years, was finally forced to resign.

Walpole was succeeded as first minister by Lord Carteret, and a month later, in March 1742, when the Duke of Argyll resigned all his offices, John, Marquess of Tweeddale, became Secretary of State or Scotland.

On 30 June 1742 Horace Walpole wrote to his friend Sir Horace Mann.

'I hear news came last night that the States of Holland have voted forty-seven thousand men for the assistance of the Queen [of Hungary]...This seems to be the consequence of the King of Prussia's proceedings – but how can they trust him so easily?'[88]

Then, after detailing some of the social gossip of London he wrote,

'The town has talked of nothing lately but a plot. I will tell you the circumstances. Last week the Scotch hero [Argyll] sent his brother two papers, which he said had been left at his house by an unknown hand [but] he believed it was Colonel Cecil, agent for the Pretender…He desired Lord Islay [sic] to lay them before the ministry. One of the papers seemed a letter, though with no address or subscription, written in true, genuine Stuart characters. It was to thank Mr Burnus (D. of A) for his services and that he hoped he would answer the assurances given of him. The other was to command the Jacobites, and to exhort the patriots to continue what they mutually so well began, and to say how pleased he was with their having removed Mr Tench. Lord Islay showed these letters to Lord Orford, and then to the King, and told him he had showed them to my father. "You did well Lord Islay," said the King, "Lord Orford says one is of the Pretender's hand…" A few days afterwards, the Duke wrote to his brother "that upon recollection he thought it right to say, that he had received those letters from Lord Barrymore" who is well known for General to the Chevalier'.[89]

James, Lord Barrymore, at that time nearly eighty, was a staunch supporter of the old Pretender, or James VIII and III, as he was known to the Jacobites.

In August, Tweeddale asked Lord President Forbes to support him in drafting a bill to control the Highlands, where the likelihood of a rising in aid of the exiled Stewart king, was still on most people's minds. Tweeddale had in fact already told General Clayton, in command of the army in Scotland, to confer with Forbes who now responded that nothing could be done effectually unless more money was forthcoming. As a result, the line between Fort William and Inverness, where now runs the Caledonian Canal, was garrisoned by regular troops, supported by a body of Gaelic speaking Highland soldiers, under Clayton's command.

Then towards the end of the year rumour began to run wild that the Highland regiment (the six independent companies now united as the 42nd) were to be ordered to march to England prior to being sent abroad to fight the King's war in Flanders. Immediately there was uproar. Scotland was to be left undefended, open to invasion from France. Forbes, writing to Clayton, told him that 'In the event of a French attempt to revive the Jacobite cause, the Pretender's emissaries would have a free hand to cajole, to promise to pay, to concert' [90] How, he argued, could regular soldiers, unfamiliar with the Highlands, hope to contend with a French invasion? They would be lost or at worst over-run.

His protests were nonetheless ignored. The Highland regiment did march south with the prospect of serving under Cumberland abroad. Several men deserted but despite his obvious involvement Tweeddale laid the blame upon Stair. Forbes, however, was not to be silenced, proclaiming that,

'The country adjacent to the Highlands suffers extremely by the absence of the Highland troops, [obviously cattle lifting was rife] nor is it possible to obviate the mischief but by the same or other forces of the like nature'.[91]

Lord Orford, himself had several times received letters from the Pretender 'making him the greatest offers'. He had promptly shown them to the King asking him to endorse them before handing them back.

Now it was obvious that the exiled Stuart monarch, having heard of the rift between Orford and Argyll, was trying to win the Scottish nobleman to his cause.

'Numbers of Jacobites had joined in the Opposition to the late Ministry…the enemies of the Duke of *Argyle*, tho' there could be nothing more improbable, endeavoured to fix this character on His Grace; and to strengthen this surmise, procured a letter under the Pretender's own hand to be addressed to him; the purport of which I will not pretend to know; but they were disappointed in their design, for as soon as his grace received it, he immediately communicated it to His Majesty's ministers'.[92]

According to Walpole, The Duke of Argyll, 'Red John of the Battles' in his old age was suffering from melancholia and confusion to the point where, shortly after this incident, he could barely write his name. In fact his eldest daughter Caroline's marriage to the Earl of Dalkeith had to be postponed because her father could not be prevailed upon to sign the necessary documents. [93]

It would seem that the Duke was afflicted by Parkinson's disease. His biographer, Robert Campbell, states that: 'His Grace had been for many years seized with a paralytic disorder which now increased'.[94] From 1742 onwards he lived the life of a recluse. He died on 3rd September in the following year to be succeeded by his brother, Lord Ilay, who became the 3rd Duke of Argyll.

Meanwhile, in the previous autumn of 1742, London was full of rumours that the King himself was going to Flanders to lead his troops against the French. In doing so he was acting in defiance of the now Tory dominated parliament and of his son Frederick, Prince of Wales. Horace Walpole, writing to his friend Sir Horace Mann, on 15th November told him that:

'Our army is just now ordered to march to Mayence, at the repeated instances of the Queen of Hungary; Lord Stair goes with them, but almost all the officers that are in parliament are come over, for the troops are only to be in garrison till March, when it is said, the King will take the field with them. This step makes a great noise, for the old remains of the Opposition are determined to persist, and have termed this a Hanoverian measure'. [95]

The chief reason for the King's unpopularity in 1742 was because the main purpose of sending British forces to Flanders, was to protect the independence of Hanover. However, public opinion, changed almost overnight in his favour when it was learned that the King, by then a man of almost sixty, was going to the Continent to lead his army himself.

Among the many officers who, despite being Members of Parliament, had volunteered to go abroad on active service, was John Campbell of Mamore, Colonel of the 21st Foot, now in command of three battalions of infantry with the rank of Brigadier. [96]

Chapter 14
Return of Heroes

In May 1743, when the grass had grown long enough for horses to graze, the Pragmatic Army, a combined force of British, Austrian and Hanoverian soldiers, marched from Flanders to Bavaria. There they encamped at Aschaffenburg, around the village of Klein Ostheim, on the north bank of the river Main. A large French Army, commanded by the Duc de Noailles, was entrenched on the south bank of the river.[74]

It was on the 9th June by the old calendar, or on the 19th by the Gregorian Calendar only adopted in Britain in 1752, that His Britannic Majesty, King George II, arrived to join them. With him came his younger and favourite son, William Augustus, Duke of Cumberland, who, together with Lord Stair, was to command the British section of the Pragmatic, or Allied Army of British, Austrian and Hanoverian soldiers under the supreme orders of King George.

The Royal pair, father and son travelled with an enormous equipage. A column of carriages, together with about six hundred horses, blocked the local roads for days. Reaching the town of Mainz, the King halted for a short time to attend the church services and civic functions which precluded the election of a new archbishop.

Then suddenly came news of impending catastrophe. The French had cut the route by the Rhine and Main rivers by which the British army was supplied from Flanders. The soldiers were without proper bread for a week until, on 16th June, [or 27th] the King ordered a retreat.

The route, which he intended his army to follow, was up the north bank of the Main, west towards Hanau and Frankfurt, from where the army could head north into Flanders. Three miles ahead lay Dettingen, a village surrounded by marshland draining into the Main. From there scouts came galloping to report that the French were now in occupation. During the night a contingent, commanded by the Duc de Grammont, had crossed the river by a bridge of boats. They now held the place in strength.

The plan of the Duc de Noailles, was to move part of his army quickly back along the south bank of the Main to cross the river at Aschafenburg before converging upon the Pragmatic Army from behind. De Grammont was meant to hold Dettingen but, in defiance of orders, he surged forward to attack.

Meanwhile the British, Austrian and Hanoverian troops formed into a battle line between the Main river on the left and the Spessart hills to the right. The manoeuvre was still in progress when the French appeared marching towards Aschaffenburg on the opposite bank. At sight of this the British and Austrian Foot Guards were dispatched back to confront them.

Hardly had this happened before, from across the river, the French guns opened fire. Then, almost instantaneously, contrary it would seem to the orders of their commander, the French cavalry made a wild, undisciplined charge out of Dettingen.

The infantry, equally disorganised, followed hard on their heels to be repulsed by the Pragmatic foot soldiers who drove them back towards the village. There, as the panic-stricken French tried to recross the river, one of the bridge of boats collapsed and many of them were drowned.

The Pragmatic Army was victorious, largely through the incompetence of their foes. The Duc de Noailles told Louis XV that the allied infantry 'were so superior to ours that they cannot be compared'.[97]

Indeed it was the foot soldiers, the three battalions commanded by Major-General John Campbell amongst them, who won the day, standing firm as their enemies advanced. The horses of the Blues and the King's Horse, terrified by the gunfire actually charged through the ranks of the Royal Scots Fusiliers who nonetheless held their ground. Amongst the young officers was John Forbes, son of Duncan Forbes of Culloden, who fought bravely throughout the campaign. [98]

More famously it was another Scotsman, Lieutenant-Colonel Sir Andrew Agnew of Lochnaw, in command of General Campbell's former regiment, the Royal Scots Fusiliers, who told his men not to fire before they could 'see the whites of their een'. The same man, renowned for his dry wit, was ready with a reply when the King, after the battle, rebuked him for letting a French cavalry charge break into his Regiment's square: 'An' it please Your majesty they did'na gang oot again!'

King George had his fair share of adventure. His grey stallion, maddened, by the thunder of the guns, bolted towards the enemy. Fortunately, a foot soldier grabbed its reins just before it carried its rider into the French lines.

Frederick the Great, a brave man himself, who admired the English King, in his 'Histoire de mon Temps' describes how 'The King then dismounted and fought on foot, at the head of his Hanoverian battalions. A large figure, conspicuous in his red coat emblazoned with decorations, a cocked hat on his wig, with his sword drawn and his body placed in the attitude of a fencing-master, about to make a lunge in carte, he continued to expose himself, without circling, to the enemy's fire'.[99]

Despite the importance of his victory King George failed to pursue the enemy to consolidate his triumph. His generals were quarrelling. There was no fixed plan of campaign; even the arrival of reinforcements in the form of an Austrian army commanded by Prince Charles of Lorraine, did not inspire him to action. Four months later, in October, when the Pragmatic Army returned to the Netherlands, the French General de Noailles told King Louis XV that 'we are heavily indebted to the irresolutions of George II'.[100]

Nonetheless, despite his failure to exploit his victory, the King returned to England amidst most glorious acclaim. Church bells rang. Celebratory dinners were held in inns throughout the country and Handel composed his Dettingen Te Deum, which was played in a special service of thanksgiving in the Chapel Royal. More significantly, the public who had so recently derided him, now saw him as their hero king. The real victory of Dettingen was that of the German born monarch over the hearts of his subjects.

Horace Walpole was ecstatic. Seizing his pen at noon, on 29th July, he conveyed his excitement to Sir Horace Mann, the British Resident in Florence.

'I don't know what I write – I am all a flurry of thoughts – a battle – a victory! This instant my lord has had a messenger from the Duke of Newcastle, who has sent him a copy of Lord Carteret's letter from the field of battle. The King was in all the heat of the fire – and safe – the Duke is wounded in the calf of the leg, but slightly; [Cumberland's injury in fact was to trouble him for the rest of his life]…The French passed the Mayne [sic] that morning with twenty-five thousand men, and are driven back. We have lost two thousand and they four – several of their general officers, and of the Maison du Roi, are taken prisoners. The battle lasted from ten in the morning till four…I don't know what our numbers were; I believe about thirty thousand, for there were twelve thousand Hessians and Hanoverians who had not joined them. O! in my hurry, I forgot the place you must talk of – the battle of Dettingen!'[101]

Chapter 15
'Follow Me Gentlemen'
The War in Scotland Begins

On 9th January 1744 a young man rose in darkness from his bed in Rome saying that he was going hunting. He rode off through drifting snow to Massa, in Tuscany. From there he headed north to France.

On 11th January 1744 Sir Horace Man, writing from Florence to the Duke of Newcastle, told him of his meeting with Prince Charles Edward, son of the exiled James III and VIII. He described the prince as 'above the middle height and very thin'. His face was long and his complexion clear but rather pale, the forehead very broad, the eyes fairly large, blue,[2] but without sparkle, the mouth large with the lips slightly curled; and the chin more sharp than rounded'.

From Paris Prince Charles wrote to his father telling him that Marshal Saxe would shortly invade England and that he would be going with him, determined, at whatever risk, to somehow win back his throne.

Preparations for an invasion of England were in fact under way. Admiral Roquefeuille, in command of the French fleet, mistaken in his belief that the British navy was congregated in Portsmouth, ordered Marshal Saxe with his land forces, accompanied by Prince Charles, to set sail from Dunkirk. Accordingly, seven thousand French troops embarked on the waiting transports.

In the meantime, Admiral Roquefeuille, sailing up the English Channel, had almost collided with the English fleet. At sight of it, realising his ships to be greatly outnumbered, he had headed for the French coast only to find that most of his ships had been put out of action by a ferocious following gale. The wind swept into Dunkirk harbour. Some of the transports sank. Others were driven onshore. Most of those, which had already put to sea, were lost with all hands-on board.

The vessel carrying Marshal Saxe and Prince Charles, however, managed to return safely to Dunkirk. They landed amidst despondency; the Jacobites believing that the near destruction of the French navy must put an end to all hopes for the invasion of England and the restoration of King James III. Only the Prince remained buoyant. With the optimism born of boundless energy he swore he would try again.

In Scotland the Lord President Forbes received a letter from the Marquis of Tweeddale telling him that a squadron of twenty ships, with an estimated 15,000 musketeers on board, had sailed from Brest on 26th January and were heading towards the north. Forbes refused to panic. Replying to Tweeddale, he told him that, while he considered the estimate of the number of soldiers to be exaggerated, he thought that, in any case, it was highly unlikely that a Jacobite rising in the Highlands would be contemplated at that time of year. In conclusion he could not resist pointing out that he had warned General Clayton a year ago, that by moving the Highland regiment to England, he was placing Scotland in jeopardy.

Following the defeat of the naval expedition, which he commanded, to restore the Jacobite king in Britain, Marshal Saxe took command of the French army in Flanders. In 1745, the red-haired and blue eyed French general, so famous for his charm, laid siege to Tournai, the medieval city in the southwest of Flanders on the west bank of the Scheldt.

On King George's return to England his son, William Duke of Cumberland, although only twenty-four, had succeeded him as Commander-in-Chief of the Pragmatic Army. He now deployed his entire force, numbering about 50,000 men, to the relief of the Dutch garrison in Tournai.

Marshal Saxe divided his larger army, estimated at 56,000, between three fortified positions to the east of the Sheldt. Two in the villages of St Antoine and Fontenoy were at the top of a hill. The third, concealed by trees at the edge of a wood, was called the Redoute D'eu.

The Pragmatic army under Cumberland advanced through burnt out villages to the foot of the hill. The English cavalry then attempted to attack the French positions above them but were driven back with great losses from lethal cannon fire.

The army then encamped, but next morning, the infantry attempted an advance. Once again, the cannons belched out a hail of death. Through the smoke and in the confusion John Campbell, now a Major-General, saw men in the dark green tartan of the Black Watch fall amongst the red coats of the other regiments of the line. To the left they could see the flash of the guns at Fontenoy. Then to the right, the well-hidden batteries of the Redoute D'eu joined in the devilish destruction.

Still the column of infantry, with death defying bravery pushed on. Amazingly the men reached the top of the hill before, with eyes filled with sweat and dazed by sheer exhaustion, they saw the whole might of the French army before them on flat ground lying ahead. Thousands of infantry and cavalry surged forward in waves of annihilation. They fought on in a desperate conflict until, as fresh regiments of Irish mercenaries, fighting for the French, appeared they were finally overwhelmed.

Those who survived retreated, stumbling with exhaustion, some supporting the wounded, down the blood-soaked slope of the hill. Mercifully Marshal Saxe did not pursue the defeated Pragmatic army but later, that year, he captured other Flemish cities including Tournais and Ghent.

Meanwhile, across the Channel in England people lived in dread of invasion. At the end of June, Duncan Forbes, then in London for the sitting of Parliament, received a letter from MacLeod of MacLeod, chief of his clan in Skye, and a loyal supporter of the crown. MacLeod wrote with some anxiety,

'I cannot help informing you of an extraordinary rumour spread hereabouts…which is that the Pretender's eldest son was to land somewhere in the Highlands in order to raise the Highlanders for Rebellion…I shall spare no pains to be better informed and if it's worthwhile, run you an express'.[102]

On 2nd July Forbes told Lieutenant-General Sir John Cope, now Commander-in-Chief of the few forces remaining in Scotland, of the warning he had received. Cope immediately passed it on to Tweeddale, but by the 16th MacLeod, after extensive inquiry, was still unable to verify the warning he had received.

There was much rejoicing in England when news came that in May, a New England colonial force supported by the British navy, had taken Louisbourg, capital of the French province of Ile-Royale, as it then was known, and renamed thereafter Cape Breton.

On 26th July Horace Walpole told Sir Horace Mann that,

'The French make no secret of their intending to come hither...their Mediterranean fleet is come to Rochfort, and they have another at Brest. Their immediate design is to attack our army, the very lessening which will be a victory for them. Our six hundred men, which have lain cooped up in the river till they had contracted diseases, are at last gone to Ostend. Of all this our notable ministry still make a secret: one cannot learn the least particulars from them. This anxiety for my friends in the army, this uncertainty about ourselves, if it can be called uncertain that we are undone, and the provoking folly that one sees prevail, have determined me to go to the Hague. I shall at least hear sooner from the army and shall there know better what is likely to happen here. The moment the crisis is come I shall return hither, which I can do from Helvoetskuys in twelve hours.

You may judge of our situation by the conversation of Marshal Bellisle; (taken prisoner by the English while going from Cassel to Berlin through Hanover) he has said for some time, that he saw we were so little capable of making any defence that he would engage, with five thousand scullions of the French army, to conquer England – yet just now they choose to release him! He goes away in a week. When he was told of the taking of Cape Breton, he said, "He could believe that because the ministry had no hand in it." We are making bonfires for Cape Breton, and thundering over Genoa, while our army in Flanders is running away and dropping to pieces by detachments taken prisoners every day; while the King is at Hanover, the regency at their country seats, not five thousand men in the island, and not above fourteen or fifteen ships at home! Allehujah!'[103]

But the crisis did not occur – at least not in the way of the large invasion expected by the hour. Neither did Walpole find it necessary to go to Helvoetsloys; his attention was diverted elsewhere.

On 16th July, ten days before his letter to Sir Horace Mann was written, Prince Charles, together with only six companions, had set sail on the French ship *Du Teilley* from the Island of Belleisle off the estuary of the Loire. Wearing the black clothes of a student of the Scots College in Paris, he had let his beard grow to complete his disguise.

On 23rd July he had landed on the west coast of the little island of Eriskay that lies between Barra and South Uist. There, walking up and down the beach, fidgeting with impatience as he waited for MacDonald of Boisdale to sail over to meet him from South Uist, he famously scattered the seeds of the pink convolvulus from his pocket, which took root in the sandy soil.

Later Horace Walpole was to write, giving the date inaccurately,

'The Pretender has landed with a few followers in the Highlands of Scotland, on the 25th of July. His appearance at this time is thus described by Mr Eneas MacDonald, one of his attendants.

There entered the tent a tall youth, of a most agreeable aspect, in a plain black coat, with a plain shirt not very clean, and a cambric stock, fixed with a plain silver buckle, a plain hat with a canvas string, having one end fixed to one of his coat buttons, he had black stockings and brass buckles in his shoes. At his first appearance I found my heart swell to my very throat, but we were immediately told that this youth was an English clergyman, who had long been possessed with a desire to see and converse with Highlanders'.[104]

Alexander MacDonald of Boisdale begged him to sail back to France. No one in Scotland would join him. He was only courting disaster. Charles, however, was adamant. He had set foot in the country of which he was born to be King. On the night of the 24th he left Eriskay to head for the mainland. The next day the *Du Teillay* dropped anchor in Loch-nan-Uamh, the sea loch which runs into the Sound of Arisaig between South Morar and Moidart.

The news of his arrival was sent by Mr Lauchlan Campbell, the Presbyterian minister of Ardnamurchan, to Campbell of Auchindoun, the Duke of Argyll's factor in Ardnamurchan, who was then at Mingary Castle where he was busily recruiting men for the Earl of Loudoun's Highland Regiment of Foot, of which General Campbell's son Jack had recently taken command. Auchindoun at once wrote a letter, which he dispatched with a messenger over to Mull to Donald Campbell of Airds, the Duke's factor in Morvern, known to have been on the island at the time. Airds hastily sent another missive to Archibald Campbell of Stonefield, the Sheriff-depute of Argyll, which was taken from Mull by a messenger who, landing most probably on Kerrera, would then have crossed by ferry to the mainland to follow the old drove road which crossed Loch Awe by another ferry to Portsonachan, this being the shortest route. From Loch Awe he galloped on to Inveraray, crossing the hill to the south. There he found the Sheriff-Depute, Campbell of Stonefield, who at once sent it on to Andrew Fletcher, Lord Milton, the Lord Justice Clerk, whom he knew to be at the Duke's house of Rosneath.

Once again the fastest way to travel was on horseback to Lochgoilhead and thence by boat to the Gare Loch to land on the southeast shore, where he found, not only Lord Milton, but the Duke and his young cousin Colonel Jack. Duke Archibald, unlike his brother 'Red John' who had been a man of action, ever a soldier at heart, was an academic, and bibliomaniac, obsessed by a passion for planting, development and design. Nonetheless, he reacted to the emergency with promptitude while Lord Loudoun, already informed by Lord Milton of the rumour that the Prince had landed, ordered Colonel Jack 'to assemble all the men that were raised in the west Highlands and to send them directly to Stirling'.[105]

On 1st August a proclamation was issued offering a reward of £30,000, an astronomical sum for those days, for the capture of the young prince.

Two days later Macleod of Macleod. From his castle of Dunvegan in Skye, wrote to the Lord President Forbes telling him that the Prince had indeed landed, reputedly with one ship, manned with sixteen or eighteen guns and with about thirty Irish or French officers on board. Forbes did not receive the letter until the 9th, just a day after he had himself written to Tweeddale to tell him that by now he had decided that rumours of the Prince's landing were, in his opinion, totally untrue. On receipt of MacLeod's letter, Forbes hurried to find Cope who was just about to head north.

To Tweeddale he reported that none of the Highland gentlemen, who had anything to lose, would be likely to rise for the Prince unless substantial foreign aid was forthcoming. He pointed out that, whereas in 1715, those loyal to the Government had been well supplied with arms, now, thanks to the Act of Disarmament which had followed that rebellion, there were none except those hidden unlawfully under the thatch. Most importantly he reminded the Secretary of

State that men like his own brother who, in the previous emergency had lent money to the State, had never been repaid.

'What I therefore submit is whether it may not be fit at this juncture to lodge with some proper person, or persons, money or credit sufficient for such occasions to be accounted for'.[106]

In writing this Forbes perhaps foresaw that unless a substantial sum of Government money was released to fund an emergency, he would be forced to arm his tenants at his own expense. Comparatively well off at that time, having succeeded to the estate of Culloden on his brother's death, he was to lose most of what he possessed in pledges that were never redeemed.

Forbes sailed back to Scotland, and after landing at Leith, reached his own home of Culloden near Inverness on 13th August. On the next day Cope, by now in Edinburgh, sent instructions to the officers of Lord Loudoun's Regiment in the north. Referring first to Forbes's record in 1715, when he had showed himself conspicuously loyal to the Government, he wrote that,

He] thought proper to put that part of the Earl of Loudoun's Regiment in the north of Scotland under his command; whose directions you are to follow'.[107]

On the same day, from Culloden House, Forbes wrote to the Highland chiefs in his area urging them to stand by the Government so that rebels would realise that they had little or no hopes of success. He wrote with the wisdom of hindsight having witnessed the misery and loss of possessions suffered by those who had joined the Rising, raised by the Earl of Mar for the Princes' father in 1715.

Most distressing of all to him was the news that Cameron of Lochiel, the 'gentle laird', had pledged himself to Prince Charles. Writing to Cope, to tell him this, he mentioned that, on that very day Lord Lovat, who had been to dine with him, had sworn that 'no hardship, or ill-usage that I meet with, can alter or diminish my zeal and attachment for His Majesty's person and Government'.[108]

Forbes, from experience, treated this sworn affiliation with the scepticism it deserved. Within a month Lovat was writing to Loch Eil, an epistle illuminating the character of the man, known by his contemporaries, to be as 'slippery as an eel'.

'I fear you have been over rash in going out ere affairs were ripe. You are in a dangerous state. The Elector's General Cope, is in your rear, hanging at your tail with 3,000 men, such as have not been seen here since Dundee's affair, and we have no force to meet him. If the MacPhersons would take the field, I would bring out my lads to help the work; and 'twixt the twa, we might cause Cope to keep his Xmas here; bot only Cluny is earnest in the cause, and my Lord Advocate [Duncan Forbes] plays at cat and mouse with me. But times may change, and I may bring him to St Johnstone's tippet [the gallows rope]. Meantime look to yourself...I'll aid you what I can, but my prayers are all I can give at present. My service to the Prince; but I wish he had not come here so empty-handed; siller will go far in the Highlands. I send this by Ewan Fraser, whom I have charge to give it to yourself, for were Duncan to find it, it would be my head to an onion,

Farewell
Your faithful friend
Lovat'.[109]

Lovat's letter is interesting, not only as a revelation of the character of this extraordinarily devious man, but as an illustration of the dilemma in which, due to their conflicting loyalties, so many leaders in the Highlands now found themselves placed. Forbes had in fact offered him the command of one of the new companies, which he had been commissioned to raise, but Lovat, prevaricating as usual, had so far failed to reply.

Cluny MacPherson's position was in fact more traumatic than most, for he actually held a Captain's commission in the Earl of Loudoun's Regiment. On 19th August he wrote to Forbes, telling him that the advancing army of the Jacobites, who [on 16th August] had just defeated two companies of Government troops on the march between Fort Augustus and Fort William, were approaching his land where 'they would burn and slay'.[110]

'If the Government does not forthwith protect us, they must either be burnt or join…What to do, to save this poor country from immediate ruin, is a very great question to me…I leave your Lordship to judge, as force has often made people commit that which was no choice'.[111]

As things turned out Cluny, having taken offence at what he saw as Cope's dismissive attitude when he asked leave to call up his men to fight for the Government, was then taken prisoner in his own house by the Jacobite army. Held prisoner for over a month he decided, in the words he had written to Forbes, to 'commit that which was no choice', by joining forces with his captors. Forbes, pleading for him later, said that 'partly by persuasion, partly by violence, [he was] prevailed with the greatest of his kindred, to the number of about 300, to go along with him to the Highland Camp, which they reached before the rebels left Edinburgh'.[112]

That the government was alarmed in London but that action was hindered by the procrastination of Lord Stair is proved by Walpole's affirmation that,

'The regency are all come to town to prevent an invasion – I should as soon think them able to make one – not but old Stair, who still exists upon the embers of an absurd fire that warmed him ninety years ago, thinks it still practicable to march to Paris, and the other day in council prevented a resolution of sending for our army home…they seem determined to send for ten thousand – the other ten will remain in Flanders, to keep up the bad figure that we have been making there all this summer…

There is a proclamation come out for apprehending the Pretender's son; he was undoubtedly on board the frigate attendant on the Elizabeth, with which Captain Brett fought so bravely; the boy is now said to be at Brest'.[113]

Walpole proceeded to tell Horace Mann that he had put off his journey to The Hague 'as the sea is full of ships, and many French ones about the siege of Ostend. I go tomorrow to Mount Edgecombe (in Cornwall.)'

Little did he know, as he wrote from his house in Arlington Street, in the heart of London, that the Prince, with a price of £30,000 on his head, far from being safely in France, was actually on Scottish soil.

On 19th August Prince Charles raised his standard at Glenfinnan in Inverness-shire. He was joined by Cameron of Lochiel with a force of about 700 and MacDonald of Keppoch with approximately 350 men. On 22nd August he moved from Glenfinnan to Kinlochiel where he wrote a great many letters, to those he believed to be supporters in Scotland, asking them for money and for arms. Also from there, he sent 150 stands of arms, each comprising a gun and a bayonet and a broad sword with a brass handle like a small sword, to the Stewarts of Appin and the MacDonalds of Glencoe, who were waiting in Duror to join him when he reached Lochaber.[114]

The Stewarts of Appin found him at Invergarry. Their chief had refused to declare for the Prince but his kinsman, Charles Stewart of Ardsheal, a giant of a man riding a white stallion big enough to bear his weight, brought 260 Appin Stewarts to augment his force. So also, to this rendezvous came further parties of MacDonalds from Knoydart and Morar.

It was at this juncture that Frazer of Gortleg, an envoy of Lord Lovat appeared. He came with a message from Lovat, who, firstly having apologised for his men being unready to rise, requested commissions for a dukedom and for the Lord-Lieutenancy of Inverness for himself. Most importantly he asked for a warrant to murder his so-called friend and neighbour, whom he nicknamed his 'dear General', Lord President Forbes.

The enormity of these demands was extraordinary. Nonetheless, the Prince, aware of Lovat's influence in the north, made him a Lieutenant-General while sending him a warrant specifically for the arrest, but not the assassination, of Lord President Forbes.

Leaving Invergarry the Jacobite army crossed the Corryarrack Pass on the south side of Loch Ness and marched onwards into Atholl. The Prince stayed several days at Blair Castle, where he approved of some recent restoration and tasted pineapples, apparently for the first time in his life.

On 29th August General Cope arrived in Inverness. Forbes, although much relieved that the capital of the north was now held by regular soldiers, was none the less aware that the way lay open for the rebel force heading for the south. On 5th September, Tweedale's undersecretary, Andrew Mitchel, sent Forbes the welcome news that twenty independent companies were to be raised in the Highlands of which Forbes was to name the officers. The subsistence and pay of the new companies was to be provided by the Paymaster-General of the army in London. On the same day came word that a large contingent of the rebel army, reputedly 1,800 men, had passed Blair Atholl heading for Edinburgh, news which prompted the Government, now in a state of near panic, to order ten battalions of the British army from Flanders.

In fact, on 4th September, Prince Charles had already captured Perth, where, joined by William Duke of Atholl and his brother Lord George Murray amongst others, his army almost doubled its size. From there it was but twenty-four miles to Edinburgh where he took the city, although not the Castle, where the garrison defied him.

On 21st September, he faced the Hanoverian army commanded by General Cope, who had marched down the coast route from Inverness, at Prestonpans. Here, once again, Charles's personal courage and charisma inspired his men, 'The Prince' wrote Lord Mahon 'put himself at the head of the second line, which was close behind the first, and addressed them in these words. "Follow me, gentlemen, and by the blessing of God, I will this day make you a free and happy people."'[115]

By this time there was terror in London as it became plain, that what had been thought to be a minor insurrection in the distant Highlands of Scotland, was in fact a full-scale invasion threatening the country as a whole. 'They are not such raw ragamuffins as they were represented'. wrote Walpole, in trepidation, to Sir Horace Mann.

Returning from his visit to Cornwall, he apologised for not answering his letters because he had been 'so constantly upon the road, that I neither received your letters, had time to write, or knew what to write…

The confusion I have found, and the danger we are in, prevent my talking of anything else. The young Pretender at the head of three thousand men has got a march on General Cope, who is not eighteen hundred strong, and when the last accounts came away, was fifty miles nearer Edinburgh than Cope, and by this time is there. The clans will not rise for the Government and the Dukes of Argyll and Atholl, are come post to town, not having been able to raise a man. The young Duke of Gordon sent for his uncle and told him that he must raise his clan…The Duke flew in a passion; his uncle pulled out a pistol and told him it was in vain to dispute. Lord Loudon, Lord Fortrose and Lord Panmure, have been very zealous, and have raised some men; but I look upon Scotland as gone! I think of what King William said to the Duke of Hamilton, when he was extolling Scotland: "My Lord, I only wish it was a hundred miles off, and that you was king of it!"'

There are two manifestos published signed Charles Prince Regent for his father, King of Scotland, England, France and Ireland. By one he promises to preserve everybody in their just rights; and orders to all persons who have public moneys in their hands to bring it to him; and by the other he dissolves the union between England and Scotland. But all this is not the worst! Notice came yesterday, that there are ten thousand men, thirty transports, and ten men-of-war at Dunkirk. Against this force we have – I don't know what – scarce fears! Three thousand Dutch we hope are by this time landed in Scotland, three more are coming hither. We have sent for ten regiments from Flanders, which may be here in a week, and we have fifteen men-of-war in the Downs'.[116]

'One really don't know what to write to you the accounts from Scotland vary perpetually, and at best are never certain. I was just going to tell you that the rebels are in England; but my Uncle [has] at this moment come in, and says, that an express came last night with an account of their being in Edinburgh to the number of five thousand. But this capital is an open town, and the castle impregnable and in our possession. There never was such an extraordinary a sort of rebellion…never was so desperate an enterprise'.

Rumour, magnified by the distance from the scene of action, made people nearly incoherent with terror. On 27th September, on news of Cope's defeat at Prestonpans, Walpole wrote again.

'I can't doubt but the joy of the Jacobites has reached Florence before this letter' he began 'Cope lay in face of the rebels all Friday; he scarce two thousand strong, they vastly superior though we don't know their numbers. The military people say that he should have attacked them. However, we are sadly convinced that they are not such raw ragamuffins as they were represented. The rotation that has been established in that country, to give all the Highlanders the benefit of serving in the independent companies, has trained and disciplined them…Our dragoons most shamefully fled without striking a blow, and are with Cope who escaped in a boat to Berwick…We have lost all our artillery, five hundred men taken and three killed and several officers as you will see in the papers. This defeat has frightened everybody but those it rejoices, and those it should frighten most, but my Lord Granville still buoys up the King's spirits, and persuades him it is nothing…Marshal Wade is marching against the rebels; but the King will not let him take above eight thousand men; so that if they come into England, another battle, with no advantage on our side, may determine our fate…I don't believe what I have been told this morning , that more troops are sent from Flanders, and aid asked of Denmark'.[117]

The first part of the rumour was entirely true. Nine thousand Dutch and English troops were being sent to Scotland at once under Marshal Wade. Lord Loudoun was coming to Inverness to take command of the army in the north and the Marquis of Tweedale, the Secretary of State, ordered the rather extraordinary sum of £4,290 6s and 3d to be sent for the subsistence of the twenty independent companies which Forbes had been commissioned to raise.

How close Prince Charles was to victory at a time when, with nearly all the army in Flanders, England was left open to invasion, is shown by a letter from Mr Henry Fox, to Sir. C.H. Williams, written on 5th September, in which he tells him 'England, Wade says, and I believe it, is for the first comer; and if you can tell whether the six thousand Dutch, and the ten battalions of English, or five thousand French or Spaniards will be here first, you know our fate. The French are not come, God be thanked! But had five thousand landed in any part of this island a week ago, I verily believe the entire conquest would not have cost them a battle'.[118]

There was sudden panic in England. In another letter, this time to his regular correspondent Sir Horace Mann, dated 4th October 1745, Walpole says,

'The good people of England have at last rubbed their eyes and looked about them. A wonderful spirit is arisen in all counties, and among all sorts of people. The nobility are raising regiments, and everybody else is being raised. Dr Herring, the Archbishop of York has set an example that would rouse the most indifferent, in two days after the arrival of the news of Cope's defeat, and when they at every moment expected the victorious rebels at their gates, the bishop made a speech to the assembled county, that had as much true spirit, honesty, and bravery in it, as ever was promoted by an historian for an ancient hero'.

Just as men of influence in England were raising regiments to fight the Jacobites, a weary, dust covered dispatch rider, his horse shining with sweat was crossing the flat Flanders land. He was heading for the small town of Vilmorden, a few miles north of Brussels, to which place Cumberland had withdrawn following the capture of Ghent by the French.

Coming in sight of buildings, drawn by the sound of English and Scottish voices, the messenger soon found himself surrounded by red-coated soldiers, busy about their business, in the British army camp. Delighted to see a stranger, bringing as they hoped news from home, there were many who offered directions as to where the headquarters of the commanding officers could be found.

It was only on receiving a report drawn from the carrier's saddlebag, that Major-General John Campbell, in command of his regiment, suddenly realised, that with the greater part of the British army being sent abroad Britain itself now lay open to a cleverly planned attack. The Jacobite Rising in Scotland, at first dismissed by Tweedale, as 'a lot of fuss about nothing' was in fact an imminent, ever increasing, danger. Scotland had been left defenceless, bereft not only of soldiers but of any competent commander. There was not a single general in the Highlands of Scotland under the age of seventy.

Urgently, the General begged his commander-in-chief, to allow him to return to Scotland. The Duke gave his assent and John Campbell wrote to Lord Harrington, Secretary of State for the Northern Department, asking for endorsement of the order.

Harrington, on 20th September replied favourably,

'His Majesty was pleased to express a very particular satisfaction in your zeal for his service; and has ordered Mr Pelham [Carteret's successor as First Minister]

to endeavour to manage the matter with the Duke of Argyll...the King approving entirely himself, that you should be employed upon that commission'.[119]

Chapter 16
Raiders in the Night

Meanwhile in Argyll there was much alarm. In a letter headed *Intelligence from Argyllshire,* dated September 1745, Archibald Campbell of Stonefield, Sheriff-Depute of the county, said that he had heard from a reliable source that a number of Jacobites, who had assembled in Kilmichael Glassary, were waiting to be joined by armed men from Mull before declaring for Prince Charles. The people there did not want to rise but 'dare not refuse, being overawed by Sir James Campbell of Auchinbrake and his creatures'[120] who ordered them to gather at Castle Lachlan on the east coast of Loch Fyne. This was the fortress of the chief of Clan Lachlan, another staunch Jacobite, who had already recruited men in Ireland to fight for the Prince.

It was disturbing news. Campbell of Auchinbreck was an eccentric elderly man, who, although born of Presbyterian parents,[3] had converted to Catholicism and become a Jacobite. With land stretching from the Sound of Jura to Loch Fyne, he could call many men to arms. Nonetheless, as Stonefield reported, Colonel Jack Campbell by sending 'a party of 40 men under the pretence of recruiting there' had the situation under control. Also, as a further safeguard, the young colonel intended to 'seize all the boats upon the lake [Loch Fyne] to hinder their assembling or march towards Edinburgh'.[121]

Jack Campbell, remembered even today as 'Colonel Jack of the Forty-Five', the eldest son of General John Campbell of Mamore, was the same age as his father had been, when as A.D.C to the second duke, he had fought in the Rising of 1715. Now twenty-two and a soldier by profession, he was also Member of Parliament for the Glasgow Burghs.

'The Earl of Loudoun has written to Colonel Campbell that he was going to Inverness to take upon him the command of 8 companies of Guise's Regimt. 2 of Lord John Murrays, and 20 companies raised or to be raised out of the well affected clans and Lord Loudoun proposes that the three companies at Inveraray should join him as soon as possible, which the gentlemen in Argyllshire remonstrate strongly against because there are 600 or 700 of the rebels, come back to reside in the country which these companies must pass through, and if these companies are taken away, the disaffected in Argyllshire would have nothing to overawe them, besides that these companies have hitherto no arms, but a few that had been left in the Castle of Inveraray ever since it was besieged in the year 1715, and these out of repair.

Colonel Campbell has applied to one of the captains of the vessels stationed upon the coasts to come up Lochfyne and visit the Castle of McLauchlin which is the resort of the disaffected people of the shire, and where they keep a constant guard'.[122]

The fears of the Sheriff-Depute were soon realised when, in the first week of November, Gregor MacGregor of Glengyle, a nephew of Rob Roy, a man commonly known as Gregor Ghlun Dubh, because of a black birthmark on his knee, advanced with a party of his men into Cowal. He intended to head for Castle Lachlan to join forces with Sir James Campbell of Auchinbreck, but stopped at Lochgoilhead, where, being fond of a dram, he revealed his plans to one Duncan Campbell, who promptly wrote them down and sent them to a friend in Inveraray.

Colonel Jack Campbell informed by the 'friend', wasted no time. Marshaling his three companies of Loudoun's regiment, he sailed across Loch Fyne to land in Cowal. Gregor Ghlun Dubh had let slip that he was heading for Castle Lachlan by the 'head of Glendaruel' and it was hereabouts that Colonel Jack and his men confronted him and sent him packing out of Cowal.

It was only a small incident. Colonel Jack lost just one soldier although two of the MacGregors were killed, fourteen wounded and twenty-one made prisoners. Nonetheless it proved the young Colonel's authority while the hopes of the Jacobites in Argyll were then further destroyed by the arrest of Sir James Campbell of Auchinbreck in his house at Lochgair.

Incriminating papers found in his pockets and elsewhere, proved him to be in league with the insurgents. Further investigation revealed his true duplicity. Not only had he been in correspondence with the Prince's father, the Old Pretender, for many years but, in 1741, he had actually been one of the seven signatories of the document giving surety to Cardinal Fleury that Scotland would rise in support of an invasion. Imprisoned in Dumbarton Castle, he was, however, released eventually on the grounds that he was by then too old and frail to be considered a threat to the government. [123]

Farther north, in Inverness-shire, the Lord President Duncan Forbes narrowly escaped being kidnapped by men trying to kill him. On the 15th October, at three o'clock in the morning, a party of Frasers attacked Culloden House. They were led by James Fraser of Foyers, who carried a warrant, apparently issued by Prince Charles as Regent of Scotland, England, Ireland and the Dominions, signed by the Princes' secretary, Murray of Broughton. The assailants told to capture the Lord President himself and to bring him before the Prince, failed to get into the courtyard and break down either the shutters or the doors of the well-defended house. Frustrated they turned their attention to the fields and drove off sixty of Forbes's own sheep and twenty-nine cattle belonging to his tenants, as well as robbing his gardener and a poor weaver of nearly all they possessed.

Forbes tried to make himself believe that Lovat was not involved.

On 19th October he wrote to him,

'The people loitered at Essich for some hours to taste my mutton in day-light, and by these means were all known; but let them do no more harm, and I freely forgive them...And if they do not send the tenant back his cattle, I must pay for them'. [124]

Replying a week later Lovat merely craved sympathy as the wronged father whose son insisted on joining the rebels. He had, so he claimed, succeeded in rescuing eight of the purloined cattle although the others 'unfortunately' had been slaughtered. He promised, however, that Forbes's lands would not be raided again and that he would compensate both the gardener and the weaver. [125]

Lovat was so plausible that Forbes hated to doubt his word. Others, more realistic, thought otherwise. Norman Macleod of Macleod, writing to Forbes from Skye to tell him that 'the Independent Companies were reported to be getting on but slowly owing to the bad weather' added that he hoped he might be spared 'from the treachery of pretended friends or the open attacks of known enemies'.[126]

Murray of Broughton claimed that the attack on Culloden House had failed because no clear order had been given to take Forbes dead or alive. Had this been given, he insisted, Forbes could easily have been killed and his death would have put an end to MacLeod's mustering of the northern clans.

But Forbes remained very much alive! On 24th October he instructed Sir Alexander MacDonald of Sleat and MacLeod of MacLeod to bring their companies to join those then converging upon Inverness. Once there the men would be armed with weapons just arrived on the sloop *Saltash* and, so he assured the commanders, all expenses would be met.

Forbes, now ever more convinced that with such a huge contingent of Government troops coming from abroad, the Jacobite Rising must end in failure and ruination to those who supported it, wrote,

'I in my conscience think that measure will determine several of our neighbours to save themselves'.[127]

However, despite his warnings, his own grandnephew, young Forbes of Pitcalnie, influenced by 'villains who seduced him' went off to join the rebels. Then on top of this came a letter from Lovat still playing the aggrieved father, saying that his own son the Master of Lovat, had also joined Prince Charles. Forbes, at least pretending to believe Lovat's protestations of loyalty, urged him to beg his son to 'forsake the dangerous course', but Lord Loudoun, in no doubt at all over the perfidy of the old chief, told him bluntly, 'You have now pulled off the mask that we can see the mark you aim at'. Describing the strength of the Government army, he advised him to recall his son and his men immediately if they wanted to save themselves and their families from destruction.

He might have saved himself the trouble. Lovat, believing he could get away with it, continued, despite these warnings, to play a double game.

By the middle of November, when the north of Scotland, lying deep in snow, was enduring one of the worst frosts on record, MacLeod of MacLeod, with four hundred men, was billeted in Inverness. Forbes hoped fervently that their presence there would deter the Frasers from marching south. He and Loudoun between them had a force of seven hundred Highland men in Inverness and more recruits were coming in. However, at the beginning of December the Master of Lovat marched off to join Prince Charles, as his father, still pretending to be a Loyalist, informed Forbes.

Loudoun, on hearing this news, marched off over the ice-packed ground to relieve Fort Augustus then held for the Prince by the Frasers. Meeting no opposition, however, he returned to Inverness to be met with the news that the Jacobite army having reached Derby, were now retreating back to Scotland.

Lord Loudoun then persuaded Lovat to live under house imprisonment in Inverness until he should bring in all the arms of which the Jacobite clans were possessed. Lovat agreed to do this, protesting that he could not control his son who by this time had reached as far as Perth. As there was no concrete evidence linking Lovat to his son's defection, Loudoun gave him the benefit of the doubt but, as time went by and arms failed to be surrendered, he put sentries on the gate of his house until he could be held, with greater security, in the castle.

This seemed a sensible precaution. Lovat was deemed too old and corpulent – his body was swollen with dropsy – to be capable of trying to escape. Nonetheless his attendants discovered a back entrance and carried him, on their shoulders, out of the house and the town from where he somehow got back to his own district of Morar on the northwest coast.

On 23rd November MacLeod was defeated at Inverurie by Lord Lewis Gordon, fighting with some of the troops Lord John Drummond had brought from France. Gordon, son of the Marquess of Huntly, then held all the country from Aberdeen to the Spey for Prince Charles, while MacLeod, driven back to Elgin, was deserted by many of his men. The situation in the north was thus so precarious that the result of the Rising might still go either way. All now depended on the efficacy of the Government force.

Chapter 17
The General Takes Command

By 15th October Major-General Campbell had arrived in London to be summoned almost immediately to an audience with the king, who, prevented only by his ministers from returning to the battlefield in Flanders, was desperate to hear every detail of the recent campaign. He received General Campbell in his closet, where the two old soldiers, whose acquaintance now spanned over quarter of a century, could talk privately as friends.

It was largely on John Campbell's insistence that the King authorised his cousin, Archibald, Duke of Argyll, to seize the boats and the castles of the rebels, to gain all intelligence that was possible and 'above all things to have in view the restoring of peace in our kingdom by the immediate reducing the rebels by force of arms'.[128]

General Campbell himself was forthwith directed,

'To go to the West Highlands by way of Liverpool, and to raise eight independent companies of 100 men each with proper officers; and likewise to arm 16 such companies more without the charge of commissioned officers who are to serve without pay, to be raised from the Duke of Argyll's and Earl of Breadalbin's countreys for His Majesty's service'.

The total cost of supplying these companies for a period of three months was reckoned to be £4,859 18s.,but such was the sense of urgency that the Duke of Newcastle, in charge of the Treasury, agreed to an unlimited credit for the public service during the state of emergency.[129]

On 5th November General Campbell wrote to his son.

My dear Jack,

I write to you by Mr Neil Campbell [a son of the Principal of Glasgow University, who was clerk to the survey at Woolwich][130] who went from here early Yesterday morning for Liverpool, to take upon him the charge of 500 arms, and ammunition in proportion which I hope will be there by Wednesday morning ready to be embarked. I shall follow very soon with upwards of three thousand stand of arms, and money to pay such men as can be raised from the Duke of Argyll's lands or from those of the Earl of Braidalbanes.[131]...The Lord Glenorchy ought to be informed of the steps I have taken towards joining his interest to that of the Duke of Argyll's by which means a considerable number of men may be enlisted for the eight Independent Companies before my arrival...You will observe that the private men are to be regularly allotted to serve for one year or till such time as an end is put to this unnatural Rebellion...I desire you will like an officer take care to have good intelligence by employing such as can inform you of which the Lord Glenorchy and the Sheriff must be the best judges. Spare no reasonable expense for this material service'[132]

On 23rd November General Campbell wrote to Captain John Fergussone, Captain of H.M.S *Greyhound,* telling him that,

'My present orders to you is, that without loss of time, you proceed to Spithead. I shall set out on Monday, so as to be at Portsmouth on Tuesday. Admiral Stewart will assist me in getting to your ship, and by this means I may be advised as soon as the Greyhound appears'.[133]

Captain Fergussone, aboard the *Sovereign,* the flagship of Commodore Smith, then lying at the Nore, replied the next day. He firstly prevaricated against the shipment of arms for the newly raised forces in Scotland being sent via Liverpool to the Clyde.

'Having advised with some gentlemen that perfectly know the Country, [they] are of opinion that it will be the safest and most expeditious way to send them directly by sea to Borowstonness [Bo'ness] which is not above 22 miles from Glasgow by exceeding fine road…I shall be ready to receive you on Thursday nixt, the Commodore is of the same opinion with me, that it will be both the safest and best way for you to embark here or at Deal'.[134]

General Campbell left the city of London in a state of general alarm. Prince Charles was known to be approaching at the head of an army of wild Highland men who, would, so it was rumoured, murder and rape every mortal being and pillage everything they found. When news came that the Prince had reached Derby there was panic. Fielding, author of the *True Patriot,* described how.

'When the Highlanders, by a most incredible march, got between the Duke's army and the metropolis, they struck a terror into it scarce to be credited'.

The result was a precipitate rush upon the Bank of England, which reputedly only escaped going bankrupt by dolling out money in sixpences to gain time.[135]

Almost alone amongst his subjects the King was unconcerned. Tales that he was packing his bags to flee to Hanover are totally untrue. Greatly disappointed at not being allowed to return to Flanders he was now longing to confront the Jacobites. Declaring that he 'would put himself at the head of those troops that are assembling on the northern road' he was raring to defy the foe.[136]

But, as it turned out, he was never to have the chance.

Prince Charles arrived at Derby in high spirits, reflecting that he was now within a hundred and thirty miles of the capital. Accordingly, that evening at supper, he studiously directed his conversation to his intended progress and expected triumph – whether it would be best for him to enter London on foot or on horseback, in Highland or in English dress. Far different were the thoughts of his followers, who, early next morning, laid before him their earnest and unanimous opinion for an immediate retreat to Scotland, Charles said, that, rather than go back, he would wish to be buried twenty feet under ground'.[137]

It was on the morning of Thursday 5th December, that Lord George Murray, burst into the Prince's bedroom in Derby to tell him that the general consensus of opinion amongst his commanders was that his army must retreat. The reasons he gave were that with General Wade advancing from Newcastle, the Duke of Cumberland, now overall commander of the Hanoverian army, in Staffordshire to the south, and a third force forming in London to defend the city, his entire army, now only about 4,500 strong, must inevitably perish in the pincer movement that would result.

On 6th December, the day to be called Black Friday, General Campbell, waiting at the Nore to board the warship *Greyhound,* was not to know, any more than did King George, that Prince Charles, although ranting in fury, had succumbed to the demands of his advisors to return the way he had come.

Chapter 18
Militiamen and Spies

On 9 December, Walpole was able to tell Sir Horace Mann of all that had occurred.

'The Duke (Cumberland) from some strange want of intelligence lay last week for four-and-twenty hours under arms at Stone, in Staffordshire, expecting the rebels any moment, while they were marching in all haste to Derby. The news of this threw the town into great consternation, but his Royal Highness repaired his mistake, and got to Northampton between the Highlanders and London. They got nine thousand pounds at Derby…Then they retreated a few miles, but returned again to Derby, and got ten thousand pounds more, plundered the town, and burnt a house of the Countess of Exeter. They are gone again and got back to Leake, in Staffordshire, but miserably harassed, and it is said, have left all their cannon behind them and twenty wagons of sick. The Duke has sent General Hawley with the dragoons to harass them in their retreat, and dispatched Mr Conway to Marshal Wade, to hasten his march upon the back of them. They must either go to North Wales, where they will probably all perish, or to Scotland with great loss. We dread them no more…Though they have marched into the centre of the kingdom, there has not been the least symptom of a rising…excepting one gentleman in Lancashire, one hundred and fifty common men, and two parsons at Manchester, and a physician from York'.[138]

The general had a terrible voyage. The *Greyhound,* having rounded Land's End, met a tempest in the Irish Sea. The ship was so badly damaged that she had to put in to Carrickfergus. Writing to John Maule, secretary of his cousin the Duke of Argyll, he told him,

'We met with a storm at sea on Wednesday evening and all that night which shook the rigging of the *Greyhound* man of war so that it was absolutely necessary to put in here to set her masts upright and repair the small damage that was done and likewise to examine the state and condition of the *Charles* and *Sandwhich* tenders [139]… I am on shore in perfect good health after having got two nights rest which I had not had for three before…There's a report here that the Duke [of Cumberland] has beat the rebels'.[140]

What in fact was happening as the *Greyhound* with the general on board was battling through the Irish Sea was that the Jacobite army, retreating from Derby, was forcing its way through the worst of the winter weather towards the north. 'They must either go to North Wales, where they will probably all perish, or to Scotland with great loss. We dread them no longer' wrote Walpole, on 9th December, to his friend Sir Horace Mann in Florence. [141] Only later was the general to learn the details of that fateful march back to Scotland as described by one who took part. James Johnstone, known as the Chevalier de Johnstone, described how on leaving Derby before daybreak,

'The Highlanders, believing at first they were to march forward to attack the army of the Duke of Cumberland, testified great joy and alacrity; but as soon as the day began to clear in the distance, and that they perceived we were retracing our steps, we heard nothing but howlings, groans and lamentations throughout the whole army to such a degree as though they had suffered a defeat'.

The Prince sulked and quarrelled with Lord George Murray, his commander-in-chief, who later described the change in his character.

'His Royal Highness, in marching forwards, had always been first up in the morning, and had the men in motion before the break of day, and commonly marched himself afoot; but in the retreat he was much longer in leaving his quarters, so that, though the rest of the army were all on their march, the rear could not move till he went, and then he rode straight on, and got to the quarters with the van'.[142]

Prince Charles, despondent as most of his men, reached Macclesfield before continuing to Manchester, where arriving with his army on 20th December he found himself confronted by a hostile mob. Likewise, the people of the countryside, hitherto friendly, now resented the Highlanders, who their discipline relaxed, plundered the farms and villages through which they passed.

Pursued by a detachment of Wade's army commanded by Major-General Oglethorpe, the Jacobites moved on to Wigan, from thence reaching Preston, on 11th December. Continuing to the north, by way of Penrith to Shap Fell, they won a brief victory in a skirmish fought by moonlight at Clifton where forty of the pursuing dragoons were killed. Then with the enemy pursuit briefly halted, on 20th December, the Jacobites managed to reach Carlisle.

Leaving the heroic garrison of the city to their fate, the Highlanders crossed the Border Esk, marching shoulder to shoulder through the flooded river to reach Scotland on the far bank. On 22nd December, Prince Charles was at Drumlanrig Castle, seat of the Duke of Douglas, where he spent the day shooting, bagging two pheasants, two partridges, and a deer, while, at Inveraray Castle in the far west of Scotland, General Campbell, newly arrived, was eagerly waiting for news.

One can picture the General, fuming with impatience at Carrickfergus, as he waited for the ship to be repaired. Immediately she was ready, he went aboard as she sailed into the wind driven Irish Sea. The familiar landmark of Ailsa Craig loomed through clouds to the east. But again, the storm increased, so that the captain, fearing for the masts, put into Campbelltown harbour until it was safe to put back to sea. Then from Kilbrannan Sound the *Greyhound* beat her way through the Kyles of Bute, into Loch Fyne.

At last, on 21st December, General Campbell, thankfully came ashore on the jetty of the old town of Inveraray, near the head of that long inlet from the sea. Landing, he was met with the news that the Jacobite army, having crossed Shap Fell, had reached Penrith. Then of more immediate danger came word that chiefs from the Highlands and the Isles were bringing large numbers of men to reinforce the Rebel army at Perth.

In Inveraray itself he was to find, that because of the emergency, work on the new castle being built by his cousin, Archibald Campbell, Duke of Argyll, had been brought to a halt. The old castle, a hall-house of four storeys and a garret, was by now almost uninhabitable as proved by a report of the previous year.

'Slits or cracks quite throw the wall to that Degree that the Air Passes sensibly throw...There are other cracks or bulgings in the wall particularly in the South east

Gevell which in Severall places are half a foot swelled out from the Perpendicular and Some Stones in a Manner threatening to Drop'.[143]

The building lived in by only a few old retainers, and used as a storehouse for the town's arms, had been declared by the town's architect, William Douglas, to be beyond repair; this being the reason why the Duke had brought Roger Morris with him to Inveraray to design a new castle in the previous year. Then they had stayed in what was called 'the pavilion', a house of two stories and a garret, built adjacent to the castle as temporary accommodation by Duke John in 1720-2. Here his namesake, the General, thankful to be on dry land, if not supremely comfortable, could at least warm his aching limbs.[4]

Outside all was confusion. General Campbell, again writing to John Maule, the Duke's confidential secretary, described how he had stepped off the ship into a scene resembling a nest of swarming bees.

'Upon my arrival here I found upwards of 600 men brought together, a vast number of gentlemen with their followers, and no thought of how they or their men were to live, other than to swallow the little money I had brought with me'. [145]

The cause of the pandemonium was that two months before, on 22nd October, the Duke of Argyll had called out the Argyll militia. Since then the quiet little town of Inveraray had come alive with men shouting in Gaelic, the neighing and stamping of horses with iron-shod hoofs, and the thud of many human feet. From the windows of the castle, looking to the southwest, the General could see the market cross of Inveraray, a Celtic carving mounted on a pedestal, to which the fencible men (those eligible for military service) had been ordered to muster.

Under the leadership of local lairds, and in some cases black-garbed ministers, the men wearing the kilt or clad in homespun trews, were marching down from their glens carrying what weapons they possessed. Most clutched the rusty swords and flintlock guns, which had been kept hidden since the last rising of 1715, of thirty-five years past. Some even carried pitchforks, lethal when used with dexterity to hamstring the legs of a horse.

On reaching Inveraray, however, they were armed with the weapons brought out of the castle and with the muskets and broadswords sent by the Government from Liverpool at the request of Colonel Jack, and of Archibald Campbell of Stonefield, the Sheriff-Depute of Argyll.

Almost as he arrived the General sent 600 men to Dumbarton from where, as the Jacobites approached, they could be moved to defend the main cities of Glasgow, Stirling and Edinburgh. In Inveraray itself, with a further 600 men encamped adjacent to the town, and another 2,000 about to arrive, the problems of supply became acute. To meet the emergency General Campbell dispatched an urgent demand to a firm of merchants in Greenock for 'any quantity of oatmeal that can be supplied for His Majesty's service…You will please order 2000 lb. weight of bisket to be baked immediately'.[146]

His request was complied with thanks to Sir John Shaw of Greenock, laird of the little Clyde side town, who with his wife (a cousin of the Earl of Stair) was a staunch supporter of King George. Lady Shaw, writing to the General on 28th December told him that 'from 2 to 300 bolls meal is in its way towards you. I assure you it was most inconvenient for the place to spare it, we shall soon be in want ourselves'. She then adds the electrifying news that,

'The Chevalier came to Glasgow about noon yesterday, and lodges in the house late Shawfield's. I don't hear that all his people together exceed 5,000 first and last'.

The house she referred to, was the one raised almost to the ground by a mob in Glasgow, protesting about the Malt Tax, in 1725. (see p.53) 'Big Daniel' Campbell, with the compensation granted by the Government, had then bought the island of Islay from where he now sent 'a fine body of men' fully equipped for warfare at his own expense'.[147]

Assured now, of at least one supply of oatmeal, the General had to turn his attention to a letter he had received from the Sheriff-depute, dated 18th December 1745, relaying the report of one of his spies.

'The Camerons and some others about 4 or 5 hundred in whole are come from Perth to Crieff, and march'd from there this morning to Dunblane, Doun [sic] and about as many more of the Highlanders are come to Crieff this night, and march the same way tomorrow; I am informed that the McIntoshes and several others are in Fife and Angus uplifting cash and are not yet returned: nor do I hear of L^d Jo: D---s [Lord John Drummond)] being come to Perth…there is none of his folks yet come to Perth excepting about 120 whereof a good many are English who were made prisoners abroad, and several of them have deserted to Stirling. They say Lord John and the rest of his people come to Perth tomorrow, I shall send someone I can trust that lenth [sic] and when he returns shall send you an express. I have conversed with a man in this neighbourhood, one of the D. of P---s [Duke of Perth's] men, but as he was forced out can trust what he says the more easily.

…I had a party of the MacDonalds, Glengary's folks at my house this night searching for horses and their officer assured me they had 2,000 at Crieff, but I do assure you, all that was there last night do not amount to half of that number…I cannot stir abroad myself, for my horse would be seized, and consequently my journey at an end, but shall send a sensible fellow to Perth who will not be suspected, and upon his return you shall have more from me'.[148]

General Campbell himself sent a report to the Duke of Argyll,
Inveraray 21st December 1745.
'State of Intelligence from the north land

We have had a man at Perth for two nights, who reports that the numbers do not exceed 2,000. That the great numbers landed from France with Lord John Drummond… were chiefly prisoners taken at Fontenoy, and some men have left them and come in lately to Stirling, that they have 2 mortars and 3 cannons…There passed 150 of Clanranald's men by Fortwilliam upon 18th. They are transporting some money landed lately in Moydart said to come from Spain and these men were to be joined by some of Keppoch's men at Highbridge and proceed together to Perth.

We are advised from the Isle of Mull that some of the McLeans are upon the point of rising in arms, being encouraged by the money and arms lately landed from the Spanish ship'.[149]

This letter was followed by another, to which the Duke, in his own hand, replied.

'I have yours of the 23rd from Inveraray and am very glad you have got there safe after such a troublesome voyage.

You have had a melancholy false report of the Rebel Army, and the Detachment you sent I hope will get safe back again, which is all that can be done till Hawley's army comes to Scotland.

I find all the King's ships are in the Clyde, whereas some of them would be of infinite more use on the western coast near Mull and Fort William. One man-of-war and a sloop would do, and if a small-armed vessel or a tender was joined to them it would be much the better, they should be victualled for a considerable time to prevent their so frequently returning into the Clyde on that pretence. I mention this the rather, that not only some Spanish ships have come there but that towards the end of this Rebellion that coast will be of great consequence to guard on many accounts… pray take all possible care to please Hawley, I believe he will be civil to you as he is an old friend of mine. I shall by the next post write him a letter of [unreadable]

I was with the King today and he is very well pleased that you are arrived'.[5]

Rumour ran wild…On 22nd December a Government spy in Perth sent a messenger to General Campbell, then newly arrived in Inveraray, to give him details of the guns held by the Jacobites in that city and to tell him that,

'All the French that came last to Perth, do not amount to above 140. They came in under night and were all quartered in the Muirhouse and Ballhenzie. This I have from the Quarter Master who gave out the billets, so that whole who came first and last do not amount to 260 or 270 at most There are none other marched than those formerly mentioned, who lie about Doon or Dunblane; and the whole of these including Glengyle, will not exceed 1200. In short the whole army above the Forth will not amount to above 2500 men…and a good number of them are still deserting; and I apprehend there is a stop to the march of any more from Perth by the news of the defeat of their friends in England…this they laugh at, and give out that there was only a small skirmish between the country people and their stragglers by which they had lost some few men, and that the P…e is at or near London, and joined by the Earl Mareschall and great numbers of men.

This they give out they had by express the other day. It is necessary to say something to keep their men together at this time until they resolve on what is to be done, which they are certainly at a loss to determine themselves in…They have brought in the water on the south side of the town of Perth in to a canal or ditch, which they have made where the town has no walls, and have in some measure repaired that old fortification called the Mount, at the head of the South Inch, which is all earth thrown up, and a trench round their artillery [which] consists only of five cannon, two of which are 16 pounders, two twelve pounders, and one 8 pounder. One of their two largest sunk the boat, and is in the bottom of Tay, they were working to get it up last day but did not succeed…As for that monstrous piece always talked of, she is not yet come up, nor never will I daresay'.[151]

Who was this Government spy? An ever-intriguing question hangs over the identity of the man who corresponded with the Campbells, both the General and the Sheriff, on what would seem to be fairly familiar terms. Obviously, he was educated as the phrasing of his letters and the accuracy of his spelling prove. Fearful for his safety he does not reveal his name – letters were often intercepted usually at the point of a sword – but the fact that he knew how many men had come with Lord John Drummond, mostly of them prisoners from Fontenoy, suggests that it might have been James Mor MacGregor, Rob Roy's eldest and profligate son, who, his own name being proscribed, had taken the name of Drummond to gain the protection of the Duke of Perth. James Mor had been badly wounded in the previous September, his pelvis cracked by a cannon ball, when fighting for Prince Charles at Prestonpans.

Now destitute and with a large family to support, he is known to have worked as a double agent, desperate for money in any way it could be found. He concludes his letter to the General by asking him to pay the bearer. A further indication that this may have been the case lies in the fact that James Mor's younger and equally dissolute youngest brother, known for his youth as Robin Oig, had been taken prisoner at Fontenoy, and thus would have known the numbers of captives released by the French to return to Scotland to fight the Hanoverian monarch with Lord John Drummond.

This must remain speculation but because James Mor, when later held for questioning, was to assert that General Campbell knew his family, it does seem probable that some sort of correspondence, either written or verbal, had taken place.

Be that as it may it is not surprising that, in the depths of winter of 1746, the spy in Perth, whatever his name, was unaware that Prince Charles was already back in Scotland, after fording the river Esk .The slowness of communication in those days must also account for the fact that, on the very day of his writing, he also had no idea that the Duke of Cumberland, summoned from Flanders to take command of his father's army, was laying siege to the town of Carlisle. On 3rd January 1746, Prince Charles and his army left Glasgow to head for Stirling. Defeated by its defences he failed to take Stirling Castle. Meanwhile, on 6th January, General Henry Hawley, who had succeeded Marshal Wade in command, reached Edinburgh.

Chapter 19
The Battle of Falkirk

General Campbell, told that the Prince had left Glasgow and was heading to the north, sent his son Colonel Jack to take command of the army he had assembled in Dumbarton.[152] On 10th January the General, while still himself at Inveraray, wrote to the Duke of Argyll explaining his own difficulties in providing for the militia who were still marching in to the assembly point of the Market Cross at Inveraray.

> 'My Lord
> I send your Grace enclosed a copy of a letter of this date to General Hawley from which you may see the difficulty I labour under, and that for the present it would not be safe to inform your Grace of the situation of affairs in this part of the country. I shall in a few days venture to send you a very particular account.
> I have upwards of 2,000 men in arms including the detachment under Lt Col Campbell's command and as the whole must be paid I beg your Grace to solicit some provision further than what was put into my hands when I left London. I have been very cautious in the distribution of what has been given out, all which will appear from the papers I shall send you very soon. I have sent out several commands to intercept the rebels, who as I am informed begin to steal homewards. I have taken up some few all without arms and one or two of them appear to be spies, there will be some expense in maintaining them and a difficulty in securing them.
> I have a command at Castle Kulhorne [Kilchurn] of 100 men and if I may be allowed to make some small expense in fitting up some cover and laying in firewood there, it is within 10 miles of Inveraray and but 10 miles from Tayndrom [Tyndrum] a very considerable pass…'

Having signed the letter he added a postscript excusing the fact that, in the cold damp weather, he had been forced to allow the soldiers to burn some of the wood stored for building the new castle, the foundations of which had already been laid.

> 'Your Grace may expect to suffer in your timber laid up for building and in your plantations 2,000 men who have been assembled here must have firing but I have settled such regulations as I hope will preserve what you most value'.[153]

Some of the wood intended for the new castle had in fact been taken to shore up the defences of Kilchurn, the castle belonging to the Earl of Breadalbane, built by his ancestor, Sir Colin Campbell of Glenorchy, to defend his lands at the east end of the great inland waterway of Loch Awe. A barracks, added to the castle in 1690, was currently garrisoned by a force of twelve officers and two hundred militiamen under the command of Captain Colin Campbell of Skipness.[154] On 1 January Breadalbane's son, Lord Glenorchy, had brought in his militiamen to Inveraray thus adding to the crowding in the town but as General Campbell told John Maule he was so 'pleas'd with his men I order'd them to goe with Colonel Campbell as being the best appointed'.[155]

On the morning of Wednesday 15th January, General Campbell wrote to General Hawley.

'By an express I received late last night, I find that you have given your orders that Lieut. Colonel Campbell should march forward to join you and left it to his direction which route he should take. By his letter to me I find he goes to Glasgow, which is what I wish, and I hope he will meet with your approbation, as I am persuaded he knows what he is about.

The reinforcements he brings you besides the three Companies of the Earl of Loudoun's Regiment, will be upwards of 800 men exclusive of officers, sergeants, corporals and pipers. I flatter myself that when you see them you'll be led to think better of them than common militia, each man has, or ought to have, eight rounds of ammunition with him.

I have sent 4,600 balls and flints on proportion all in cases and loaded upon five horses, a man to lead each horse…

There's an old saying set a thief to catch a thief but the best of Highlanders are not to be depended upon for laying hold of a rebel without arms for which reason I have this day ordered a detachment of their officers and fifty men of my own regiment, now at Dumbarton Castle, to march hither directly.

I have a command of 500 men at Castle Kulekchorn, [Kilchurn] ten miles from hence, with orders for out parties to lay hold of such rebels as are returning, but they have done little.

My scheme is to send out another command of 100 men to Tayndron, [Tyndrum] partly regulars and officers at their heads that will have no regard to a Highlander that is or has been in arms against His Majesty. Tayndrum is within 24 miles of Fort William to which place they will be 'a porte', in case of its being attacked from the land, which by a letter I had from the Lieutenant Governor he is very apprehensive of. It is for this purpose that I have sent for a command from Dumbarton Castle, at the same time let me assure you that I shall take care of that important place by supplying it with men to defend it, as I have with provisions.

Could I have found provisions to send forwards or to carry it properly equipt Colonel Campbell would have joined you with double the present numbers. Could I have had only oatmeal, tho in this I might have been to blame, by the hint given me in the Lord Justice Clerk's letter, which was only to send you about 800 men including the Regulars.

PS. I forgot to tell you that I have sent forward to join the command a surgeon with two small travelling medicine chests.

If you think it for the service I can send you another Battalion, but I cannot answer for the officers in regular service, though they really may be depended on with their own people and on the hills'.[156]

On the day that this letter was sent, the recipient, General Hawley, was preparing to leave Edinburgh. The train of heavy cannons, brought down from the Castle, to bombard the enemy who were besieging Stirling Castle, was already pulling out of the city. The next day General Hawley followed, and, together with Cobham's Dragoons reached Falkirk.

Here, only two days later, on the morning of the 17th, he was joined by Lieut. Colonel Jack Campbell of Mamore with three companies of Lord Loudoun's Regiment, one of Lord John Murray's (the Black Watch) and twelve of the Argyll Militia. With these reinforcements General Hawley now commanded about 8,000 men.

Colonel Jack arrived almost as the battle began. His men, posted to the right of the regular infantry, were barely involved in the scrimmage as the Jacobite army, with the wind driven rain at their backs, drove the 14th and 15th Dragoon Regiments through the infantry lines. Some of the militia men panicked, one survivor claiming afterwards that he could not fire his musket for fear of hitting the redcoats as they ran before the Highland charge.[157]

The Jacobites were triumphant. The Hanoverians despondent. General Hawley, having retreated to Linlthgow, wrote to the Duke of Cumberland,

'My heart is broke…such scandalous Cowardice I never saw before. The whole second line of foot ran away without firing a shot'.[158]

Meanwhile in Inveraray General Campbell waited for news of the battle in an agony of mind. Bereft of any word as to what had happened, he poured out his frustration at the lack of information and his own feeling of inadequacy due to his poor health. In a letter to John Maule, the Duke of Argyll's secretary, he wrote,

Inveraray, Monday, 20th January 1746.

'I have met with many rubs, I have suffered in my health but I don't feel the want of spirits tho' I have a cough and night sweats. If I can but last to see the end of this rebellion by assisting to extirpate the race of rebels, I shall think my time well spent…

Inveraray is, as far as I can see from the window and posts I thought necessary to take possession of, a charming pretty place. But ther's so great difficulty of access to it, so many ferries, and when heavy rains come, which are very frequent, ther's no having any intelligence, which at present makes it very unpleasant to me'.[159]

At last, almost as the courier bearing his missive to John Maule departed, another messenger, on a tired horse, clattered over the arched bridge into Inveraray. He brought a confused account of the battle of Falkirk, which the General took to be largely inaccurate. Then, to his great relief, a short note came from his son. Dated Saturday morning [18th January 1746], it was written in the formal tone used even amongst family members at that time.

'Dear Sir, We had a skirmish Yesterday evening. Our dragoons behaved very ill and we were obliged to retire to our camp. At night we marched forward to Linlithgow and are now marching out towards Edinburgh. Our loss is very inconsiderable; General Hawley told me that we were obliged to go to Edinburgh for want of ammunition.

I am Sir
You're most obedient son and servant
J.C'.

'Our militia was not engaged but as half of them dispersed and deserted we have been terribly fatigued'.[160]

The Hanoverian army, as Colonel Jack reported were now heading towards Edinburgh. General Hawley, once in the city, justified his soubriquet of 'Hanging

Hawley' by having thirty-two of his soldiers shot for cowardice. Those who were executed were unfortunate. His tyranny was not to last. On 30th January, the Duke of Cumberland, who had travelled from London in only six days, arrived to take over command.

On the previous day, when the news of Cumberland's impending arrival reached Stirling, Lord George Murray together with the most influential of the clan chiefs, faced with a rapidly deteriorating situation as many of their men deserted, had presented a petition to Prince Charles.

'If yr R.H. should risque a battle and Stirling Castle not in your hands: we can forsee nothing but utter destruction to the few that will remain'.

They urged that he should return to the Highlands, assuring him that there,

'We can be usefully employed the remainder of the winter, by taking and mastering the Forts in the North'.

The Prince, on receiving this letter, was so furious that he banged his head against the wall. He protested most fiercely against retreating, insisting that he had beaten the enemy a fortnight before and could easily do it again. No one it seems; believed him. His army was already heading west to cross the Forth at the Fords of Frew. Then when word came, on 31st January, that Cumberland with most of his force had already reached Linlithgow, the retreat became a rout. Carts and cannons were abandoned on the road.

On 2nd February the Highland regiments reached Crieff where, that evening, the Prince held a Council of War. The atmosphere was electric – allegations of cowardice and even of treachery being thrown about – but eventually, after heated altercation, it was decided that the whole army should march north for Inverness.[161]

Cumberland followed in the Prince's tracks. Leaving Linlithgow on 1st February, and travelling through Stirling up to Crieff, he reached Perth, just a day after Prince Charles had left it, on the 6th. He then stayed there for the next two weeks, sending out foraging parties to gather stores from farms and terrorising local landlords, known to be Jacobites.

General Campbell, at Inveraray, was preparing to visit his troops at Dumbarton. Writing to his son, Colonel Jack, on 31st January he told him,

'I am very weak but still entirely free from any fever of rheumatic pains. Order the messenger to call at Dumbarton when he returns for I intend going thither'.[162]

On 3rd February General Hawley, now serving under the Duke of Cumberland, wrote from Stirling,

'As the measures of the rebels seem now to be entirely disconcerted, there remains for us only to pursue and punish them in the manner they deserve, for which purpose it will be proper that you come this way with all the force you can get together, and as you must be the best judge which route to take, his Royal Highness leaves that, and everything relating to it, to you. Your son hath sent for the people from Dumbarton Castle.

They are still flying'.[163]

Chapter 20
A Poor Plunder'd Country

Major General Campbell was just about to leave for Dumbarton, to inspect his troops, when, on the orders from General Hawley, he changed his plans. Subsequently, he sailed immediately from Inveraray to Greenock, where, with Captain Thomas Noel, of the Royal Navy, he discussed the best ways in which the warships could be put to use. The Duke of Argyll had already emphasised, in his letter already quoted, that the ships should be patrolling the western coast, particularly round Mull and up Loch Linnhe, instead of lying idle in the Clyde.[164] Captain Noel acquiesced with the General's suggestions, instigated as they were by the Duke, whereupon three sloops, the *Terror,* the *Serpent* and the *Baltimore*, promptly put out to sea to sail up the northwest coast.

General Campbell, having carried out his cousin's commission, himself then crossed the Clyde to Dumbarton. From there, with four companies of the Argyll Militia, he went north to Stirling where, told that the house of Mr Henry Stirling had been ransacked by Government troops, he issued a stern order forbidding all forms of looting.[165]

The exact location of the Jacobite army, thought to be heading either north or west, was at this point unknown. It was also widely believed that the army so long expected from France, was about to land.

On 8th February, one Donald MacLean, the barracks master in Glen Elg, (who was later arrested as a spy) wrote from Kirkibost, in Skye, to Old Clanranald, chief of the MacDonalds of Clanranald, who lived in Benbecula, the island between North and South Uist. Revealing his true colours he told him that,

'By letters I received from Trotness last week, was informed that the Prince when joined by the forces in Perth (at Bannockburn) amounted to 5,000 men and I hope in God he has had as good success as some of his predecessors have had some time ago in that place. Was likewise told [that] General Ligonier, who commanded the King's forces, was at Lithgow with 2,000 men, so that an engagement was unavoidable, my anxiety to know the Princes' success, and my tender regard for my friends and countrymen oblige me to send you this express hoping you'll favour me with the particulars of the action and of any other extraordinary occurrences. I am afraid the Prince was overpowered with numbers, but notwithstanding am still inclined to believe that he has obtained a victory…

There was a French landing under the Duke of Richelieu hourly expected in England from Dunkirk and some Hessians from Williamstat to Scotland and its thought the former must have landed some time ago or to have been dispersed.[166]

Bernera has about 60 of MacLeods men taken at Inverurie among whom is McCoumen the piper, four of them that deserted about Stirling and were telling that the Prince's party were in high spirits. They were likewise telling that there was then a French landing in England but as that news came not from C---n [Cameron?] we have not faith enough to believe it. Rasay fell off his horse some mile without Perth, whereby one of his legs was hurt which obliged him to return to Perth'.[167]

On the same day Alexander Campbell, the old Governor of Fort William, wrote in a state of panic revealed by his shaking hand, to tell General Campbell that he had just received.

'Certain intelligence that the army of the Rebels are within thirty-two miles of this garrison, in Badanoch, and on their retreat to this country, most of their Chiefs being already arrived...

I humbly beg you will send me one hundred more men or as many as you can spare and likewise that you will give your positive orders to a King's ship to come here if the Capt^ns will not think proper to comply with my request'.[168]

Cumberland had decided to deploy part of the Argyll militia in manning several small garrisons throughout Perthshire with the purpose of preventing men of doubtful loyalty, in a countryside where many were nearly starving, from raiding the local towns.

On 7th February, Colonel Jack Campbell, in command of the militia, wrote to his father,

'I am ordered by His Royal Highness to leave 420 of my command to be posted', according to the enclosed list which he then enumerated as follows, together with the number of men installed.

Blairfetty 60
Kynachan 100
Glengoulin and Cushavile 60
End of Loch Rannoch
Clachan of Balquidder
And west end of Lochearn 50
Dunkeld 50

General Campbell, with his four companies of Argyll militia joined the Duke of Cumberland at Perth on 9th February. The next day the three remaining companies, marching from Dumbarton, reached Crieff. The commissariat, the department in charge of provisioning the army, could not contend with such numbers in a country already stripped bare of food for both men and horses by the Jacobites. General Campbell, after all his efforts to provide the force, which he had been asked to raise, was now ignominiously dismissed.

On 11th February he wrote to the Duke of Argyll's secretary, John Maule,

'The last division came to Crieff on Monday, so that there is no less than 1200 of the Argyllshire militia in the neighbourhood. Believe me it is no easy matter to provide for such a number of men in a country the rebels have left and our troops have past, so that I may say I fought my way hither and I am now to scramble back with about 500 the best way I can, His Royal Highness judging that I may possibly be of more service in the West Highlands, and only chooses to have about six or seven hundred men, under the command of Colonel Campbell which have hitherto formed the van of the army...I take it for granted that his Royal Highness will dismiss me in a day or two, so that I shall have a pretty jaunt back to Inveraray'.[169]

The General accepted his orders without complaint. Resentment, however, emerges in a letter, written on 12th February, to the Duke of Argyll.

'I am far from being well but hope to scramble back to Argyllshire. I must return by a poor plundered country and carry provisions with me till I can get to Dumbarton where I have made a small magazine of meal beside what I laid up for the defence of the castle'.[170]

The real reason for the general's dismissal, as shown by the Duke of Cumberland's correspondence, was that he did not trust the men he commanded. On 10th February, he wrote to the Duke of Newcastle, the King's Secretary of State,

'General Campbell came hither to meet me and has brought with him four companies of Western Highlanders. He assures me that they will show no favour or partiality to the other Highlanders, as he knows them best he must answer for this, for my own part I suspect them greatly, for those who were with us here before these came, absolutely refused to plunder any of the Rebel's houses, which is the only way we have to punish them or to bring them back'.[171]

Cumberland was no fool. His assessment of the character of Highland men, who, even if constantly feuding with each other were loyal to their own kind, was true to the mark. He knew, for example that even in Morvern, where the people were all tenants of Argyll, there was hardly a man of them who was not faithful to Lochiel. Prince Charles had in fact ordered that the houses of those who would not come out for him should be burnt. There was little or no mercy on either side.

General John Campbell, travelling back to Inveraray, was stricken with a recurrence of the rheumatic fever, (probably malaria) which left him weakened and in great pain. Unable to ride, he was forced to stay two nights with the Lord of Session, Patrick Campbell of Monzie, 'and take his chariot to Stirling'. [172] Already depressed by his illness and by Cumberland's flagrant ingratitude, he reached the village of Gargunnock in an exhausted state, to be met with instructions which drove him nearly to despair.

Cumberland now demanded, what in modern terms would be described as ethnic cleansing, or in other words the total devastation of all that the Jacobites possessed.

The General, on opening the dispatch and realising the import of the words, knew that as a soldier, he had no option but to obey. From Gargunnock, later on that same evening of 22nd February, he wrote with an aching hand, to the Sheriff, Archibald Campbell of Stonefield,

'His Royal Highness has ordered that strong parties should be sent to burn and destroy all the rebel's country as far as they can go, and drive their cattle. My notion is that this should be carried into execution the moment they march out not before lest that they should be made desperate too soon...'

Having thus found a good reason for Cumberland's orders to be delayed until men were actually proved to be rebellious, he gave instructions regarding the three companies of his own troops returning to defend Inveraray. 'Boats should be provided to ferrie the men over [Loch Fyne] from St Catherine's for they must be greatly fatigued'.

Then reverting to the subject so heavily on his mind, he continued,

'If the intelligence I have this evening received is true the rebels must have left their country and in that case I am of the opinion all ought to be burnt and destroyed but be that as it will I have His Royal Highness's positive orders for so doing. In the Isles the ships ought to land some of their men and doe the like, for which purpose I desire you will acquaint the several captains with His Royal Highnesses's commands – the plunder they will have a right to excepting arms'.[173]

The Sheriff, on receipt of this letter, wrote immediately to the Duke of Argyll, telling him that there was 'not a shilling of rents recovered since ever the rebellion broke out' from his estates in Morvern and in Mull. Nonetheless he was deeply concerned over Cumberland's policy of scorched earth.

'The inevitable consequences of the execution of this order, is that the tender innocent babes must suffer with the guilty and that it will probably introduce a horrible scene of murder, blood and rapin, not only in the rebels' country, but likeways into all those countries that unluckily happen to be in their neighbourhood.

It seems reasonable to wish that this order was not carried to execution, till once the rebels were thoroughly dispersed, and a strong force brought into their country, lest they should in revenge fall upon His Majesty's loyal subjects…Men reduced to absolute despair will attempt anything, it is not unlike they may direct their resentment against Argyllshire for their dutiful and loyal appearance… The order being in general to burn the houses and drive the cattle of the rebels, may infer, that it is to be execute against the tenants in rebellion tho' the landlord is loyal and acting for the Government or leaving [sic] peaceably at home'.

The Sheriff, having given such good reasons for why reprisals should be delayed then pointed out that, in any case, it would barely be feasible to drive off the cattle until after Whitsunday [traditional date for putting the cattle on the hills] 'when they may have strength to travel and grass fixed for them'.[174]

The Duke replied from London,

"I was sorry to see by you[rs] of the 25th February the measure approved of, which I like as little as you do for I am altogether of your opinion."

But, like his cousin in command of the West Highland Forces, who was actually on the scene, there was little or nothing that he could do to prevent the destruction ordered by Cumberland on the authority of his father King George.[175]

COLONEL JOHN CAMPBELL, *of Mamore & Ixora*

Who Succeeded to the Dukedom of Argyll in April 1761.

The 4th Duke of Argyll

Duncan Forbes of Culloden

John Campbell, 2nd Duke of Argyll

George II, King of England

Caroline of Brandenburg Ansbach

Charles Edward Stuart

Donald Cameron of Lochiel

Prince William, Duke of Cumberland

Flora MacDonald

John Campbell, 5th Duke of Argyll

Elizabeth Gunning

Chapter 21
The Fall of Inverness and the Atholl Raid

Meanwhile part of the Jacobite army, under the Duke of Perth and Lord Cromartie, were approaching Inverness where Lord Loudoun, in joint command with Lord President Forbes, of the Government forces in the north, prepared for an expected attack. A ditch had been built around the city and cannons strategically placed, although their force now numbered about 2,000 men most were untrained recruits drawn from the clans in the area which, largely due to Forbes's influence, remained loyal to King George.

On 9th February, three ships sailed in to Inverness. One was HMS *Speedwell,* a naval vessel commanded by a Captain Porter, which was escorting two transports, the *Helen* and the *Margaret* loaded with cargoes of arms, munitions and a huge sum of money, reckoned at between £5,000 and £6,000 to be delivered to 'Duncan Forbes Esq., Lord President of the Session'.

Such was the state of emergency, however, the enemy with a force far outnumbering the garrison, being only about twenty miles away, that it was decided to entrust both the arms and the money to Captain Porter who would lie off the coast in the *Speedwell* to be ready to sail to the attack.

The crisis soon came. On 16th February Prince Charles arrived at the House of Moy, only seven miles from Inverness. Here he received a royal welcome from 'Colonel' Anne, wife of the chief of Clan Mackintosh who, while her husband fought for the King, herself led a contingent of their clansmen to join the Jacobite army.

That same night Lord Loudoun, informed of the Princes' arrival, attempted to take him prisoner. Marching out of the city in darkness at the head of 1500 men, Loudoun suddenly heard an explosion of fire from a detachment about a mile from his left. It turned out that the troops had seen running figures and fired.

The enemy proved to be five men, headed by the local blacksmith who, yelling, "Advance my lads! Advance! We have the dogs now!" So terrified Loudoun's young recruits that, thinking Satan's host was upon them, fired blindly at the fleeting forms.

Meanwhile Prince Charles, awakened by the racket, fled from Moy House in his nightcap and slippers, and wearing only a nightshirt, caught a chill in the frost and damp. Laid low in bed, for some days, his illness postponed his army's advance on Inverness.

Lord Loudoun and Forbes in the meantime, knowing that with their largely untrained soldiers, many of whom were deserting, they could not hold Inverness, decided to resort to strategy. Their plan rested on the fact that Cumberland, known to be approaching with a large army, would find his way unimpeded should the Jacobites be lured across the Beauly Firth, as he advanced upon Aberdeen.

The ruse worked. Forbes was a prime target for the Jacobites who claimed that had he not kept so many clans, namely the MacDonalds, the MacLeods of Skye, the MacKenzies and some of the Frazers, out of the Rising, London could by now have been theirs.[176]

On 18th February Loudoun withdrew from Inverness, sacrificing the town and the castle to the enemy in accordance with their plan. Captain Porter, having mustered a great number of boats, was ready to carry the troops across the Firth to Kessock on the Black Isle. The first men were aboard when a party of Jacobites, with horses trotting flat out, dragged three cannons into position to fire on the boats below. Cannon balls and bullets crashed down churning the water into foam, as the petrified young soldiers cowered in the bottom of the boats in their first experience of heavy fire.

Providentially no boats were sunk and no one killed, but many, once on dry land, deserted – it is said two hundred in all. However, the next day Loudoun moved what remained of his army, some across the ferries at Cromarty and some by a land route to Tain. Forbes's meticulous accounts, kept even in times of emergency, show that he had his horse shod and his boots mended at Alness, each for the price of 6d. [177]

From Tain, on 23rd February, the army crossed the Dornoch Firth by the Meikle Ferry to Sutherland where the little town of Dornoch then became the headquarters of the loyalist army and Tain, on the south side of the Firth, that of the Jacobites.

Loudoun and Forbes, convinced of pursuit, placed guards on all the ferries and the fords across the river Shin and seized boats on the Moray Coast, from where, as Loudoun rightly deducted, an attack was most likely to come. Forbes, by now at Overskibo, got information of what was happening from the ferryman at the Meikle Ferry, who was later to pay for his loyalty when the Jacobites destroyed all his boats.

Late at night on 10th March Lord Glenorchy sat down by the light of a candle to write to General Campbell, by this time back in Inveraray. He gave him a list of the disasters, which had overtaken three of the outposts garrisoned on the orders of the colonel, his son. The commanders were both Campbells. Glenorchy gave reasons to excuse their alleged incompetence.

'You must certainly think it very odd to receive a letter from me telling you that all the posts in the country about me were quiet and unmolested, when the bearer of it would inform you that three of them were forced. This apparent absurdity requires explanation.

I wrote on Sunday night and gave the letter to Barcaldine to send away next morning, when I came thither. He kept the man a little while after I was gone, to write by him; and in that time the account of the Rebels having attacked these posts came to Taymouth. I don't yet know the particulars, but in general the whole party commanded by Glenure, a Lieutenant in Loudoun's regiment, is said to be either killed or taken except a very few, and the other posts at Kainachan and Blarfetty under the command of Knockbuy. I don't yet know the particulars but in general the whole part commanded by [Campbell of] Gleneure, a lieutenant in Loudoun's Regiment, is said to be either killed or taken except a very few, and two other posts at Kainachan and Blarfetty under the command of [Campbell of] Knochbuy had the same fate. Knockbuy was that night with Colonel Stewart at the Bridge of Tay and Gleneure, having writt several letters for meal, of which he began to be in want, went on Sunday to settle a regular method of being served with it. In the evening he came to Taymouth to see his brother Barcaldine who has the gout, where he stayed all night, and went from thence next morning to his post, but came too late. [178] He told me the night before that all danger was over, and many of the country people who had appeared in arms in the hills on his first coming there were come down to their houses, but he said the post could not possibly be defended if attacked in the night, for his men were scattered in different houses or huts at a distance from each other'. [179]

Soon after this account came hither, another arrived that the rebels had invested and taken Blair Castle, the latter part is not true, but we think the other is, for there is no communication with it, the pass of Gillikrankie [Killiecrankie] being guarded by them, and 'tis said the advanced party of the garrison is certainly taken. If they have surrounded the Castle, they can hold out no longer than their provisions last…for there is no marching to it by the Pass where the road is cut in several places, and the other way by the Kings Road is impracticable, the Bridge of Kainachan being broke. [180]

The Duke of Cumberland had arrived in Perth on 6th February. After spending some time there, he moved northeast to Aberdeen which he reached on the 25th. However, from there, in the middle of March Lord George Murray returned to Blair Atholl.

The family of Murray of Atholl, like so many others in Scotland, was divided in loyalty. William Murray, Duke of Atholl, had joined Prince Charles. His estates and title being forfeited, he was known as the Marquis of Tullibardine, while his younger brother John, loyal to King George, was acknowledged as the Duke of Atholl. Lord George, still younger, was Lieutenant-General of Prince Charles's army.

Lord George returned to Blair Atholl to find the castle held by a garrison of Hanoverian troops. Lord Glenorchy's letter continues,

"We have often been alarmed here with different reports. Yesterday we had certain intelligence that Lord George Murray had invested Blair with 2500 men and that the like number was on their march by the King's Road to attack Castle Menzies. I doubted of the latter part of the news because I had not heard it from Taymouth, where Barcaldine has assembled some men for the defence of the House…The former part relating to Blair is certainly true, and the last account from thence say that they have two cannon with which they have damaged the roof but had not then made any impression on the walls, but that they were building a furnace to heat the bullets. Lord George Murray who is there has ordered all the men of Atholl down to Dunkeld."

Writing again on 19 March, in reply to a letter from General Campbell, Glenorchy told him,

'The account I had from Taymouth of the forcing three posts by surprise in the night, I can't yet learn who did it…Some say it'was the Macphersons, others say Lord George Murray was there. Blair is likewise said to be invested …and a report is now spread that the Rebels are come to Dunkeld…

A letter from the [Government] army, which came here today, mentions their being at Aberdeen and nothing of their moving from it. I saw a letter today just come from a good hand (whom I know) assuring me that the Rebels are between 8 and 9,000 including 2,500 who went after Ld Loudoun that all the MacDonalds, MacPhersons and some others to the number of 600 had left his Lordship when he went from Inverness. That the Frasers and MacPhersons are still in their own country from whence I imagine that the latter, with some additional forces, attacked the posts.

That the rebels have placed cannon on the banks of the Spey and seem desirous to have the Duke advance, and that they have sent ten thousand bolls of meal to Fort Augustus and would send as much more. I hope half of this is not true, but I fear it'.[181]

On the morning of 20th March Lord Loudoun rode off to inspect his outposts on the Shin just as a Jacobite force, commanded by the Duke of Perth, came in from the sea. Shrouded in thick fog the Jacobites sailed across from Tain to take Dornoch where some houses were burnt on the order of young Ross of Pitcalnie, Forbes's own great-nephew, who was now a colonel in the rebel army he had begged him so earnestly not to join.

From Dornoch they marched on towards Overskibo, like hounds on a trail, every man of them lusting for the blood of the Lord President Forbes, whom they held mostly responsible for holding the north for King George.

They failed to catch him. Forbes, warned of their coming, escaped. Joining the Earl of Loudoun, together with many men of the Independent Companies, he reached Loch Carron, from where, in small boats, nearly swamped in a choppy sea, they crossed the Minch to Skye.

Here, on 31st March, they were joined by Sir Alexander MacDonald of Sleat. Desperate for news of what was happening on the mainland, Forbes sent a note, asking for information, to the chief of Clan Chisholm, concealing it in the lining of his messenger's coat. Chisholm's reply, if he sent one, must have been destroyed. Meanwhile Forbes and Loudoun, had neither money to pay, nor provisions to feed, the nine hundred men under their command.

On 29th March, Forbes sent another message to Major-General Campbell telling him all that had occurred and asking for aid for his own and Loudoun's detachment. General Campbell, prostrated by 'a very severe fit of the rheumatism', could not himself reply, but forwarded the letter immediately to Andrew Fletcher, Lord Milton, who in turn passed it on to the Duke of Newcastle. Meanwhile the General sent a ship loaded with meal for the relief of the near starving men. He also sent ammunition, first across land and then 'by the boat that carried your messenger'. [182] He also told Forbes that he would find it impossible to import meal from Ireland but that plenty [at a price] could be had at ports on the Clyde where large cargoes had been landed from Liverpool and Bristol.

'The General wished much to have the E. of Loudoun and your Lordship with any officers you have with you, to assist him to carry on His Majesty's Service in the West parts'. [183]

Chapter 22
Conflict Without Mercy

Glenorchy's news of the Government army holding Aberdeen was certainly true. It was even known in England where Horace Walpole, writing to Sir Horace Mann, said,

'I have no new triumphs of the Duke to send you he has been detained a great while at Aberdeen by the snows. The rebels have gathered numbers again and have taken Fort Augustus and are marching to Fort William. The Duke complains extremely of the loyal Scotch says he can get no intelligence, and reckons himself more in an enemy's country than when he was warring with the French in Flanders. They profess the big professions whenever he comes, but, before he is out of sight of any town, beat up for volunteers for rebels'.[184]

From Aberdeen the Duke of Cumberland himself wrote to General Campbell on 18th March.

'As you are already apprised of the march of Captain Patton, with his detachment, I have only to give you notice of that of the two companies of Johnson's from Edinburgh for Glasgow, who are to take in a quantity of biscuit and potatoes there, and then throw themselves into Fort William. My Lord Chesterfield [Lord Lieutenant of Ireland] has been also written to send more ammunition of all kinds. As I look upon Fort William to be the only fort in the Highlands that is of any consequence, I have taken all possible measures for the security of it, as by your letters you seem to have done on your part. I doubt not but that you will do everything that is within your power, for the preventing of it falling into the Rebell's hands.

I am very glad you have sent thither Mr Russell as he may be of great service to Captain Scot'.

The ageing and fearful Captain Alexander Campbell on Cumberland's orders to General Campbell, had already been replaced as Governor of Fort William, by Captain Caroline Scott, an ambitious and efficient young man who, as commander of a company of Guise's regiment, was already notorious for his cruelty towards Jacobites.

Cumberland continues,

'The opinion I have of Captain Scott and the precautions we have taken, set me safe about this important place, but if it were possible that all this should fail, I would have you, as you will know it long before I can, immediately communicate it to my Lord Chesterfield, to prevent the stores being sent, and you will likewise acquaint the officers of His Majesty's ships or sloops stationed there, that it is expected of them, they give all the assistance possible to His Majesty's garrison there, to annoy the Rebells in all manner of ways.

As to your present situation, tho' a disagreeable one, I hope it will not be found so, to the extent you seem to think, for I flatter myself that the Rebells will not be in a condition to make any attempt upon you, tho' I would have you continue to take all kinds of precautions, and I heartily wish you success if it should come to a trial. I am your affectionate friend.

William'.[185]

Cumberland's fears for Fort William were soon justified. The Jacobites laid liege to the town on 19th March. On 2nd April the garrison at Blair Castle was relieved when on the point of starvation. On the same day Captain Caroline Scott, desperate for supplies, wrote from Fort William asking for salt beef to be sent from Glasgow or Greenock as a ship expected from Ireland had not arrived.[186] The very next day, however, the siege was raised as Prince Charles withdrew his troops to meet Cumberland's expected advance from Aberdeen.

On 7th April Lord Loudoun sent instructions to Lieutenant John Campbell of Captain McLeod of Bernaras Company telling him to take fifty men from Broadford and proceed with them immediately to the island of Canna. From there he was to sail with Captain Fergussone, of His Majesty's ship *Furnace* to Barra and then to South Uist 'in order to seize and carry along with you from thence all the arms and boats together with such money as you can get intelligence of that may be in those parts for the Pretender's service'.

Ferguson would take extra crewmen to carry off the boats that Campbell would seize on the islands. On landing on Barra, however, he was to show respect to MacNeil, the Laird, 'as he has behaved dutifully' and to tell him that he was under orders 'not to destroy or distress the country provided the people gave up their arms and ammunition and the boats with their sails and tackle and what foreign money they possessed'.[187] If MacNeil refused, however, he was to be seized and put on board the ship of war.

From Barra Campbell was to sail to South Uist to deliver a letter from Captain MacLeod to Clanranald stating much the same terms. He was to show all due respect to MacDonald of Boisdale, leaving him 'just a boat for his own convenience in expectation of [his] intelligence and assistance'.[188]

Finally, Lord Loudoun told him that Ferguson, on landing on Canna, had orders to sink the boats of any men who had come from either Barra or South Uist to prevent them from returning before they could be disarmed. Should assistance be needed more men would be sent from Skye.

On 8th April John Maule, the Duke of Argyll's secretary wrote to General Campbell from London telling him that there was enormous resentment in England over a military expedition being sent to Cape Breton 'when we have so formidable a Rebellion at home'. He added that national anxiety was increased by uncertainty as to 'what part the Dutch are to take, if they are to make a peace with France…[The French Foreign Minister D'Argenson had put forward peace proposals after the battle of Fontenoy and again in the following September] some think that notwithstanding of the disadvantages Sardinia has had in Italy he'll [Charles-Emmanuel, King of Sardinia] take the benefit of it to make peace with France'.[189]

Thus while the international situation hung in the balance and with invasion from France still a strong possibility, the war in Scotland, then so remote from London, let alone the rest of Europe, might be decided from abroad.

The main part of the Government army left Aberdeen on 8th April. Colonel Campbell's regiment of Argyll militia leading the van [190] The Duke of Cumberland is claimed to have used the militiamen as a shield for his regular regiments. However, thanks to the Jacobite forces being largely occupied elsewhere, no opposition was met with even when crossing the Spey.

Prince Charles meanwhile had taken possession of Duncan Forbes's house of Culloden where he is known, at least on the nights of the 14th and 15th of April, to have slept in Forbes's own bedroom in his large four-poster bed.

In fact, it was not until 14th April that the two armies actually sighted each other near the village of Auldearn, the scene of Montrose's victory a hundred and one years before. A first hand witness of all that was then to ensue was Mr Donald Campbell of Airds, the Duke of Argyll's factor in Morvern, he who had passed on the message of Prince Charles's arrival in Scotland only nine months before. From his account it becomes obvious that the men of Cumberland's army were in much better condition to fight a battle than were their adversaries, Prince Charles's tired and hungry men.

'April 16th; a glorious Day. The army decamped early, officers and men in the highest spirits. The Campbells with a party of Kingston's light horse were kept before, to secure the woods and roads, the army marching in three columns.

When within a mile of Culloden, we halted for the army. When come up H.R.H. put them in battle order, and having advice of the enemies being on a muir and rising ground above Culloden, he marched up the hill, that he might attack them in front, and prevent them giving him the slip either to the right or left, so as to get the advantage of the weather which favoured us as it blew in their faces with sharp showers.

The orders H.R.H gave Colonel Campbell was to divide his men on the right and left wings of the army and so to march on till the engagement began when they were to retire to guard the baggage. Captain Campbell of Balliemore with his company, the Glenorchy, Achnaba's and Dugald Campbell's companies of militia were detailed to the left, the Colonel with the rest being on the right'.[191]

Colonel Campbell, sticking to his orders, remained in charge of the baggage train, but the companies on his left advanced into the battle.

The Jacobite gunners opened fire before, about two minutes later, Cumberland's own batteries, manned by well-trained crews, responded with murderous accuracy cutting swathes through the opposing lines.

Then as the Prince's army made its doomed but heroic charge, the Hanoverian cavalry, commanded by Major-General Bland, began the encircling movement of the right wing, which proved a decisive factor in the outcome of the conflict. For a short time, Bland was halted, finding his entrance to a field blocked by stoutly built stone walls 'high stone park dykes' as Airds called them too high for the horses to jump.

At this point the Argyll men, most of them sturdy farmers, had their moment of glory as charging the walls on both side of the field with pikes and axes they sent stones crashing to the ground leaving gaps through which the horsemen galloped onto the muir to charge into the Highland ranks. Simultaneously, the Argyll militiamen, levelling their muskets on the remains of the second wall, fired at the enemy's second line and 'killed and destroyed great numbers of them' although suffering casualties themselves.

In the aftermath of the battle, the Duke of Cumberland, exalted at his victory, summoned Colonel Jack on the battlefield and thanked him for all that he had done.[192]

Later that evening, from Inverness Colonel Jack wrote to his father:

'I have just time to inform you that we have gained a complete victory over the rebels. The main body of my corps was ordered as a guard for the baggage by which means I had no opportunity of seeing the affair distinctly...part of our men were engaged and behaved comparatively well amongst whom Balliemore was killed and Achnaba dangerously wounded. I believe there are above a thousand dead of the rebels on the field and five hundred prisoners – on our side about 40 men killed no officers of note but Lord Robert Kerr'.[193]

Chapter 23
The Chase Begins

On 20th April General Campbell, who had just heard the news, wrote to congratulate the Duke of Cumberland.

'I most heartily congratulate Your Royal Highness on the complete victory you have lately obtained over His Majesty's rebellious subjects near Culloden, which has at once not only put an end to the present Rebellion, but in all probability will prevent the like daring attempts for the future. If anything could add to the joy this important news gave me it was Your Royal Highnesses safety, and the loss of so few of His Majesty's loyal subjects'.

The General then enumerated his plans for preventing the Jacobites escape from Scotland. He told him that he had made an encampment of from six to seven hundred men in Glenorchy. In another letter to the Duke of Argyll he wrote 'There's no doing without tents' explaining that, in the absence of straw, the tents had to be covered with heather which could afterwards be used to heat the camp kettles. [194]

'Glenorchy being a good place for intercepting such of the rebels as may attempt to get into the Western Islands, is also in some measure centrical for marching where any of their chiefs may be skulking till an opportunity for their getting off.

I propose myself to go to Fort William where I shall expect the honour of Your Royal Highnessess commands…I propose to scour the Western Islands, from which I think the Rebells (as being the most rational rout) will attempt getting out of Britain, and therefore in my humble opinion great attention should be placed to secure all the passes leading thither.

I would also incline to have Colonel Campbell with me…my reason for proposing this, is that he is better acquainted with the Highlanders than anybody I have and knows better than I how to manage them.

As I have for some time had this island expedition in view, I prepared two vessels with provisions which are now ready to sail to Dunstaffnage, and will always be a 'porte' to supply me wherever the exigencies of affairs may require I should go'.[195]

General John Campbell, as he wrote this, was totally in ignorance of the terms of capitulation that were to shock him to the depth of his soul. Only afterwards was he to learn that Cumberland, when asked for his orders regarding his fallen enemies, many of whom lay wounded upon the field, had written, it is said on the playing card, the nine of diamonds, the mortal words 'No quarter'.

Within a few days, however, he was to hear more details from Lord Glenorchy, writing from Taymouth on 20th April, who told him:

'I have this moment received an account from different hands that the rebels were entirely defeated by the Duke on Wednesday last. I have not yet heard the particulars, but all agree there was a great slaughter of them and that our army has suffered but not near so much. One of my people whom I sent out for intelligence met Lord George Murray with only two with him retiring to the hills…What confirms the defeat more than all I've heard from the common people, is that a gentleman of character told a person who told it to me, that he with four other gentlemen had accompanied the young Pretender some miles. and that he desired them to shift for themselves, and that the fewer were ever seen together the better…I'm told the cries and the howlings of the women of Culdares's Estate can be heard for some miles, cursing him for forcing their husbands who would have stayed at home if they durst for him'.[196]

That Prince Charles had escaped and was in Moydart seems to have been fairly common knowledge. Captain Caroline Scott, writing from Fort William on 27th April affirmed that,

'Charles is certainly about Koydart with a very small retinue'. He added that 'Lochyiell [Lochiel, who Glenorchy reported as dead] is shot thro' the foot, and lay all night a few miles from the field of battle under a craig. Next day he was carried off and is now in Badenoch amongst the MacPhersons in some obscure place'.[197]

Unaware as he was that the Prince had escaped from the mainland, Captain Scott, like his commanding officer, the Duke of Cumberland, had small sympathy for prisoners. Nonetheless some were treated with humanity as is proved by the correspondence between General Campbell and the Marquess of Tullibardine, de facto the Duke of Atholl.

After the battle of Culloden, Tullibardine wandered south with a few other survivors who included Michelle Vezzosi, Prince Charles's Italian valet. Exhausted and starving he finally gave himself up near the southeast shore of Loch Lomond, to William Buchanan, younger of Drumakill. Buchanan wrote to General Campbell, telling him how at about seven o'clock in the morning, a servant had come running to say that there were travellers at the gate who were seeking a guide. Going out, he had found a pathetic party, riding miserable horses, who briefly revealed who they were. The Marquess said he wanted to surrender to General Campbell but, in his absence, thankfully came into Drumakill house where he gave Buchanan his sword, telling him to keep it as a present.

They were certainly in a bad way. 'The Italian made no difficulty in surrendering, he has almost lost both the use of his hands and feet, and the Marquis is very crazy, and has some difficulty in walking', he wrote to General Campbell'. I gave him my word of honour that he would be civilly used'.

Moved to pity he gave them dinner. A message was sent to Dumbarton Castle and subsequently, in the afternoon, Lieutenant Duncan Campbell of the Scots Fusiliers, appeared with an escort of soldiers to take the prisoners by boat to Dumbarton where Tullibardine was treated, on the specific orders of General Campbell, not as a rebel but as a prisoner of war.

On 28th April, phrasing his letter in accordance with the civilities of the time, General Campbell, wrote to Tullibardine,

'My Lord,
Being informed that you have surrendered as a state prisoner, I have given directions to the Lieut. Governor of Dumbarton Castle to receive you as such, and to accommodate you in every shape, so as to make your confinement as easy as possible till such time as His Majesty's pleasure is known.

What depends upon me, which is being treated as becomes one of your high rank, you may expect from. [198]

My Lord
Your Lordship's most obedient
Humble servant as far as law the laws permit
John Campbell'.

Immediately Tullibardine replied:

'Sir

With much satisfaction I had the pleasure of yours from Inverary of Yesterday's date and cannot but thank you kindly for your no less oblidging than politely friendly expressions which shall never be forgot.

The Deputy Governour and everybody in whose hands I am here is extremely complesent which leaves nothing further to be wished in my unfortunate situation then never falling into less agreeable hands therefore cannot desire any change of quarters nor of the honourable treatment given.

Sir,
Your Most Obedient Humble Servant in so far as truth permits
Atholl'.[199]

Hardly had the General received this rather sad letter from the Marquess of Tullibardine than another came from Lord Glenorchy asking him to use his influence to procure the release upon bail of Doctor Archibald Cameron, brother of Lochiel, the now hunted chief, who was known to be badly wounded, Glenorchy vouched for Doctor Archie's character saying that,

'I am earnestly importuned by Mr John Cameron of Fassifern, Locheil's brother, to mention his case to you. It is certain that he left Lochaber and came into this country before the young Pretender came there who lodged a night in his house. He did not return home till the rebels had gone from thence. Sometime after his brother the doctor came into Lochaber to assemble the men who went home, and came to his house …Upon this Mr Cameron was taken up and kept prisoner in Fort William, till his case was laid before Council at Edinburgh and was found bailable, and his uncle Sir Duncan Campbell [of Barcaldine] gave bond for his appearance when demanded' till the 5th of May.

'I know all these circumstances as to his leaving the country before they [the rebels] came into it and not returning till they were gone, to be true. As to private inclinations no man can know them, but he certainly has had no public connection with the rebels. If you'll procure his release upon bail' twill be a very good natured action, if you have no objection to it'.[200]

Glenorchy, in the same letter, gave a pathetic description relayed to him by a man who brought letters for intelligence who said that he saw 'near 500 of the rebels, most of them wounded and some of them dying, in huts on the road between Inverness and this place [Taymouth.] but adds on a more cheerful note that' the Macgrigors marched into Balquhidder with colours flying'.

He then relates a curious story,

'Yesterday morning about 9 o'clock I was informed that a person of distinction with three servants on horseback had passed, not very far from hence three hours before. I immediately picked out some of the nimblest fellows in the neighbourhood, gave them what arms I had and sent them after them. The chase lasted near 15 miles when they came up with them and seized them. It proved to be the Count Mirobel, the Engineer General, he produced his commission from the French King. The gentlemen who I sent with the party searched his pockets and clothes bags and those of his servants for papers but found none. In every other respect I directed that he might be treated with great civility, and this day I have sent him with a guard to Lord Craufurd. One of his men had a black-haired girl behind him, whom the commander of my party knew to be an Argyllshire girl. She told him she was going to Glasgow, and the Count said he knew nothing about her, though probably his servants might, and seemed ashamed of that part of his equipage, for she was not handsome enough to carry with him openly. My people left her on the road to shift for herself'.[201]

Chapter 24
Men Living like Foxes in Caves

On 20th April, as General Campbell, unaware of his fateful order to spare none of the defeated Jacobites, was writing to Cumberland, congratulating him on his victory, Prince Charles was hiding in the house of Alexander MacDonald of Boisdale, in Arisaig.

He was there when John Hay of Restalrig found him. Hay brought news that both Fort Augustus and Fort William were now strongly garrisoned with Government troops. Shortly after this he heard that Lord Loudoun, who was commanding the Government soldiers in Skye, had been ordered to head for Fort William through the districts of Arisaig and Moidart, burning the country and driving off the cattle, as he went.

The Prince, at Arisaig, dictated two letters to John Hay. The first was to Sir Thomas Sheridan, his former tutor, who had sailed with him to Scotland. The second, post-dated, to be opened after he had left for France, was to the Highland chiefs. To them he said,

'When I came into this Country, it was my only view to do all in my power for your good and safety. This I will always do as long as life is in me. But alas! I see with grief, I can at present do little for you on this side of the water, for the only thing that now can be done, is to defend your selves till the French assist you'.[202]

Captain Scott was not to know until much later, that on the very evening of 26th April, prior to the writing of his letter from Fort William warning that the Prince was in hiding somewhere in Moidart, Prince Charles, walking alone in a wood at Borrodale near Arisaig, the place of his landing just over a year before, had come across a worthy seaman, Donald Macleod of Galtrigal in Skye.

According to Donald, the Prince asked him,

"Are you Donald MacLeod of Gualtergill in Skye?"

"Yes," said Donald, "I am the same man, may it please your Majesty at your service. What is your pleasure wi'me?"

"Then," said the Prince, "you see Donald I am in distress. I therefore throw myself into your bosom, and let you do with me what you like. I hear you are an honest man and fit to be trusted."

Charles then said to Donald,

"I hear Donald you are a good pilot that you know all this coast well, and therefore I hope you can carry me safely through the islands where I can look for more safety than I do here."

Donald then replied that he would do anything in the world for the Prince. He procured an eight oared boat and on 26th April they went on board 'in the twilight of the evening'.[203]

A storm was coming up and the sea was already so rough that Donald begged the Prince to postpone sailing until it calmed down. But Charles insisted that they should leave at once and through the darkness they went, into the wind and waves so high that the boat very nearly sank. But miraculously they reached the coast of the island of Benbecula, between North and South Uist, and landed at Rossinish in the dawn. There on the morning of 27th April, they found a hut where they made a fire to dry their clothes, and the Prince, utterly exhausted, went to sleep on an old sail spread on the ground.

Sick and sore from the sea journey after months living rough in the hills, searched for by Cumberland's Red Coats, eager as blood hounds to claim the great prize of £30,000 for arresting him, Charles spent two days at Rossinish, that remote spit of land between North and South Uist, MacDonnell of Clanranald's land. The chief's eldest son had joined the Prince's standard on his landing in Moidart in July of the previous year while Clanranald himself had stayed in his house of Nunton, on the west side of the island some six miles away. This was for two reasons, one being his age, the other that, as in any civil war, the policy of most families was to have members on either side thus ensuring that land and possessions would not be forfeited whoever won.

There were cows round the hut and Colonel O'Sullivan, one of the prince s companions who had come with him from France, was told by the Prince to shoot one which he did while Charles promised to pay the owner when found. It may have been the smoke rising from the fire while they cooked steaks cut from the carcass of the cow, or because he realised that the animal was missing, that a watchful herdsman ran over the flat land of Benbecula to warn Clanranald, that men who he did not recognise had landed at Rossinish from a boat pulled up on the shore.

Reaching Clanranald's house of Nunton, he found him dining in the company of Neil MacEachain, who, having trained at the Roman Catholic seminary at Douai for the priesthood, had abandoned his vocation to become tutor to Clanranald's younger children. Also, there, unfortunately, was John Macaulay, the Church of Scotland minister for South Uist, a staunch Presbyterian amongst Catholics and a fervent supporter of the government, who listened with great interest as the herd boy, in great excitement, gabbling in his native Gaelic, poured forth his tale…

Clanranald at once sent his younger son, with the herd to guide him, to find out what had occurred. He was unaware that the minister, hastening from the table, then covertly sent one of his own flock, to ascertain the identity of the strangers who had come so surprisingly ashore. His messenger, while pretending to come from Clanranald, managed to extract the information that the Prince was indeed amongst the men, who had landed so mysteriously from the boat, and that he meant to go on to Stornoway, on Lewis, to wait for any ship that might possibly take him to France.

Clanranald, in the meantime, with Neil MacEachain beside him, walked over to Rossinish to find, as they had half expected, that the Prince was waiting in the hut, or as some claim in an empty boat. Bowing to Charles, Clanranald swore to serve him and between them they agreed to quash any local rumours, by claiming that he and his companions were the crew of a merchant ship, wrecked off the coast of Tiree, who were now trying to get home.

But word of the Prince's escape from the mainland was already known. Ships of his Majesty King George's navy were patrolling the seas of the Hebrides, with lookouts searching for any sign that could possibly show where he was. It was therefore decided that to stay in Benbecula was too dangerous. He had to move elsewhere.

Thus, it was, that at first light, on the morning of 29th April, just as General Campbell, leading a heavily armed force to look for him reached Appin, a northern outpost of Argyll, that Prince Charles and his companions were once again boarding Donald MacLeod's boat. With Donald himself at the helm they intended to sail to Stornoway, where they believed the Prince could hide until one of the French ships, which he knew were coming to rescue him, should reach the little Lewis town.

Meanwhile, on the mainland of Scotland, those of his soldiers who had survived the slaughter of Culloden were trying to find their way home. Amongst them was Charles Stewart of Ardsheal, a massive man, over six feet high and equally wide in proportion, who sat astride the huge grey stallion, which, taken out of the lines before the slaughter started, had survived Culloden.

Charles Stewart of Ardsheal had commanded the Appin Regiment, in place of his chief, Stewart of Appin, who, on the excuse that his father had been attainted in the Rising of 1715, thereby losing all he owned, had refused to rise for Prince Charles.

Ardsheal's survival seemed miraculous. Although famed as a swordsman – he had actually once defeated the legendary Rob Roy – the target of his huge frame must have been almost impossible to miss.

His escape is said to have been due to his being shadowed throughout the battle by Allan Breck Stewart, foster-child of his half-brother, a mysterious rascal of a man, widely believed to be a spy, who was later to achieve notoriety as the main suspect in the famous Appin Murder.

Reaching his home of Ardsheal, lying in the shelter of the mountains of Appin on a green stretch of meadowland on the south side of Loch Linnhe, Charles Stewart at once ordered the house to be stripped. Everything of worth was buried or otherwise hidden. His children were made to change clothes with those of a local family with whom they were sent to live. Ardsheal himself then hid in a cave in Glen Stockdale while his wife Isabel stayed in Ardsheal House waiting, as they both knew, for the retribution bound to come.

Sure enough, in the third week of May, a party of Redcoats, from the barracks at Fort William, arrived. They drove away all the cattle, which as elsewhere in the Highlands were the mainstay of life.

Captain Caroline Scott, who, two months earlier, on Cumberland's specific order, had been made commander, of the Government troops at Fort William, was already notorious for his cruelty. Shortly he was to commit an appalling atrocity, when three men, who were actually coming in to surrender their weapons, were, on his orders, hanged over a mill-spout with the ropes of a salmon-net.[204]

Ardnamurchan was to be ravaged but was providentially saved as reported in *The New Statistical Account.*

'A ship of war came to lay waste to the country, but the minister and factor succeeded, by their representations, in saving the inhabitants from the indiscriminate cruelties to which the Highlanders were at this time subjected'.[205]

The minister, thus, named was in fact none other than the Reverend Mr Lauchlan Campbell (who had first passed on the word of Prince Charles sailing in to Loch-nan-Uamh while the factor was Donald Campbell of Auchindoun, the Duke of

Argyll's tacksman (tenant) in Ardnamurchan, who had sent on the minister's message on that fateful day of the previous July.

Colonel Jack Campbell arrived at Fort William on 24th May. He joined his father the next day. On the morning of the 27th they left Dunstaffnage on the *Charles* tender to sail up the Sound of Mull to Tobermory. Re-crossing the Sound they made their way up Loch Sunart to the little township of Strontian, which became the General's temporary headquarters.[206]

The correspondence of this time reveals the terrible situation in which General Campbell now found himself placed. All contemporary accounts acclaim him a fair and humane man. A Highlander himself, although he had spent much of his life in England, he was horrified by Cumberland's orders to literally exterminate 'the rebels' who had threatened his father King George.

Cumberland's own attitude is hard to understand. He was not entirely oblivious to the feelings of the common man. His own soldiers adored him. He was a hero in their eyes. The most obvious, in fact the only explanation, is that he was entirely ignorant of the minds of Highland men. He failed to comprehend the bonds of loyalty which bound them to their chiefs. To him they were savages who deserved no mercy. Only by brutal treatment could they remain submissive to the point where the spirit of defiance would be forever subdued.

General Campbell, however unwilling, could only obey the orders of the Commander-in-Chief. Ever practical, and concerned for the comfort of his men, he wrote from Inveraray to Captain Scott at Fort William on 2nd May telling him to find roofing for tents pitched out in the fields.

'I know there is no such thing as straw near you so when there comes a fair day pray order out regular Command with an Officer to pull heather to serve about 500 tents, what is pulled ought every night to be stacked up and properly covered. Stick up a short pole and stick it round. I need not have said so much to you, you'll see that even after it is used within the tents it may serve to heat the ovens'.[207]

On 5th May he wrote to Sir Everard Fawkener telling him that he hoped to be in Fort William in three days' time. He added that, just a week earlier he had been told that MacDonald of Glencoe, one of the Rebel chiefs, was in his native glen. He had ordered two detachments of eighty men to make a pincer attack but the plan had failed, because, thanks to appalling weather, the assault had been delayed so that the soldiers arrived in the night to find that 'the bird was flown, both man woman and child with all their cattle having retired to the mountains which are inaccessible'.[208]

However, there the story did not end. Glencoe, warned of Cumberland's merciless treatment of Jacobite prisoners, wrote a personal letter to General Campbell offering to surrender and 'begging you'll please befriend me in my great extremity and interpose your good offices with His Majesty in procuring my remission and sparing a life that is in all probability near an end'.[209]

The General sent a copy of this missive to Sir Everard Fawkener, adding that Glencoe was ill whereupon Cumberland instructed Fawkener to tell him to use his own judgement 'he might be very well left where he was, a guard being placed about him to prevent his escape, if he should recover'.[210]

From Inveraray, during the first week of May, General Campbell marched to Appin. He stayed at Port Appin, in Airds House then newly built by Donald Campbell of Airds, in its lovely position looking out over the sea.

It was at this point that he asked for a reinforcement of regular soldiers, preferably from his own regiment the Royal Scots Fusiliers, to be sent to replace some of the militia so that they could 'return to their little farms'.

No one knew better than the General that the lives of almost all people in northwest Scotland depended on the produce of the land. Cattle were the mainstay of existence but in early summer crops had to be planted, and in the absence of enclosures, the cows driven to the hills. In a letter to Sir Everard Fawkener, written from Fort William on 15th May, he said,

'I gave orders to receive such arms as were brought in, taking down the names and place of abode of such as surrendered, that the common people should be allowed to return home, but if any gentlemen they should be civilly treated and kept prisoner, till such time as I should know of it'.[211]

General Campbell had no option but to obey Cumberland's orders. These included specific instructions that the cattle of the rebels should be taken from them with the object of reducing their resistance by starvation. The cattle taken were sold and the money used to provide for his own soldiers. Nonetheless he was all too aware of the suffering this imposed upon people whose very existence depended, in most cases, upon the few beasts that they owned. Cattle were still the chief currency of the Highlands. Also, particularly in the months of winter and spring, they were the main source of food.

The General, who probably guessed at Ardsheal's whereabouts, also knew that his wife and young children were left with little or nothing to keep them alive. On the 25th May, he wrote to Isabel Stewart. Using what he took to be her husband's mistaken loyalty, as an excuse to come to her aid.

'Madam, Your misfortune and the unhappy situation Ardsheal has brought you and your innocent children into, by being so deeply concerned in this unnatural rebellion, makes my heart ache. I know the King to be compassionate and merciful. I know the brave Duke under whose command and orders I act, to have as much humanity as any man on earth, from which, and my own inclination, I have taken the liberty of ordering back your milk cows, six wethers, and as many lambs; the men who pretend a right to them shall be paid. I have taken the freedom at the same time of ordering two bowls of meal, out of my own stores, to be left here [i.e. at Airds] for you, which I desire you accept for the use of yourself and your little ones, and if what I write can have any weight, I most earnestly entreat you to bring up your children to be good subjects to His Majesty. I wish your husband, by surrendering himself to the Duke of Cumberland, had given me an opportunity of recommending him to His Majesty's mercy. I feel for you, and am, Madam your most obedient and humble servant.

John Campbell'.[212]

Thus, Isabel Stewart and her children believed themselves to be saved. Alas it proved wishful thinking. Retribution, cruel and unmerciful, as yet unforeseen, was to come.

On 30th May the Duke of Cumberland wrote to General Campbell telling him of the steps he had taken 'In order to root out the remainder of the Rebels that are in arms'.

'And that no part of the country may pass unexamined I should have you march with your body to sweep in everything that lies in Swyreord[?] and Morvern, you will serve the same orders already given you with regard to those in arms and make constant reports to me.

I am your affectionate

Friend

William

As there is a report (though' I believe with no foundation) that the Pretender's son is still in the Country, you must be as exact as possible in your search'.[213]

On 31st May, the General, by then in Strontian in Morvern, wrote to Sir Edward Fawkener. His letter sets alight the mystery of the whereabouts of the gold, sent from France to help the Jacobite cause, which remains unsolved to this day. The information came from Alexander Cameron of Dungallon whose letter, offering his surrender, he enclosed. Vouching for his character the General writes.

'He seems a bashful modest man extremely sensible of his crimes and gives a very ingenious and satisfactory answer to such questions as I have asked him. The most material intelligence I had the honour of sending His Royal Highness proves there was £35,000 in gold landed, about 3,000 stands of arms and ammunition in proportion, but he says that the chest of arms were broke open and most of them carried off by the country people, together with a considerable quantity of brandy and one of the cases of gold which was afterwards recovered with the loss of about 300 Louis. The person entrusted with the money, one Brown, brother of the Colonel, who was taken on board the Hazard sloop, was obliged to leave it on shore, that it was committed to the care of Mr Thomas Sheridan and Mr Murray.

That the Pretender's son attended only by Mr Sullivan went off from Arisaig about two or three days before the arrival of the French ships to some of the Isles, but as to this he cannot be positive having only heard it from others.

On the 29th after it was dark, I sent a detachment of 150 men to Moidart with orders to drive all the cattle they could meet with, to search the houses for arms, but not to burn them as I intended to go there myself. The party arrived by break of day but Captain Fergusson of the Furnace, having the night before landed Captain Miller with his command consisting of eighty regulars and 120 of the Argyllshire Levies which gave the alarm so that all the cattle were drove to inaccessible mountains. Kinlochmoidart House plundered and afterwards set on fire together with all the little huts in the neighbourhood so that the party sent from hence having no cover were forced to return with only three horses belonging to Lord Elcho and a little fresh meat for themselves'.[214]

On 7th June the General replied to his letter from the Duke of Cumberland.

'In my last to Sir Everard Fawkener [sic]I advised him of two brothers of Kinlochmoidart viz. Aeneas and Allan, the first formerly a banker of Paris was one of those that came over with the Pretender's son and intrusted with all his money and affairs. I did not think it proper to trust them on shore, or even in this loch. So, ordered them on board Captain Hay's sloop the same night, under the care of Lieutenant Lindsay, and finding I could draw nothing of moment from either, I ordered the ship to sail next morning for Tobermory, and there remained 'till further orders giving Lindsay a strict charge not to suffer any person to speak with them but when he was present. The banker being put on board and suddenly finding the ship under sail the next morning has had the desired effect, for he now begins to squeak, and told Lindsay that he knew where the French money was hid, but will not discover it under any other conditions than that of his pardon, which if he obtains he will certainly subscribe to banishment.

He further says that the Pretender's son had once got to the Lewis Island, but was soon obliged to leave it and forced back to the Continent, this intelligence of his may be with a design to prevent searching the Island of Lewis but be that as it will, I intend to take one of the wherries I have here, and go to Tobermory to see what I can make of the Banker, and at the same time send notice to the Ships of War of what I have learned.

I humbly submit to Your Royal Highness whether you will not think it proper to allow me to promise him his pardon provided he discovers where the money is hid, or where the Pretender's son may be apprehended. If he performs either of these, I am resolved to promise largely and shall leave it to Your Royal Highness to bring me off afterwards'.[215]

Sadly, for the people of those days and for posterity, Aeneas MacDonald either managed to conceal his knowledge or was actually unaware of the location of the hidden treasure. The General, having cross-questioned him minutely, declared himself to be 'greatly disappointed'.[216] He was not helped by the fact that Cumberland bluntly refused to collude with Campbell's suggestion of trading secrets for a pardon.

Two days after the General's arrival, H.M.S. *Furnace* commanded by Captain Fergusson, sailed into Tobermory Bay. On board was Lord Lovat, who, at the age of eighty, had been induced to join the Rising on the offer of a dukedom from Prince Charles. Captured by Government soldiers, when hiding in a hollow tree, Lovat was now on the first part of his journey to London to stand trial for treachery to the King. He had married the General's sister Primrose, to whom, by all contemporary accounts, he had been excessively unkind. Nonetheless the General, having persuaded him to write a statement in his own defence, sent it with a letter to Sir Everard Fawkener calling him 'My dear brother Lovat' and asking for mercy to be shown.

Likewise, when Cameron of Dungallon (who had offered to surrender and given useful information about the landing of gold and arms from France) together with old MacDonald of Glencoe were sent to Inveraray, the General wrote to the Sheriff:

'I beg you will order them to be well used but when they go abroad that an officer may attend them. Such letters as are directed to them and such as they write ought to be looked into'.[217]

On the following day the General summoned Captain Fergusson, together with other Naval personnel, including Commodore Smith, newly made senior naval officer in the West Highlands, who the General thought to be 'a most judicious sensible humane man'. News had just come in that some of the most sought after Jacobites were hiding in the remote island of St Kilda and thither the General proposed to go.

He went on board the *Furnace* on 15th June. With him, on this and several other small craft, he took 50 men of his own regiment, the Royal Scots Fusiliers and 120 of the Argyllshire levies. They first sailed to Loch Moidart, then to the island of Eigg only 'to find nothing there'.

This was hardly surprising as Captain Fergusson, in addition to taking 132 prisoners, had already taken all that the remainder possessed. Even the boats had been seized, so that the unfortunate people, deprived of their cattle, could fish only from the shore.

The neighbouring island of Canna, so recently searched by Captain Fergusson, was the next port of call. From there they set forth for the Western Isles. Rounding the north end of Lewis, they thrust into the rolling swell of the Atlantic, for St Kilda, where, as General Campbell's A.D.C. reported, their arrival caused the inhabitants to fly in terror from the shore.

'The 19th we came near St Kilda, and landed part of our troops, and some sailors, but after searching the island found nothing but the miserable inhabitants whose aspect, dress, and sentiments, sufficiently denote their remote situation and the little commerce they have with the continent. At St Kilda we parted with the Commodore who made for his rendezvous off Barra head'.[218]

The next day General Campbell set sail again, heading east for Pabbay, an island between Harris and North Uist. Then he continued to Bernera where he landed about 100 men. Convinced that the 'young adventurer' as he called him, was somewhere on the Long Island he determined to make an exhaustive search of the Uists from north to south.

Chapter 25
The Irish Spinning Maid

On Friday 20th June, Captain Caroline Scott, landed with a strong force on the shore of Loch Boisdale only two miles from where Prince Charles was hiding. Alexander MacDonald of Boisdale, Clanranald's younger brother, who despite initial misgivings was a staunch supporter of the Prince, was arrested and held prisoner aboard the warship H.M.S. *Baltimore.*

A local man, breathless and terrified, came running to tell Prince Charles and his companions of the danger in which they stood. Captain Scott had seized Boisdale's house. He had tortured his wife and servants, gagging them and tying their hands behind their backs, while his men ransacked the building.[219]

The Prince did not wait. Together with his companions he scrambled into a boat. Pushing out from the shore they sailed to the head of Loch Boisdale to land, probably at Aurotote or at Loch A' Bharp.

The mouth of Loch Boisdale was watched by two fast sailing men-of-war, so the only escape route lay across the hills to the west. The Prince said farewell to the boatmen and with Felix O'Neil, a mercenary soldier who had been with him since Culloden, was guided by Neil MacEachain, the tutor of the children of Clanranald, to a cave behind Beinn Ruigh Choinnich.

According to MacEachain, a small man bent in the shoulders for the fiddle playing for which he was renowned, it was while they were hiding in the cave that a messenger from Hugh MacDonald of Armadale came to tell them that the Prince must somehow reach Skye. Once there, Lady Margaret MacDonald who although the wife of a staunch Hanoverian was secretly a Jacobite, would protect him.

Hugh apparently put forward the amazing plan, that Charles, disguised as a maid, should travel with his stepdaughter Flora MacDonald. The Prince was greatly excited and at sunset he and Neil set off to what must have been a pre-arranged meeting.

Flora, according to tradition, was sleeping in a hut, guarding her brother's cattle, on a shieling (a summer grazing) on the northeast slope of Sheaval overlooking Loch Eynort. This is verified by the accounts of both Neil MacEachain and Felix O'Neil, but a girl of Flora's social position would not, in reality, have been herding cows on a mountainside alone at night. Therefore, it must be taken that she was keeping an assignment.

The hut is believed to have been built against the side of the lower of two large boulders on the west side of the burn, which runs down the hill from the Pass of Unasary. (773273 0.S. Map sheet 22).[220]

The night of Friday 20th June was clear, it being only a few hours short of the Summer solstice, a time in the North West Highlands, when darkness is little more than dusk.

The three men climbed the hill cautiously, glancing over their shoulders to watch for signs of pursuit. Where possible they clung to the shadows, for a full moon shone over the island casting her light on land and sea. Neil MacEachain went first, with the Prince and O'Neil creeping behind until, as they approached the shieling, Neil edged forward on his own. He spoke through the door to Flora, who hastily threw on some clothes, and then, coming out into the moonlight, was introduced to the Prince.

The conversation between them, apparently at the back of the hut, resulted in the proposal being put to Flora that she should take the Prince by boat to Skye, in the disguise of a spinning maid, supposedly Irish, on passports provided by her stepfather. Flora demurred, saying firstly that his wife, Lady Margaret's involvement in the plot might result in ruin for her husband, Sir Alexander MacDonald of Sleat, and secondly that she feared for her own reputation on account of malicious gossip. On the first point O'Neil assured her that Sir Alexander, as a serving soldier then in Fort William, would not be held responsible for his wife's actions, and on the second he promised her that 'if she feared for her character he would marry her without hesitation'.[221]

This is what he reported, but Flora herself was later to say that it was the sight of the Prince, in the Highland dress which Clanranald had provided, now torn and stained with peat, and of his features tense with anxiety, which moved her to try and save him. Thus, did the instinctive kindness of a brave and determined young woman lead to a historic rescue.

Following her meeting with Charles, on Saturday 21st June, Flora, accompanied by Neil MacEachain, travelling in the disguise of her servant, set out for Nunton, the Clanranald's house on Benbecula. The ford at Carnan, which they had to cross from one island to the other, was guarded and Flora, without a passport, was promptly arrested by the militia and held in custody in a guard-house on the far side for what appears to have been two nights.

Finally, her stepfather, Hugh MacDonald, the commanding officer, appeared and after he and Flora had breakfasted together, he gave her passports for herself and Neil and for another woman. In addition, he provided her with a covering letter to his wife in Skye, telling her that he was sending Flora with an Irish maid who was a very good spinster, to help her with a large amount of lint which she had amassed, apparently, at Armadale. He then put forward the suggestion that Flora should meet the Prince at Rossinish, from where they could embark for Skye. On the strength of this Neil returned to the Prince's place of hiding on South Uist to tell him of what was planned.[222] Flora then went to Nunton, where she found Lady Clanranald. From there she contrived to send a message to the Prince telling him that all was well.

Neil MacEachain, in the meantime, knowing that the ford was closely guarded, managed to find some local fishermen who, for a sum of money, agreed to take the three of them, himself, the Prince and O'Neil, to Benbecula. From there they struggled through bogs in darkness and in pouring rain to the cottage on Rossinish where they hoped to find Flora.

The people there, however, denied seeing her. Furthermore, they warned that a body of the Skye Militia was encamped nearby. Despite this daunting news, Neil managed to find shelter in the house of a tenant of Clanranald, who, not only welcomed the Prince but set him before a fire to dry his clothes. Next morning Neil set off for Nunton to tell Flora that the Prince was waiting. He returned to say that all was not yet ready and Charles, to his utter fury, was forced to remain in hiding while messages went to and fro Nunton, for another three days.

Ostensibly the reason for the delay was that the clothes for the supposed spinning maid took a long time to cut out and sew. In fact, from the evidence available, it now seems clear that the real reason was that a system of deception was being organised to ensure that the voyage across the Minch would be free from detection and pursuit.[223]

It is at this stage of the story that Donald Roy MacDonald – who was destined to play such an important part in the Prince's escape – first appears on the scene. Donald Roy, the brother of Hugh MacDonald of Baleshare in North Uist, was at that time recovering in Skye after being wounded in the foot fighting for the Jacobites at Culloden. He now went openly to the island of Flodda Chuin, off the north end of Trotternish, carrying six shirts belonging to Sir Alexander MacDonald (whose wife Lady Margaret probably organised the plan). The sharp-eyed watchers were deceived into thinking that he was taking them to the Prince and consequently the search for him was intensified in the northeast corner of Skye, rather than on the west coast, which had been under constant surveillance.

The greatest risk of capture still lay in crossing the Minch, where naval ships patrolled constantly, and stopped any vessel afloat. An Irish boat called *The David*, which carried meal between the islands, suddenly disappeared and rumours were spread that the Prince was aboard and was making for the open sea. Commodore Smith, sailing from St Kilda in the *Eltham*, was stopped off Barra Head and informed. He immediately ordered an intensive search of the seas around Barra upon which the ships left the Minch to join in.

Thus, was the sea-lane cleared for a safe passage to Skye. Nonetheless the problem remained of entering Loch Snizort, where a landing was intended, without being discovered by the guards on Waternish Point.

This seemed almost impossible. However, once again the intrepid MacDonalds formed a conspiracy in which a lady was involved. This time it was Mrs MacDonald of Kirkibost, in North Uist, whose husband, a cousin of Sir Alexander MacDonald of Sleat, commanded an Independent Company.

On Friday 27th June, she sailed from North Uist to visit Lady Margaret at Mugstot, and to tell her all that was planned. But on landing she was searched with a thoroughness bordering on indecency, in case she was the Prince in disguise. As a lady of some importance, she professed to be greatly insulted, as her skirts were pulled up and her stays, enforced with whalebone, prodded by none too gentle male hands.

Her protests were voluble, but it seems that the whole incident was a well-played out charade. Accusations of slackness could not be levelled against the guards. Somehow, in a low voice she managed to warn the officer of what was likely to occur. He then whispered back an assurance that, in the immediate future, he would not show excessive vigilance in stopping unrecognised craft.[224]

Meanwhile as this was happening on Skye, the Prince's situation in Benbecula was becoming increasingly desperate. The government troops, which had landed on both North and South Uist, were continuing their systematic search and it now seemed almost inevitable that he would shortly be captured.

According to a long-established tradition, by the morning of Friday the 27th of June, he had become so despondent that he was about to send Felix O'Neil to

General Campbell to offer him his surrender. Then as he reached the depths of despair John and Rory MacDonald, cousins of Flora's who were to form part of the crew, reached him with a message from Flora that the boat was ready.[225]

Flora herself came from Nunton to Rossinish with her brother Angus, his wife Penelope (Lady Clanranald's eldest daughter), and Lady Clanranald herself. They arrived there to find the Prince waiting on the shore. Having greeted her with great courtesy, he handed Lady Clanranald to the farmhouse, the home of her husband's tenant. There a supper was prepared, with the Prince, now restored to his usual enthusiasm for even the simplest task, taking part in the cooking of the roasted liver, heart and kidneys of a bullock. Then they all sat down in high spirits to enjoy the impromptu feast.

Hardly had they begun, however, before a boy came running with a message that General Campbell had landed at Gramsdale, only two miles away. The party immediately ended. Everyone leapt to their feet. Grabbing whatever they could carry, they hastily boarded the boat and crossed to the south side of Loch Uskevagh where they finished their supper in the dawn.

Then came another message from Nunton. General Campbell had arrived at the house. Captain Fergusson had even had the temerity to sleep in Lady Clanranald's bed. Furious, but apprehensive, Lady Clanranald returned home at once to be closely cross-examined by General Campbell as to her whereabouts during the night. She told him that she had been visiting a sick child, whereupon the General, in a friendly voice, told her that he proposed to dine with her but must first know the name of the child. Lady Clanranald, having given, or invented a name, told him the child was much better. Fergusson did not pretend to believe her but the General told him to be quiet.[226] Subsequently, to her enormous relief, he bade her farewell that morning before embarking with all his men to sail south to the island of Barra to search for the fugitive Prince Charles.

Later, in the evening of that fateful day of Saturday 28th June, Prince Charles together with Flora MacDonald and Neil MacEachain, with five strong trusted oarsmen, embarked in an open boat only eighteen feet long, on a night crossing of the notoriously rough stretch of sea between the Western Isles and Skye, called the Minch.

Chapter 26
'A Very Pretty Young Rebel'

From Benbecula General Campbell followed the Prince and Flora MacDonald across the Minch to Skye. On 7th July, from Watersea Bay, where the fugitives had so recently come ashore, he wrote to Captain Caroline Scot.

'Captain Campbell of Skipness who is now at Boisdale will inform you of what intelligence I have…and of the consequent disposition I ordered to be made of the troops. He has the direction of for apprehending such of the Rebel Gentlemen, as there is reason to believe are a skulking thereabouts…

You will no doubt take care that the birlings you brought from Fort William, are secured from falling into the hands of them who may be suspected to make a bad use of them, for I look upon the securing of boats on the Long Island at this time to be a matter of consequence…

As the ships of war may be necessary for your support in carrying on the public service whilst in these parts, allow me to advise you to give Commodore Smith notice of what you are doing, and let your letter be directed to him and me jointly in Watersea Bay'.[227]

From Loch Snizort, whence he had sailed, on 9th July, he issued an ultimatum addressed to 'All His Majesty's Officers Civil and Military, and to all the Leigcy [sic] Ecclesiastics or Laymen on the Island of Skye'.

'Whereas I have received undoubted intelligence that on the 28th of last month the Pretender's son crossed over from the island of South Uist to the isle of Skye disguised in women's cloths, and accompanying a daughter of McDonald of Milton. These are designing you in His Majesty's name to exert yourselves in scouring and apprehending the said Pretender's son with all his adherents. And especially to be aiding and assisting as much as in your power to the bearer Captain Lachlan McNeil and all others acting under my command in executing the said service. Given under my hand on board His Majesty's ship Furnace in Loch Snizort on the 9th July 1746'.[228]

Then on the next day, from Sir Alexander and Lady Margaret MacDonald's house of Mugstot he wrote to Captain MacLeod of Talisker, a man much feared by the islanders, who was in command of the militia on Skye.

'As there is certain intelligence, that the Young Pretender has left South Uist, and come to this island, I have sent Captain Fergusson of the Furnace sloop of war, with some of my officers and men joined to some sailors to endeavour to apprehend him, I therefore desire that you will be assisting therein, by joining to those he has, such of your command as he may find necessary which he is to signify in writing'.[229]

From Portree, on the east coast of Skye, the Prince had in fact reached the neighbouring island of Raasay. He then crossed over to the mainland, from where, after many adventures, as is so well known, he escaped at last to France.

Flora for her part, with Neil MacEachain, left Portree the next morning after spending the night at the inn. They found a boat, which took them across Loch Portree. Then, after landing on the far shore, they got horses and rode southwards to her mother's house at Armadale, a distance of over forty miles.

She must have been physically exhausted and also extremely apprehensive for she knew that the Prince's escape from South Uist would, almost certainly, be discovered. Once that had happened, the part she had played would, inevitably, be detected. She was under no doubts whatever of how she would suffer in consequence…

Flora remained at her Mother's house at Armadale but, on 11th July, she received a message from her cousin, Donald MacDonald of Castletown (a place about 4 miles away). He asked her to come to his house to meet a lawyer, who, on the instructions of a Lieutenant MacLeod of Talisker, wanted to ask her some questions about her involvement with the Prince. Donald Roy, also at Armadale warned her that this was a trap, but Flora, with typical determination, insisted that she must do as she was asked.

On the way she met her stepfather, who seems to have been unaware of what was planned, for shortly before she reached her destination, she was arrested by Lieutenant MacLeod, who appeared with a body of militia.

She was not allowed to go home or even to send word to her mother before being conveyed by boat to the *Furnace.* There, to her great good fortune, she was cross-examined, not by the merciless Captain Fergusson, but by Major General Campbell of Mamore.

The general sat behind a table beneath the low cabin roof. Resplendent in red coat and wig, he waited to interview the girl who, by all accounts, was likely to be a harridan. Expecting her to be dragged in, wild-eyed, dishevelled and screaming, he found himself instead facing a young woman, small and slight in stature, who stood erect before him. Ordering her guards to release her he briefly took in her appearance, noticing the dark hair and fair skin so typical of Celtic people. Most notably he recognised the courage revealed in the direct gaze of the fine, wide apart, eyes, calm rather than defiant, which met his own without revealing fear.

Flora answered his questions politely in the soft voice of one whose first language is Gaelic, which falls so pleasantly on the ear. She told how she had been introduced to the Prince in the shieling and of how she had been prevailed upon to help him in his time of distress. She described how she had then gone to Lady Clanranald's house of Nunton, where the blue sprigged dress and the other items of the Prince's disguise had been made for him, after which she had conveyed him in a boat from Benbecula to Skye.

She admitted that on landing she had gone to Mugstot, but she made no mention of Kingsburgh. Also, she cleverly whitewashed the involvement of Lady Margaret by saying that she herself had sent for Donald Roy MacDonald and had beseeched him to take the Prince to Raasay in the hopes that MacLeod of Raasay would help him. She then told General Campbell how they had set out for Portree from Mugstot, insisting that they had merely called in at Kingsburgh House, where, because she felt ill, they had been persuaded to stay the night. She swore, furthermore, that she had slept in one room and that the Prince and Neil MacEachain had shared another. She then described how they had continued to Portree from whence the Prince had sailed to Raasay.

General Campbell, having heard her account, told her that she must remain a prisoner. However, aware as he was of the harsh treatment of the Jacobites by some of his subordinates, he gave specific orders that she was 'to be treated with the utmost respect'.[230]

Another prisoner brought before him was old Donald Macleod of Galtrigal, captured on Benbecula by Allan MacDonald of Sleat. A slight figure, grey-haired and probably wearing the spectacles that he needed for his fading eyesight, [231] this elderly man, who had piloted the boat across the Minch on that stormy night in April and who had stayed with the Prince thereafter in his places of hiding in the Uists, now stood erect before the General who was much the same age as himself. Asked if he had been with Prince Charles, he replied in his soft Highland voice that indeed this was true. 'I was along with the young gentleman and I wanna deny it'.

"Do you know?" asked the General, "What money was upon that man's head? – no less a sum than thirty thousand pounds sterling which would have made you and all your children after you happy forever."

"What then?" said Donald, "Thirty thousand pounds – though I had gotten't, I could not have enjoyed it eight-and-forty hours. Conscience would have gotten up upon me: that money could not have kept it down. And though I could have gotten all England and Scotland for my pains, I would not allow a hair of his body to be touched, if I could help it!"

"I would not say," replied General Campbell, "that you are wrong."[232]

Flora was indeed fortunate, for thanks to the General's insistence, she was saved from the miseries endured by other prisoners on the voyage who, kept in darkness between decks and given only minimal rations, slept upon coils of rope.

They were, however, allowed daily exercise on the quarter-deck where Flora, it would seem to her surprise, encountered Felix O'Neil. He had, in fact, escaped in a French ship, but determined to find the Prince, had disembarked to search for him in South Uist where he had been arrested. Flora, on seeing him again, is reputed to have tapped him lightly on the cheek and taunted him with causing her misfortune, to which accusation he replied, "Why Madam, what you call your misfortune is really your greatest honour," words which, unbeknown to either of them at the time, were to prove to be of such great significance thereafter.[233]

O'Neil was held afterwards in Edinburgh Castle where he spoke to his visitors of Flora, for whom he is known to have had a fondness. He was never to see her again, for once freed in the amnesty of 1747, he returned immediately to France.

Flora herself, after three weeks in the *Furnace,* was transferred to the *Eltham,* the flagship of Commodore Smith, who treated her with fatherly concern. When the ship came close to Armadale, he allowed her to go ashore under escort, and on her own promise that she would not speak Gaelic, unintelligible to her guards, while she was there. Her conversation with her mother must have been restrained for Hugh MacDonald, her stepfather, was in hiding. Had he been arrested, he would have faced capital punishment.

Flora returned to the ship with some clothes and other possessions. She also took with her a girl called Kate MacDonnell, who stayed with her as her maid for at least three months, and whose company during that time of her imprisonment must have been of great comfort and support.

On 24th July, General Campbell wrote to Lord Albemarle, who had taken over from the Duke of Cumberland as Commander-in-Chief of the Government army in Scotland.

'I have got several prisoners of some distinction which by H.R.H's letter of the 13th I am directed to put on board Commodore Smith when I come up with him.

I have sent Lieut. Buchanan with two French officers taken near Loch Broom where they landed with design to inform the Pretender's Son where a ship might be heard of to carry him off. I have after hunting for her found that she went off Sunday the 12th wanting provisions, one of the officers is very sick at sea so I thought it but common humanity to send them by land to your Lordship.

I know that Col. Campbell received orders to join Colonel Conway and take it for granted that the whole command must be gone to Morar, as soon as I can pick up some straggling parties I left in South Uist which are ordered to Kinlochnedael in Skye. I shall try to find out Colonel Conway and make offer of the small command I have with me towards executing H.R.Hs orders.

I send your Lordship enclosed the copy of a letter from the present Barrack Master of Bernera, [12] which I am persuaded will justify my sending him prisoner... I would have sent your Lordship the original letter, but fearing it might be lost and as it helps to corroborate other proofs I have against Clan Donald I thought best to keep it...

Captain Campbell of Skipness who has not yet joined me from South Uist, writes that one of his prisoners, to wit the Baylie of Benbecula, was with his Master Clanranald twice in company with the Pretender's Son, upon the whole I am humbly of opinion that Clanranald should be apprehended. I shall lay hold of him if he comes in my way and take care to secure the evidence against him.

I had almost forgot to send your Lordship two paragraphs from letters wrote by Capt. Norman McLeod of Waterstein who is Capt. of one of the Independent Companies in Sky, I am afraid it will appear that many have been employed who are very unworthy. Donald MacDonald of Armadael,[13] one of the Militia captains, and step-father to Miss MacDonald my prisoner, has escaped me and gone off. I discovered him to have been very active in the Young Pretenders escape, and was so indiscreet as to give his daughter a pass for herself, and one said to be an Irish girl her servant. This villain met me in South Uist, and had the impudence to advise me against making so close a search, and that if I should for some days a little desist he made no doubt of my success. I suspected him at the time, and have given it in charge to the officers in Sky to apprehend him, plainly telling some of them that if he was not taken I should have reason to suspect them likewise'.[234]

The *Furnace* sailed south from Skye on 28th July. On board were Major-General Campbell with a body of soldiers and some prisoners, amongst them Flora MacDonald, who the General now believed to have been cruelly exploited by her step-father, a man for whom he had a particular loathing as his letter to Lord Albemarle reveals.

On the 29th, the ship anchored in Loch-nan-Uamh (Loch of the Caves) the sea-loch which runs northeast from the Sound of Arisaig between Arisaig and Moidart. It was here, on the shore of the loch, that Prince Charles had first set foot on mainland Scotland almost exactly a year before. Then when a rumour, which proved to be false, was heard of a French Naval force approaching Mull, the *Furnace* sailed away from Loch-nan-Uamh and having rounded the point of Ardnamurchan into the Sound of Mull, put into the harbour of Tobermory, where a hundred soldiers were sent ashore.

The *Furnace* then sailed on through the Sound of Mull and the Firth of Lorn to the anchorage in the lee of the island of Kerrera, just to the southwest of Oban, then much used by the Royal Navy, known as Horse Shoe Bay.

From the ship the General wrote to Neil Campbell, hereditary Captain of Dunstaffnage, the mighty fortress at the mouth of Loch Etive (about 4 miles east of Oban) an important garrison of Hanoverian troops. The General, having given him instructions, asked him to visit him on his ship. He then added a most unusual request.

'Make my compliments to your Lady and tell her that I am obliged to desire the favour of her for some days to receive a very pretty young rebel; her zeal and the performance of those who ought to have given her better advice, has drawn her into a most unhappy scrape by assisting the young Pretender to make his escape. I need say nothing farther till we meet, only assure you that I am, dear Sir, your sincere friend and humble servant.

John Campbell.

I suppose you have heard of Miss Flora MacDonald'.[235]

The answer was favourable. Flora was duly accepted as a guest, rather than a prisoner, in the two-storeyed dwelling house, which had been constructed within the northwest range of the castle as recently as 1725.

Dunstaffnage Castle, built by John MacDougall, Lord of Lorne, in the mid-thirteenth century, is one of the finest examples of Medieval architecture in Argyll. Sited on the south shore, near the mouth of Loch Etive, to guard both the great inland waterway and the surrounding country, it then stood, magnificent as, although now partly ruined, it remains today.

The castle's importance as a landmark gave General Campbell a very real excuse to take Commodore Smith to visit Flora on the afternoon of 6th August 1746. Both men openly admired her. Commodore Smith being so entranced that he was shortly to give her 'a handsome suit of riding cloths, with plain mounting, and some fine lincs riding shirts',[236] hardly practical presents for a girl who was still held prisoner on board the battleship H.M.S. Eltham by then lying in the Firth of Forth. In view of his known attachment to Flora it may, in fact, have been Commodore Smith who persuaded General Campbell to visit Dunstaffnage Castle on that late summer afternoon.

Approaching from the sea the two elderly officers of King George's armed forces climbed the outside stair, built so steep and narrow that a single man could defend it from above. The General struggled up with difficulty, pained by the arthritis in his joints. Entering the castle, they were met by the Captain and his lady, and while entertained with tea or a glass or two of wine, they were joined by Flora, a slim figure with dark hair, wearing her best silk dress, collected in great haste before leaving Skye.

Known to have been treated by her so-called jailers as their honoured guest, she stayed at Dunstaffnage for over a week, for it was not until Wednesday, 13th August, that General Campbell wrote to the Captain of Dunstaffnage to say that her visit must end.

'Sir-you will deliver to the bearer, John MacLeod, Miss MacDonald, to be conducted her(e) in his wherry; having no officer to send, it would be very proper if you send one of your garrison along with her, I am, your most obedient humble servant.

John Campbell'.[237]

Flora returned to Horse Shoe Bay where she said farewell to the General, who, as far is as known, she was never to see again. Each remembered the other with respect, and in Flora's case with gratitude. Later the General wrote from Inveraray:

'I cannot but say (that) I have a great deal of compassion for the young lady. She told me that she would in like manner have assisted me or anyone in distress'.[238]

His words can be construed in several ways. Was he in fact secretly in love with her? They had, after all, spent almost a month together in close contact. He found her very attractive as the words of his letter prove. Nonetheless, as a man of honour, he may have felt bound to conceal his feelings for a young woman, who was actually a year younger than his own daughter.

The General, who had now been a widower for ten years, was predictably a lonely man. The idea of marriage may have been prohibited by the great difference in their ages. Also, Flora, as the daughter of a fairly humble tacksman in the Outer Isles, would not have been considered suitable as the wife of a duke, which the general now seemed bound to become. Indications are that he loved her with the affection of a father rather than as an intended bride.

Flora's own feelings were conveyed in a letter written later by Captain Knowles of the *Bridgewater* to General Campbell. 'She esteems you the best friend [s]he has in the world'.[239]

Chapter 27
Return to Inveraray

Whatever their feelings for each other; Flora and the General were never to meet again. She was carried off as a prisoner, first to Leith and then to London, where thanks to his intervention and that of Commodore Smith, she was spared the misery of the prison hulks lying in the Thames.

Instead she was lodged in the house of a Mr William Dick, a government messenger who was licensed to hold political prisoners in his home. Here she became a celebrity, thanks mainly to Lady Primrose, a prominent Jacobite, who introduced her to others in her house in Essex Street off the Strand. Again, it was thanks to Lady Primrose that she went back to Scotland in a post chaise, following the amnesty of 1746. Back in Skye Flora married Allan MacDonald of Kingsborough, the house to which she had taken Prince Charles, disguised as spinning maid, before his escape from Portree.

General Campbell, for his part, having said farewell to Flora in that August of 1746, was anxious to return to Inveraray to deal with the mountain of business relating to the supply and equipment of the army raised to defend the northwest of Scotland against the Jacobite Rising.

Stormbound in Horseshoe Bay, he wrote, on 12th August, to the Sheriff, Campbell of Stonefield,

'If the Commodore can't get out it is very possible I may not be at Inveraray before the beginning of next week which I desire you to keep to yourself least I should be plagued with a parcel of idle people following me about trifles.

Duntrune has been telling me of the great hardship it is to him to have his company kept out. I'm glad H.R.H'.s orders to me impours me to make everybody easy by discharging the whole, for which reason, I beg you to forward the enclosed order by express'.[240]

He then foretold what he rightly knew would occur when the fencible men were dismissed. Cattle lifting was still rampant in the Highlands. In August the beasts, full of summer grass, would be all too ready prey for robbers.

'When the country suffers they will cry out for some small force to protect them against thieving, then will be the time to offer my opinion that some independ[ent] companies should be kept on foot – you understand me'.[241]

The General's prediction proved to be all too true. In most parts of Argyll, they were gathering the harvest but in Appin destruction continued as the Red Coats from Fort William searched relentlessly for survivors of the Appin Regiment who had fought so gallantly for Prince Charles.

Amongst them, Charles Stewart of Ardsheal, their erstwhile commander, was hiding in a cave behind a waterfall on the steep, south facing, mountain of Beinn a'

Bheithir, just above the farm of Lagnaha. As above the ridge before him, he saw a black smudge in the sky, he knew that it was no ordinary bonfire. His house of Ardsheal was on fire. Terrified of what was happening to his wife, he was to learn later that, warned of the soldiers coming, she had fled to a barn where that same night she gave birth to their youngest daughter named Ann.

Previously, when the estate had been raided in May, General Campbell had ordered the milk cows to be returned thus saving Isabel Stewart and her children from starvation. This time, however, Captain Caroline Scott saw to it that every moveable object was taken before his superior officer could intervene. In a long letter to the General, dated 25th August 1746, Isabel Stewart gave a list of all that had been taken. Her own riding horse and two ponies used for bringing in peats. Cooking pots, knives and forks, bed linen and blankets; everything useful had gone. All that remained was destroyed. Even the fruit trees in the garden had been mercilessly hacked down. Then to add insult to injury Scott had seized the young man she employed as her children's tutor and carried him off to Fort William where, despite the fact that nothing could be proved against him, all his money and possessions, except for the clothes on his back, were taken from him before he was set free. Her bitterness emerges in a postscript in which, apologising for the coarseness of the paper on which she wrote she added 'my good friend Capt. Scott having left me none better'.[242]

Meanwhile her husband, who had several times narrowly escaped capture, made a bid to escape abroad. On his great grey horse, he rode up Glen Duror into the mist. The sun broke through and the Red Coats saw him and pursued. But nonetheless he eluded them and with the help of a farmer in Kinlochetive, who reputedly hid him in his grain kiln, he somehow reached the port of Leith. From there, pretending to be a wine merchant, he sailed safely to Flanders before moving to France where, his wife having joined him, he lived in exile until he died.

Charles Stewart was just one of the many Jacobites who managed to find a haven in France. Prince Charles himself was even then waiting for news of the ships, believed to have been sent to rescue him, by the King of France.

It has been suggested by some historians that the authorities in London sent unofficial orders to the army commanders in Scotland to allow the Prince to escape. If captured, he would have been an enormous embarrassment to the establishment. He was, after all, King George's cousin. Execution would make him a martyr, a cause for a bloody revenge. Imprisonment would have been, not only expensive but another cause for retribution. It was reckoned that the French King would, almost certainly, give him sanctuary. Therefore, he would be well out of the way.

Whether or not there is any truth in this surmise it is known that by the middle of August General Campbell believed the Rising to be well and truly at an end. His first priority now was to get the men of the Argyllshire militia off the pay list and back to the harvesting on their farms.

Thanks to contrary winds it was not until 18th August that he at last reached Inveraray. Once there he immediately 'called in all the out commands and dismiss them agreeable to the Duke's order, all except a few in the castles to guard the prisoners & c'.[243]

The toll which the campaign had taken of his physical strength was revealed the next day when he once again nearly collapsed from what appears to have been a bad attack of influenza, described as 'rheumatic pains accompanied with a fever'.[244]

However, now, as in the other bouts of illness, he struggled on with grim determination, grumbling but refusing to submit to debilitating pain.

Not everyone agreed with Campbell's decision to stand down his men. On 20th August, only two days after his arrival at Inveraray, a party of Argyllshire landowners, who included the Deputy-Lieutenants, assembled to sign a memorial asking General Campbell to 'intercede for us with His Majesty that some of the independent companies in the West of Scotland may be kept on foot'. The General forwarded this appeal, together with similar requests from the lairds of Stirlingshire and Dunbartonshire, to Lord Albemarle, now since Cumberland's resignation, Commander-in-Chief in Scotland. Albemarle in turn sent them on to the Duke of Newcastle, King George's principal Secretary of State, with the pithy remark that 'as it appears to me to be a scheme entirely grounded for the defence of the Argyll country, I shall not presume to give my thoughts thereupon, but shall beg of your Grace to lay them before his Majesty'.[245]

On 23rd August, the Duke of Argyll's secretary, John Maule, wrote to the General,

'His grace offers you his best compliments, as we all do to Colonel Jack…our ministers here say they have certain intelligence that the Young Pretender is got to France'.[246]

This was in fact misinformation. Prince Charles was at that moment hiding in a wood called Torvault near to Cameron of Lochiel's burnt out house of Achnacarry.

The General himself was not deceived.

'I really believe that the Pretender's son is still in Scotland, and that the Court of France continue to make a tool of him to divert our sending our troops to Flanders', he wrote to the Duke of Argyll'.[247]

His surmise proved to be correct. The Prince was at large for another three weeks, until, on 19th September, he managed to reach Borrodale, where two French ships, *l'Heureux* and *Prince de Conti,* were lying in Loch-nan-Uamh.

The Prince boarded the *l'Heureux* immediately and, in the early hours of next morning, while still in total darkness, the ships weighed anchor and with a fair wind behind them, sailed for the open sea. Nonetheless, thanks to rough weather thereafter, it was not until 10th October that he landed safely in France.

On 24th September Lord Albermarle wrote to General Campbell with the news that from dispatches sent from Fort William he believed that the Prince had escaped. 'Which if confirmed will give you liberty to go to England whenever you shall think proper'.[248]

The General, extremely tired and still plagued by the rheumatism, which he had suffered throughout the campaign, longed, intensely, for his home in Kent. Nonetheless his work in Scotland was unfinished. There were still accounts to be done. Greatly fatigued as he was, he sat down at his desk in 'The Pavilion' and began working through the files of papers which lay piled up before him.

'The Pavilion' at Inveraray, built only as a temporary measure, in late autumn, became increasingly cold and damp. With draughts whistling round him, his arthritic fingers cramped with cold, John Campbell struggled on. Granted £20,000 by the Government for the funding of his campaign, he had also contributed £2,552, 15s 7³/₄ of his own, part of which went to pay for the meal supplied by the Barrack Master of Bernera'.[249] Determined to account for all he had spent, together with the Sheriff, Archibald Campbell of Stonefield, he laboriously listed every item of expense incurred in raising, arming, and providing for the Argyll Militia, from the start of the emergency now over a year ago.

On 8th September he wrote to the Duke of Argyll, listing his expenditure and telling him, 'I was obliged to act the part of Commissary of provisions in a country where there was none'. His work, however, was not yet done for it still took another month to number and collate the arms, handed in to Inveraray Castle, by the fencible men who were being stood down.

Burdened as he was with paper work the General now got instructions from his cousin the Duke to supervise the building of the new castle, abandoned since the outbreak of the Rising. The architect Roger Morris had designed the building in a symmetrical classical design, 'in outline a rectangle of 118 by 100 feet and at each corner a tower, 24 feet in diameter, placed as far out as possible on the angle without actually being detached. The castle was to consist of three floors and garrets, the corner towers four. The main floor containing the public rooms was to be approached by Gothic bridges on north and south, over a fosse 35 feet wide and some 9 feet deep; above were to be bedrooms and below, looking out into the fosse, the kitchen offices'.[250]

William Adam of Maryburgh, who, on the suggestion of the Sheriff, had been selected to be the master of works. Adam duly arrived whereupon the General, writing to the Duke, reported him 'slow but sure'.[251]

General Campbell then annoyed his cousin by suggesting that, the proposed new castle should be built to face Loch Fyne rather than the old avenue on the south side

'If I should take upon me to alter the Front of your House I am persuaded you'll forgive me'.

He was over optimistic. The Duke was furious, deeming such an idea to be nothing short of interference. John Maule, his secretary, did his best to patch things up. Writing to General John he said,

'I am sorry the D: was so peevish about your proposal about altering ye fronting of the house at Inveraray, which has been entirely owing to His Grace's misunderstanding your words'.

But to Lord Milton (the Lord Justice Clerk) he was more outspoken, telling him that,

"The Duke...has written to ye Sheriff, that he's displeased wt ye alterations G.Campbell and Adams proposed about ye house at Inveraray that he has expressly discharged them, and that they proceeded upon a mistake in one of ye alterations viz about the breadth of ye Gallery," which in fact would be half a foot wider than his Library at London! He soon calmed down, however, and the General was present when the foundation stone was laid on 1 October 1746.[252]

His last letter from Inveraray, written on 9th October, was addressed to the Sheriff to whom he gave instructions regarding the prisoners, still held there in the prison, and also in the island fortress of Castle Stalker in Appin.

'It is necessary that a number of men be kept in pay to guard them' he wrote before detailing the number of officers and men required with his usual regard for detail.

Then at last he was able to leave Inveraray. But first he had to go to Edinburgh, to deal with yet more paper-work concerning evidence against Jacobite prisoners. Finally, on 20th November, he wrote to John Maule telling him that he would be leaving for England the next day.

A post chase was the fastest and easiest way to travel, but the General knew that he would have to move in stages, resting in inns on the way. 'I am not well my dear John and cannot go by post'. At last he was forced to acknowledge the ravages, which the rigours of all his campaigns had made upon his health.

Chapter 28
The Winter Wind of Man's Ingratitude

General Campbell was not the only one to suffer. Duncan Forbes of Culloden, the Lord President, had returned from Skye, on 23rd April, to find his estates ruined. Both the Jacobites [including the Frasers] and the Government soldiers had pillaged and burnt without mercy. The extent of the damage, reckoned at £517, was merely the tip of the iceberg. It would take many years to repair ravaged buildings, to build up stocks of sheep and cattle, and to make the land as productive as it had been before. As Forbes' biographer states,

'It is one of the ironies of the rebellion that the estate of the mildest and most peace-loving man involved in the whole miserable business should itself have been the scene of one of the most abhorrent of the subsequent butcheries. William Rose, grieve to the Lord President, stated that twelve wounded men, carried out of his house under pretext of having their wounds dressed by the surgeon, were shot in the hollow very near the scene of the battle. The King is said, later, to have asked Forbes, "If it was true that a party of the Duke's army had killed certain supposed rebels, who had fled for safety into the court of Culloden House."

He replied: "I wish I could say 'No'." This put an end to his favour at court'.[253]

King George is supposed to have turned his back on Forbes, deaf to his pleading for clemency to the Jacobite prisoners, while Cumberland begged to be rid of 'that old woman who talked to me about humanity!'[254]

Once returned to Edinburgh, Forbes's reputation as a man who loved clemency led to him being deluged with pleas for help by those now threatened with loss of life and property for their loyalty to Prince Charles. In particular Forbes plead the case of MacDonald of Kingsburgh who, out of common humanity, had given the Prince a night's rest and shelter after he had found him 'maigre, ill-coloured, and overrun with the scab' after having been without food or sleep for two days, 'sitting on a rock beat upon by the rains, and when they ceased, ate up by flies'.[255] The case for Kingsburgh's release became more urgent when Forbes's friend, Sir Alexander MacDonald of Sleat, died suddenly on his way to Edinburgh, leaving his widow Lady Margaret (for all she was a Jacobite) without the support of Kingsburgh, who steward of their estates for nearly thirty years, was the man upon whom she most relied. Forbes with the quiet sense of humour, for which he was so well known, writing to Sir Alexander shortly before he died, enquired after Lady Margaret, whom he much admired, 'and her Infantry' as he called her brood of children![256]

Then, most famously, he championed Lady Anne Mackintosh, who as 'Colonel Anne', had led her husband's clansmen to fight for the Prince, while he himself stayed loyal to the crown thereby saving their estates. Her father, John Farquharson of Invercauld, wrote to Forbes thanking him for achieving her 'better usage, in the time of her great distress'.[257]

Forbes, in his capacity as a lawyer, was largely instrumental in drafting the Disarming Act of 1746, which forbade the possession of weapons in the Highlands. Nonetheless he considered that the loyal part of the Highlands should not be disarmed until the rebels had surrendered their weapons and the threat of a landing from either France or Spain had finally been brought to an end.

To the imposition of another act, against the banning of the Highland dress, he very strongly objected, declaring its prohibition as 'no more than a chip in porridge, signifying not one half-penny'. What really mattered, he insisted, was the prohibition of arms, 'let them dress as they liked'.[258] Forbes with his precise lawyer's mind, visualised the country which, once the Disarming Act became effectual, Scotland could become. He envisaged no difficulty in disarming the loyal clans but thought it essential that five or six garrisons should be established in areas where the people were known to be rebellious. From these military headquarters, if and when trouble arose, detachments could be sent out quickly to deal with violence into remote straths and glens. The garrisons would be self-sufficient communities containing tradesmen and weavers and even schools where women could learn to spin. Most importantly fishing would be encouraged in places anywhere near the sea, 'not only for the convenience of the troops, but for promoting the trade of the nation'.[259]

Most significant, however, of all the changes inaugurated at this time, was the Jurisdiction Bill, by which the hereditary rights of the Chiefs of the clans to administer justice was transferred to sheriff-substitutes acting on behalf of the Crown. Although drafted originally in August 1746, proceedings were held up until Lord Lovat, tried and condemned to death as a traitor, was executed on Tower Hill. Introduced by the Lord Chancellor Hardwicke, to the House of Commons, on 7th April 1747, the Bill finally became law in 1748.

Forbes, who initially opposed it, on the grounds that it gave too much power to the state, eventually became one of its strongest supporters, believing it to be a measure of great importance to the public. He did however stipulate that the power of judging petty trespass should be left to the Baron's Courts, an amendment which was accepted as a saving of great expense.

A document in his own small, neat handwriting, states that in his opinion social and economic improvements, such as existed in the more fertile areas of Scotland, were the best means of preventing lawlessness in the Highlands. He believed that it only needed one generation for people deprived of their weapons, to realise that the benefits of trade and industry were preferable to waging war. [260]

Despite all that he had done – it was reckoned that but for his influence in the Highlands over four times the number of men would have rallied to the banner of Prince Charles – Forbes died unrewarded, and near bankrupt, thanks to his service for the King. Not only had he spent great sums of money himself in arming and providing for the Independent Companies that were raised, but his factor had contributed about three years rent of his estate of Culloden, which the Government failed to refund. The remuneration of the men of the eighteen Independent Companies, which he had been commissioned to raise, had long obsessed his mind. Describing the men enlisted as 'children of my own' he had written endlessly to the prime-minister, the Duke of Newcastle, and to other leaders of the government, demanding the bare justice of the payment to them that was due.

For Forbes there was little or no reward. He left London at the end of 1746 having completed the final stages of his last great political achievement, the Heritable Jurisdiction Bill, which was to transform the life of the Highlands, His health was becoming a problem, the rough living and heavy load of responsibility he had borne during the Rising combined with heavy drinking had drained his once strong physique. In May 1747, knowing that he was ill, he decided to make a visit to the southwest counties of Scotland, hoping that he might benefit from a change of air. Then, in August, he went back to Bunchrew, the house where he was born, where there was nothing to talk about but lovely weather and a surfeit of salmon. But the autumn days shortened, and from his windows, he saw snow upon the hills.

Returning to Edinburgh in November, now knowing he had not long to live, he wrote to his only son John.

'I am very sorry for you, the great charges and expenses I have been at in supporting his Majesty in the Rebellion have far exceeded the sum I thought it would have cost when I saw you last. I would advise you to go to London where I believe I may have some friends yet. Mr Scrope, Mr Littleton and Mitchell are kind-hearted, affectionate men and they will tell the King that his faithful servant Duncan Forbes has left you a very poor man – Farewell – May the God of Heaven and Earth bless you!

Duncan Forbes'.[261]

Forbes then asked his cousin, Will Forbes, to explain to his son John the reasons for which he would find himself with little to inherit following his death. Duncan had long been a widower. His wife, a daughter of Hugh Rose of Kilravock, a neighbour in Aberdeenshire, had died very young and he had never remarried. Now John, his only son, just managed to reach him, in his house in the Cowgate in Edinburgh, before, on 10th December 1747, he died there aged only sixty-two.

Many were the epitaphs to this man so universally respected throughout the Scottish realm. Lord Monboddo, himself an advocate and a judge on the Scottish Bench, called him 'the greatest judge that has been in Scotland in our time'.[262] None, however, are more touching than that of his devoted servant John Hay, who throughout his illness had barely left his bedside. Writing to Forbes's sister, Grizzy, Mrs Rose of Kindeace, he said,

'I have not words to express the grief that is among all the people here on account of his death…I can write no more from grief but ever am the family of Culloden's and your affectionate servant.

John Hay'.

Chapter 29
Retirement – Tragedy and Triumph

General Campbell retired to Combe Bank his home in Kent. Although imposing in appearance with its Palladian design, the rooms with their high ceilings were cold and inhospitable, lacking a woman's touch. According to one visitor it was hardly more comfortable than the draughty old 'pavilion' of Inveraray while a Mrs Damer, staying at Combe Bank in 1803, wrote to a friend 'This house as you know with everything that is ornamental and pretty, has little of comfort, and the cold of it is above imagination'.[263]

Some two months after his arrival, there was a family festivity when the General's only daughter Caroline married for the second time.

In 1739, only three years after her mother's death, Caroline, at the age of eighteen, had married (as his third wife) Charles, 4th Earl of Elgin and 3rd Earl of Ailesbury. He had died leaving her with only one daughter. Now, on 19th December 1747, she married the Honourable Henry Seymour Conway, brother of the Marquess of Hertford, and first cousin of Horace Walpole with whom, he had a strong and lifelong attachment, being one of the main recipients of the many letters Walpole wrote.

Conway, an outstandingly handsome man, was also possessed of a charming personality. 'No man of his time was more generally liked. While he was a man of fashion, his tastes were cultivated and his habits respectable. In a period marked by political intrigue and corruption, he was conspicuous for integrity and a delicate sense of honour'.[264]

Renowned for his courage, he had fought at Fontenoy as Cumberland's ADC, before commanding the 48th Regiment of Foot, at Culloden. General Campbell in his letter to Lord Albermarle of 24th July had told him 'I know that Col. Campbell received orders to join Colonel Conway… I shall try to find out Colonel Conway and make offer of the small command I have with me towards executing H.R.Hs orders'.[14]

Conway was, nonetheless, a greater soldier than a diplomat. Walpole shamelessly manipulated him in pursuing his own ends.

Apart from the diversion of his daughter's wedding, the General, still a Gentleman-in-Waiting, made occasional journeys to London to wait on the King. It is easy to believe that the two talked mainly of the exploits of their soldier sons now both serving in Flanders to combat the French invasion of the Netherlands.

William Duke of Cumberland, by all accounts the King's favourite son, had handed over the reins of the army in Scotland to the Earl of Albermarle. Already defeated at Fontenoy he now again waited to confront Marshall Saxe, the greatest military strategist of his day. With him were both Harry Campbell, the General's second surviving son, and Harry Conway, his son-in-law.

On 2nd July 1747, the French general led his army against the combined forces of the Scots Guards under the Duke of Cumberland and of the Dutch Republic, led by the Prince of Orange, at Lauffeld (or Laffelt, now part of Reims) on the river Meuse just west of Maastricht.

Cumberland was once more overcome. Nonetheless, the battle ended with the British and Dutch forces making an orderly retreat while the French, who had lost more men, were prevented from taking Maastricht. Thus, a tactical victory for their foes was strategically a British victory.

Horace Walpole, writing to his friend George Montagu, sent him an account of the battle almost as the news reached his ears.

'Though we have no great reason to triumph, as we have certainly been defeated, yet the French have as certainly bought their victory dear…their least loss is twelve thousand men, as our least loss is five thousand. The truth of the whole is, that the Duke was determined to fight at all events, which the French, who determined not to fight but at great odds, took advantage of. His Royal Highnesses valour has shone extremely but at the expense of his judgment. Harry Conway, whose nature always designed for a hero of romance, and who is d'eplacé in ordinary life, did wonders, but was overpowered and flung down, when one French huzzar held him by the hair, while another was going to stab him: at that moment an English soldier with a sergeant came up, and killed the latter; but was instantly killed himself; the soldier attacked the other, and Mr Conway escaped; but was afterwards taken prisoner; is since released on parole, and may come home to console his fair widow, whose brother Harry Campbell is certainly killed, to the great concern of all widows who want consolation. The French have lost the Prince of Monaco, the Compte de Baviére, natural brother to the last Emperor, and many officers of great rank…

The King had a line from Huske in Zealand, on the Friday night, to tell him we were defeated, of his son not a word – judge of his anxiety until three o'clock on Saturday! Lord Sandwich had a letter in his pocket all the while, and kept it there, which said the Duke was well'.[265]

How much does this description, penned in the elegant and lively style, so typical of Walpole's writing, convey the agony of mind of those waiting for news? One senses the relief of the old King, believing, as he probably did, that his son was dead and in contrast the agonising sorrow of General Campbell, knowing now for certain that his own son Henry, or Harry as he was always known, had been slain,

Harry, who, while still in his early twenties, had shown great promise as a soldier, had been serving as ADC to General Sir John Ligonier, when he was killed. The shock and sorrow of his loss can only to some extent have been lessened on hearing that his daughter, Caroline's, new husband, Henry Seymour Conway, had miraculously managed to survive.

Although thankful to know that he was alive, Caroline had to endure long months of separation as the French refused to release him.

Again, writing to George Montagu, on 1st October, Horace, the faithful scribe, told him:

'I had a letter from Mr Conway, who is piteously going into prison again, our great secretary has let the time Slip for executing the cartel, and the French have reclaimed their prisoners'.

Nevertheless, despite his tedious incarceration, Seymour Conway, or Harry as he was known, was free by the summer and with his wife was visiting the court of the Princess Royal and her husband, William of Orange.

Horace Walpole, by this time ensconced in his villa at Twickenham, called Strawberry Hill, wrote to him on 27th June, describing his life in the country where 'in short, planting and fowls and cows and sheep are my whole business'. Nonetheless. Despite this new preoccupation, he still found time to relay the gossip of the day, items such as that the Duchess of Richmond was terrified to go out for fear of a miscarriage (this being her twenty-fifth pregnancy) and that at Vauxhall he had seen a long torchlit procession as Prince Lobkowitz' preceded by liveried footmen led Madame ambassadrice de Venise, in a green sack with a straw hat to the Prince of Wales's barge.

Is not my lady Ailesbury wary of her travels? Pray make her my compliments, unless she has made you any such declaration as Lady Mary Coke's[15] I am delighted with your description of the bed-chamber of the House of Orange…but the sight itself must have been very odious, as the hero and heroine are so extremely ugly…Adieu! Do let this be the last letter and come home'.[266]

The marriage of Lady Mary, 'this wayward, undisciplined young woman – one of those bawling Campbells fathered by the 2nd Duke of Argyll'[267] shortly came to an end 'as much through her own temperament as that of her execrable husband'.

Caroline's second marriage, in contrast, turned out to be a happy one. She had another daughter with whom, together with her older girl, she visited her father, at Combe Bank in Kent, enlivening his house with its echoing empty rooms. Their renewed companionship proved congenial to them both for she too had spells of loneliness with a husband serving abroad.

Harry Conway, meanwhile, continued to gain promotion in the army Firstly, as colonel of the 29th regiment of the line, he served with his regiment in Minorca, before being given command of a cavalry regiment, the 13th Dragoons. Returning to England he bought Park Place at Remenham, described by Horace Walpole, as one of the loveliest houses in England. He did not have much time to enjoy it before being posted to Ireland where his wife Caroline joined him, leaving their three-year old daughter with Walpole at Strawberry Hill.

The year 1747 proved auspicious for the General's family. In addition to his daughter Caroline's second marriage, he himself became a Lieutenant-General while his eldest son Jack, who had won such acclaim in the '45 as commander of the Argyll Militia and companies of the 42nd and Loudoun's Highlanders, was appointed Lieutenant-Colonel of the latter regiment. Following this, in 1749, Jack was given command of the 42nd regiment of the Line [later the Black Watch], while three years afterwards, in 1752, the General became Colonel of the 2nd Dragoons, later so famous as the Scots Greys.

By now the British army was largely based in Britain, the War of the Austrian Succession having been at last concluded with the signing of the Peace of Aix-la-Chappelle.[268] The Treaty was preceded by an armistice lasting for six weeks. The city of Maastricht, however, remained under siege but Horace Walpole relates how the Duke of Cumberland sent Lord George Sackville to Marshal Saxe, to tell that, 'as they are so near to being friends, he shall not endeavour to raise the siege and spill more blood, but hopes the marshal will give the garrison good terms as they have behaved so bravely'.[269]

147

Walpole also details the agreement, describing it as 'a general restitution on all sides'. The most important items being the allotment of Parma and Placenta to Don Philip of Spain. Of infinitely more significance to the people of Great Britain, however was the declaration that 'The Pretender [was] to be renounced, with all his descendants male and female'.[270] And that he himself was to be expelled from France.

Prince Charles replied with a public protest (in French) 0n 16th July 1748.

'We protest...against all the conventions that may be stipulated in the said assemblies, so far as they shall be contrary to engagements already entered into by us,

We declare by these presents that we regard, and will always regard, as null, void, and of no effect, everything that may be statuted or stipulated which may tend to the acknowledgment of any other person whatsoever as sovereign of the kingdom of great Britain, besides the person of our most excellent prince, James the third, our most honoured lord and father, and in default of him, the person of the nearest heir agreeably to the fundamental law of Great Britain'.[271]

His arguments proved to be futile. King Louis, although reluctant to expel Prince Charles from France, was forced by the terms of the treaty to sign an order to make him leave the country on 10th December 1748. Charles initially took no notice but eventually King Louis had him arrested at the opera and escorted to the frontier between France and Savoy.

Meanwhile in Britain the immediate result of the peace was a boom on the stock exchange. Nonetheless, as Walpole reports in the May of 1748.

'The city grows furious about the peace; there is one or two very uncouth Hanover articles, besides a persuasion of a pension to the Pretender, which is so very ignominious, that I don't know how to persuade myself it is true'.[272]

In fact nothing came of the pension so that Prince Charles was to remain in great poverty until, following the death of their father in 1766, his brother Henry, by then a cardinal, would resign to him his own pension from the Pope of 20,000 crowns, together with the small amount of money left by their father in his will.[273]

In 1748 Prince Charles must have been even more chagrined if the news ever reached him that the British Government, having refused to grant him a penny, was now granting what Walpole called 'three places for life of a thousand and twelve hundred a-year for three of his court, to compensate for their making him president of the session against his inclination' to Archibald Campbell, Duke of Argyll, now ruler of Scotland in everything but name.

In view of all that had happened, it seems barely credible that Prince Charles actually came to London in 1750. Despite the danger or perhaps even because of it – he is known to have loved taking risks – or as some think to get away from his troublesome mistress, Madame de Talmond with whom he is known to have had a violent quarrel – the Prince somehow crossed the Channel undetected. From 16th to 22nd September he stayed in London with the strongly Jacobite Lady Primrose, who had already befriended Flora MacDonald, in her house off the Strand in Essex Street.

Amazing though it may seem, the Prince walked openly round London in the company of a Colonel Brett. Reputedly, he even inspected the gates of the Tower of London and declared that he thought it would be feasible to blow in one of them with a petard.

This remark lends some credence to the curious tale told by Lord Stanhope, that Charles, who he says had gone to London in disguise, 'was introduced to a room full of conspirators'. They were all for a night attack on the palace but the Prince refused to have anything to do with it unless the safety of George II and his family was assured'.[275] Certainly he is known to have steadfastly turned down all suggestions aimed at the assassination of the man who had taken his throne, so in view of this, the story may indeed be true.

More extraordinary still is that the fact that no one betrayed him. The well-informed secret service must have known of his arrival in London therefore it does seem more than a co-incidence that, just as he managed to slip away from Scotland without detection, the authorities in London, burdened with the problem of what to do with him, now turned a blind eye. Despite the supposed secrecy of his visit the one thing which does emerge for certain is that, whatever the reasons for his apparent anonymity the Prince returned to France and his troublesome mistress, unrecognised (at least officially) and unscathed.

Chapter 30
The New Road to Inveraray

Duke Archibald, now in his seventies, continued to travel to Scotland every year. As Lord Justice General, Lord Clerk Registrar and Keeper of the Great Seal, his main business was conducted in Edinburgh, but in autumn, he proceeded to Inveraray where work on his new castle was under way. Progress, however, was slow. The difficulty of finding and transporting timber, lead for piping and other materials, proving to be a time consuming task.

One outstanding development, however, was the completion of the military road between Dumbarton and Inveraray. In May 1741 James Smollett of Bonhill had described Inveraray as 'singularly beautiful as the road is singularly bad, fit only for wild goats to scramble over'. On the Duke's previous visit in 1744, when, together with a party of friends who included the architect Roger Morris, brought to design the new castle and its surrounds, he had sailed from Greenock in a boat provided by his friend Sir John Shaw. Then, landing at Lochgoilhead, the party had mounted horses, sent to await their arrival by Archibald Campbell of Stonefield, Sheriff Depute and Chamberlain of Argyll, on which they had ridden slowly to the top of the pass above before coming down through the defile called Hell's Glen to St Catherines from whence they were ferried across Loch Fyne to Inveraray on the north shore.

Now, although the military road was still in the final stages of completion, it was possible for the Duke, by this time a man of sixty-two, to come in his carriage from Edinburgh to Inveraray.

Seven years had gone by since 1745, when, almost as Prince Charles came ashore in Scotland, 300 men of Lascelles Regiment (the 23rd of the line) had been set to work under the direction of Major William Caulfield, Inspector of Roads and Bridges in North Britain, to commence, what in the best of circumstances, could only be called an awesome task.

The weather was frequently atrocious. Caulfield himself was spared the worst of it, being called away to serve as Quartermaster to Sir John Cope, leaving men who made the best of his absence to labour as slowly as was possible. Then to crown everything as they toiled up the side of Loch Lomond, Gregor Ghlun Dhubh, of Glengyle, had swept down from the hills with a party of caterans to carry off the masons and men working on the bridges as prisoners together with all the timber, tools and other equipment which could be put to any other use.

However, despite this set-back the work had continued. Bit by bit foundations had been blasted out through Glen Croe, until on a steep zig-zag course, the road had reached the head of the glen. Exhausted, the soldiers and civil engineers commemorated their great achievement by carving 'REST AND BE THANKFUL' upon a stone.

By the summer of 1748, when eighteen bridges, some with arches fifty feet high, had been constructed, the road had reached the head of Loch Fyne. Then it continued along the north shore until, approaching Inveraray, it crossed the still unfinished bridge, with a sixty-foot arch, over the Garron Water, which runs from the Dubh Loch at the foot of Glen Shira, to Loch Fyne. Roger Morris, the architect for Inveraray Castle, had then suggested that young John Adam be put in charge of the completion of this work, made to his design, which was finished in 1749.[276]

On 23rd March 1752, the Duke of Argyll obtained a commission to buy up the forfeited estates of the Jacobites from the mortgagees, for the King to be 'colonised and civilised' thereafter presumably by himself. The Bill was passed by the House of Commons, but in the Lords, the Duke of Bedford, rightly interpreting it as a form of aggrandisement on Argyll's behalf, strongly attacked him. Accusing him of favouring the Jacobites, he produced several instances in proof of his claims which the old Duke neither refuted nor attempted to deny but instead made an almost incoherent speech, not even directed at Bedford, but at Lord Bath who had taken the government to task for allowing the Scots to pay no taxes for the last five years. The result was that twelve lords divided against eighty, who were for the bill, which subsequently became law.

In the autumn of 1752, however, controversy over the actions of the parliament in London was eclipsed by events taking place, in what at least to most people, was the remote region of Argyll. All Scotland buzzed with excitement as the trial, which has been described as one of the greatest travesties of justice ever known, took place in the little town of Inveraray. So great was the assembled crowd of lawyers, jurymen and collective dignitaries that the trial had to be held in the Parish Church for want of room in the old Court House, the town house of today.

The reason was murder. Colin Campbell of Glenure,[16] he who had been censored by General Campbell for failing to guard an outpost in 1746, now the Government factor for the forfeited Jacobite estates in the districts of Appin and Lochaber, had been shot from a long barrelled gun fired by an unknown hand.

The crime, although dreadful, in itself, was blown out of all proportion by the dread of another rebellion ever uppermost in most men's minds. Fear lent force to demands for retribution inciting the authorities to make an example of what dissidents might expect.

Appin was known to be a Jacobite stronghold, for which reason James Stewart of the Glens, a small farmer in Glen Duror, was accused of involvement in the killing on evidence largely procured by making the witnesses drunk. Argyll, as Lord Chief Justice in Scotland, with two other Law Lords, Lord Kilkerran and Lord Elchies, presided over the jury,[17] which, predominated by Campbells, condemned James Stewart to be hanged.

The enormity of the injustice imposed on the small Appin farmer is still remembered to this day. Although little excuse can be offered it must be remembered that only six years had passed since the Hanoverian dynasty had been threatened by the Rising of 1745. James of the Glens was made a scapegoat, his body left hanging in chains by the ferry from Argyllshire to Inverness-shire, to serve as a terrible warning to any who might try to rise again.

Chapter 31
'I Think I Have Some Credit with the General'

The very real fear of renewed rebellion in Scotland was based on the work of the undercover agents working both at home and abroad. Foremost amongst them, and probably the most dangerous, was a young man called Alexander Murray. His brother, Lord Elibank, outwardly a respectable laird on the Tweed, was actually, according to Walpole, 'a very prating, impertinent Jacobite'. Alexander, who is known to have liked his drink, was imprisoned in the infamous jail of Newgate for brawling in a Westminster election. Having refused to beg on his knees for pardon, saying that he only kneeled to God, he was held until, when released by the sheriffs, he was escorted by a cheering crowd, to his brother's house in Henrietta Street.

Subsequently, Murray, said to have lost his nerve, crossed the Channel to Paris where a spy, who went under the pseudonym of 'Dixon', told Prince Charles that he believed 'he can raise five hundred men for your service in and about Westminster'.[277]

The substance of the 'Elibank Plot' was that Alexander Murray would bring some of Lord Ogilvy's Regiment from France to London, where he would then secretly assemble a bunch of Jacobite supporters. The Prince himself would join them from his place of hiding, in Lady Primrose's house in Essex Street (where he had stayed on his visit to London in September 1750.) On a date still to be decided the men armed with swords and pistols, would break into St James's Palace and either kill or kidnap King George II and his family, after which Prince Charles would proclaim himself King Charles III.

At the same time James Keith, the Earl Marischal's brother, would land with a force from Sweden to rendezvous with the Scottish Jacobite chiefs at the cattle market in Crieff.

An unsigned letter, headed merely 'December 1752', thought to have been written by Young Glengarry, known commonly as Pickle the Spy, gives details of what was planned:

'The Young pretender about the latter end of September [1752] sent Mr Murray [of Elibank] for Lochgary and Doctor Archibald Cameron. They met him at Menin. He informed them that he hoped he had brought matters to such a bearing, particularly at the King of Prussia's Court, whom he expected in a short time to have a strong alliance with – that he did not desire the Highlanders to rise in arms until General Keith was landed in the north of Scotland with some Swedish troops. He likewise assured them that some of the greatest weight in England, tho' formerly great opposers to his family, were engaged in this attempt, and that he expected to meet with very little opposition. In consequence of this he gave Lochgary, Doctor

Cameron, Blairfety, Robertson of Wood Street, Skalleterr, mony and sent them to Scotland so as to meet several Highland gentlemen at the Crieff Market for Black Cattel'.[278]

An unsigned document among the Stuart papers in Windsor Castle tells how sentries were to be placed at St James's Palace, and in the adjoining park, and that two or three thousand men were to be hidden in Westminster, lodged in small groups in separate houses so as not to arouse suspicion. At a given time they were to seize the Palace and the Tower of London, to be taken by blowing in the gates, a plan believed to have been thought of by Prince Charles when walking round the city in 1750, when he said to his companion Colonel Brett that he thought it could be done with a petard.[279]

The scheme was hatched with the connivance of Frederick King of Prussia, who although a nephew of George II, saw his uncle's removal from the throne of England as a means of strengthening his association with France and with Queen Christina of Sweden, to whom the naval strength of Britain was a threat.

George Keith, the Earl Marischal, who had fought for the exiled King James in 1715 and then led the invasion of Spanish troops, which ended in defeat in Glenshiel in 1719, had found refuge in Prussia. By now an old man, he was nonetheless dispatched by King Frederick as his ambassador in the Court of Versailles, where his house in Paris became a centre of Jacobite intrigue.

Meanwhile in England the Elibank Plot to capture King George and his family, several times postponed, was finally abandoned when betrayed, it is thought by Young Glengarry, known to posterity as 'Pickle the Spy', who was constantly in touch with Henry Pelham, prime minister since 1743.

General Campbell, although avowedly living in retirement, now appears to have become involved in the machinations of the double agents working undercover in both Britain and France.

The evidence lies in a letter in the British Museum. The writer was James Mor Drummond, who had adopted the family name of the Duke of Perth while his own of MacGregor was proscribed. James Mor was the eldest son of the notorious Rob Roy MacGregor, who himself had taken the name of Campbell to gain the patronage and protection of 'Red John of the Battles'. Rob Roy had first come under suspicion as an agent of the Duke when he famously refused to lead his men into the battle of Sheriffmuir. If Rob Roy spied for the Duke, it seems logical to believe that his son did the same for General Campbell.

James Mor himself had led an extraordinary career. Fighting for Prince Charles he had been badly wounded at Prestonpans, but recovering, had fought again for the Prince at Culloden. Thereafter, a victim of ingratitude as he believed himself to have been, he had become a secret agent, spying for whoever would pay him for the information he revealed. Thought to have been involved in the murder of Campbell of Glenure, he may have produced the assassin who fired the fatal shot. Most famously, however, he had quarrelled with Young Glengarry over the question of money.

In April 1746, almost as Culloden was fought, two ships, the *Mars* and the *Bellona* had arrived in Loch-nan-Uamh. They had carried 12,000,000 livres from Spain, together with a large sum of money from France, sent belatedly by King Louis XV to help the Jacobite cause. Learning, however, that this was already lost, and that

Prince Charles was a hunted rebel, the captains had ordered their crews to unload the money and quickly put back to sea.

This was the fabled treasure about which General Campbell had so closely questioned the Princes' banker Aeneas MacDonald and his brother Allan, when he found them held prisoner at Tobermory. They had given him some information, when, as he put it 'they began to squeak', but by this time the gold had vanished.

Six caskets of coins, in fact, had been carried to Arkaig, just north of Fort William, where they were buried. The treasure was first entrusted to Murray of Broughton [Secretary to Prince Charles] who began to distribute it amongst the Clan chiefs, but when he was taken prisoner, later to turn king's evidence, the money was put in charge of Cameron of Locheil, until, when in September 1746, he fled to France with the Prince. Then it was left with Clunie MacPherson, that eternally colourful character, who remained in hiding in his famous 'cage' on Ben Alder for another eight years. James Mor certainly got some money much to the fury of Glengarry, who, having forged a letter from King James VIII & III (the Old Pretender) got away with part of the hidden hoard.

Doctor Archie Cameron, brother of the exiled Cameron of Locheil, who was serving as a secretary to King James, was sent by him from Rome to bring back some of the money. Cameron, having accused Glengarry of theft, was then betrayed by him when hiding in a house called Brenachyle near Loch Katrine. Taken to London, to be tried and convicted of treachery for fighting in 1745, Cameron was executed despite the desperate pleas of his wife who flung herself, begging for mercy, at the feet of King George.

Horace Walpole, in a letter to Sir Horace Mann told him that 'Doctor Cameron is executed, and died with the greatest firmness. His parting with his wife the night before was heroic and tender. He let her stay till the last moment, when being aware that the gates of the Tower would be locked, he told her so; she fell at his feet in agonies: he said "Madam, this is not what you promised me', and embracing her, forced her to retire, then with the same coolness, looked at the window till her coach was out of sight, after which he turned about and wept."

Walpole, having described the gruesome details of the execution – Cameron endured the medieval punishment for traitors by being hanged and beheaded, but was spared the final agony of being disembowelled while still alive – then adds a common rumour 'I cannot tell you positively that what I hinted of this Cameron being commissioned from Prussia was true, but so it is believed'.

'The populace' wrote Tobias Smollett, 'though not very subject to tender emotions, were moved to compassion and even to tears, by his behaviour at the place of execution, and many sincere well-wishers to the present establishment thought that the sacrifice of this victim, at such a juncture, could not rebound either to its honour or security'.[280]

James Mor in the meantime, having managed to reach Paris, offered to capture Allan Breck Stewart, believed to be the murderer of the Government factor, Campbell of Glenure, and to bring him back to justice in England. Summoned to London, initially for questioning, he wrote to Lord Albermarle saying that,

'If your lordship think this agreeable, I should wish General Campbell would be one of those present as he knows me and my family, and besides that, I think to have some credit with the General, which I cannot expect with those whom I never had the honour to know'.[281]

What actually did he mean? Can it be taken that he was trying a subtle form of blackmail to coerce the General into vouching for his character in return for favours – presumably information as to movements of the Hanoverian army – formerly received?

James Mor was examined in London on 6th November 1753. He told how he had gone to France in the previous May where he had met with Lord Strathalane who undertook to tell 'the Young Pretender', that a large body of Irishmen were willing to cross the sea to fight for him in Scotland. Lord Strathalane had then given him a message from the Prince telling him to go to the Scots College in Paris where Mr Gordon the Principal, would pay his expenses forthwith.

James Mor continued to affirm that there were 9,000 stands of arms lodged in Clanranald's country and that 'Doctor Cameron had taken away, without orders, 250 stands'. He added that the doctor had told an acquaintance that 'he hoped the Restoration would happen soon, for that preparations were making for it, and that he had been sent to Scotland to transact some affairs for that purpose'.[282]

In England James Mor declared that he was 'offered handsome bread in the Government service as a spy' but then added in self-justification, that he 'was born in the character of a gentleman and could only serve as a gentleman of honour'.[283] Despite these affirmations his double-dealing was exposed, it is thought by Young Glengarry, and James returned to Paris a resentful and penniless man. His last letter to William MacGregor of Balhaldie, (who also used the pseudonym Drummond) written on 25th September 1754, asks pathetically for the loan of some bagpipes so that he could play 'some melancholy tunes'.[284]

James died shortly afterwards having failed to apprehend Allan Breck who was seen some years later in Paris by young Campbell of Ardchattan when making the grand tour.

Chapter 32

A Dukedom and a
Beautiful Daughter-in-Law

On 20th October 1760, King George II suddenly died. Then six months later, on 15th April 1761, Archibald, 3rd Duke of Argyll, at the age of seventy-nine, also swiftly expired of a stroke.

Duke Archibald had no legitimate heir, his wife having died childless, in 1723. He did however have a natural son and a daughter by a Mrs Williams, his mistress for many years, to whom he was very attached. Nonetheless, under British law his son could not inherit his titles. Therefore, it fell to Lieutenant-General John Campbell of Mamore to succeed his cousin as the 4th Duke of Argyll.

Almost a year was to pass before the grandson, who succeeded George II was crowned. At the coronation of George III General Campbell, now 4th Duke of Argyll, as hereditary Grand Master of the Household, carried the gold-mounted staff, which he holds in the magnificent full-length portrait by Gainsborough in the Scottish National Portrait Gallery in Edinburgh.

As a commoner, Lieutenant-General John Campbell had been Member of Parliament for the County of Dunbartonshire from 1727, a period of thirty-four years. On succeeding to the dukedom, he was appointed as one of the sixteen Representative Scottish Peers in the House of Lords.

More locally, at Inveraray, he had already been made an honorary member of the town's borough council, an office which he now surrendered to his eldest son John, and to his younger son Frederick',[285] who had just been elected Member of Parliament for the Glasgow Burghs.

John Campbell, the General's eldest son, 'Colonel Jack of the '45', on his father's ennoblement became the Marquess of Lorne. As A.D.C to King George II, for three years prior to his death, he had been much about the court. There, like his father before him, he had fallen in love with a girl of outstanding beauty, in his case the widowed young Duchess of Hamilton.

The Duke of Hamilton had died, his system weakened by hard drinking, in January 1758. Now, just over a year later, on 3rd February 1759, his widow, who as Elizabeth Gunning, a penniless girl from Ireland, had turned all heads with her beauty, re-married Major-General John Campbell as, thanks to recent promotion, he had just become.

At the beginning of June, the Duchess of Hamilton – as until her husband's succession she was always known – was taken by her sister-in-law Caroline Conway (still known as Lady Ailesbury) and the young Duchess of Richmond, Caroline's daughter, to Strawberry Hill, Horace Walpole's Gothic mansion in Twickenham.

Walpole was enchanted to see the 'Three Graces' sitting on a shell-seat in his garden. 'No woman in the future could excel them' he avidly declared.

Soon afterwards Elizabeth Hamilton went to Ireland with her soldier husband. Returning to London in December, she gave birth to her fourth child, a daughter, who was called Augusta, in honour of her close friend the Princess Royal. In the following year of 1761 Jack Campbell was promoted to Lieutenant-General before being appointed Commander-in-Chief in Scotland.

Sadly, but in retrospect it seems inevitably, Elizabeth was plagued by the jealousy of the four surviving daughters of the 2nd Duke of Argyll, 'the bawling Campbells' as Walpole called them, who sided with her adversaries in one of the most celebrated law-suits of the time.

Known as the Douglas Cause, the controversy was based on the will of the mad old Duke of Douglas who, without a child of his own bequeathed the greater part of his large estates to Elizabeth's eldest son. Thus the little Duke of Hamilton, a boy of eight years old, through descent from the 1st Marquess of Douglas, inherited his titles although his land was not entailed.[286] The Duke of Douglas, however, did have a sister called Jane, who was married to an elderly soldier, Colonel Steuart of Grandtully, Suddenly this lady, who was living in Paris, claimed to have given birth to twin boys. Their legitimacy was very doubtful: Archibald, the elder of the two, being very dark and swarthy, whilst both his parents were fair. Consequently, the rumour circulated that they were actually the children of French beggars who had sold them to the Steuarts.

Ten years after the birth of the twins, to everyone's enormous surprise, the old Duke of Douglas, confirmed bachelor as he claimed to be, suddenly married. His bride was another Douglas, Margaret, or Peggy Douglas of Mains,[18] a buxom, vociferous lady of middle age, who, it seems largely from jealousy, persuaded her near demented husband to leave the land, promised to the young Duke of Hamilton, to his sister's supposed eldest son. Peggy bullied him relentlessly until, in July 1761, two years after he had married her, the Duke of Douglas died.

Chapter 33
Family Fortunes and a Feud

It was during their visit to Paris, in 1763, while searching for proof of Archibald Steuart's illegitimacy, that Elizabeth and her husband Jack Campbell, the Marquess of Lorne, are believed to have bought at least some of the furniture and exquisite Beauvais tapestries that remain in Inveraray Castle to this day. In doing so they were dreaming of the future. Duke Archibald's great creation being hardly more than a shell.

Duke John, who had faced the roar of cannons without fear, now found himself overwhelmed by the towering half-built house. 'Much of the principal story had no floors, the long gallery walls were not yet lathed, and the hall and other rooms were only first-coated with plaster. One of the main and one of the spiral stairs still lacked hand rails'.[287]

The blue-grey walls of the new building, built of stone from the quarries of Cregans and St Catherines ferried across Loch Fyne, rose above the old castle, which, now much dilapidated, but still housing a few old retainers, seemed to crouch beneath the shadow of a giant. Worse still the houses of the old town, also badly in need of repair, remained by the side of the river Aray where it entered into Loch Fyne.

Faced with what seemed to him as the monumental and almost insurmountable task of completing his predecessor's scheme, it is hardly surprising that the new Duke, himself now aged sixty-eight, a widower, much troubled with rheumatics and intermittent bouts of malarial fever, felt himself overawed and incapable of completing the daunting prospect on hand.

He did make some slight attempt. Hand-rails rendered the castle stairs much safer, so that he himself could get up and down, and some additions were made to the estate offices in the Cherry Park. Nonetheless he felt happier and more at home at Rosneath Castle on the Gareloch where, together with Jack, his eldest son, and his daughter-in-law, he made many happy visits largely in the summer months.[288]

The year 1765 saw Duke John, created both a Member of the Privy Council and a Knight of the Thistle, in addition to which, in honour of his military service, he was given the rank of full General.

Also, in the same year, his family achieved yet further acclaim, when Lord Frederick, the second of the Duke's surviving sons, was appointed to the Privy Council and became Keeper of the Privy Seal of Scotland. In this capacity he laid the foundation stone of Robert Adam's Register House in Edinburgh in 1774 where his portrait in full regalia, by the Scottish artist Raeburn, hangs today. [19]

In 1764, the Duke's youngest son Lord William, a Post-Captain in the Royal Navy, resigned as Member of Parliament for Argyllshire, to be Governor of Nova

Scotia, a post he resigned two years later on becoming the last Royal governor of South Carolina. Subsequently, following his father's death, on the outbreak of the War of American Independence in 1774, he served as a volunteer in the defence of Charleston. Although wounded in that action, he was given command of H.M.S. *Lion,* but died as the result of his injuries in 1778.

In June 1767, the Duke's daughter-in-law, Elizabeth (still known as the Duchess of Hamilton) left the court in London and set off for Scotland with her two Hamilton sons. Her main reason for doing so was that at last, after nearly five years, the Scottish Court had finished its examination of the Douglas Cause and the Lords of Session were ready to give judgment on the case. Excitement ran high in Edinburgh where bets amounting £100,000 were being laid on the outcome. The drama was increased by the publication of a novel called *Dorando*, which, although set in Spain, was clearly based on the Douglas Cause. The book culminated with the victory of Archibald Steuart in the courts.

Soon it transpired that the author was none other than the ambitious young son of Lord Auchinleck, the barrister James Boswell, who, through his successful authorship, hoped to gain the commission of counsel for the defence. Elizabeth Hamilton was furious. She never forgave the insult. Boswell's name lay dormant in her mind.

On 7th July the Court of Session assembled in Holyrood House to pronounce judgment on the cause. Each of the fifteen law-lords spoke at length. At last, after six days, when all had recorded their opinions, they were found to be equally divided, seven on either side. The Lord President, Robert Dundas, called upon to give his casting vote, decided in favour of the Duke of Hamilton. Dundas received threatening letters but nonetheless it seemed that the Douglas claimant had lost his case. His only hope remained in an appeal to the House of Lords.

Chapter 34
The Year of Sorrow – 1769

The case of the Douglas Cause came at last before the Lords on 19th January 1769. The proceedings, however, dragged on until, on 27th February, the final judgment was declared. In the upper chamber of Westminster Hall, no less than one hundred and five lords spiritual and temporal assembled on the benches, while both Douglas and Hamilton supporters were crowded against the walls. All held their breath as Lord Camden, the Lord Chancellor, rose to make his address.

'Is the appellant the son of Lady Jane Douglas or not?' he thundered, 'I am of the mind that he is!'

Those in attendance could hardly believe what was happening as he went on to proclaim that he believed the witnesses of the Hamiltons, including Andrew Steuart, to be corrupt. Camden was followed by the Lord Chief-Justice, Lord Mansfield, who held his audience in thrall as he spoke of the wrongs which he believed to have been inflicted on Archibald Steuart's mother, the now dead Lady Jane.

'Is it possible, my lords', he demanded, 'to imagine that a woman of such a family, of such high honour…could be so base as to impose false children upon the world?'

His words rang through the chamber, raising his audience to great emotion, which increased as, overcome by heat and exhaustion, he tottered and seemed about to fall until revived by a bottle of wine.

At last, at nine o'clock in the evening, it was agreed without a division that the verdict of the Court of Session should be reversed.

The philosopher David Hume was furious, as also was Adam Smith, who declared that the Chancellor Camden had always courted publicity while the Lord Chief Justice had succumbed to public intimidation. [289]

The Douglasses were triumphant. A bonfire blazed on Salisbury Crags, while the streets of the city of Edinburgh were thronged with triumphant revellers. Then as stones were hurled through the windows of the Lord President Dundas in Adam Square, the city guard had to be summoned from the Castle to put an end to the commotion.

Next day an advertisement was posted up for the arrest of the instigators of the riot. Amongst them, James Boswell, author of the novel so disparaging to the Hamiltons, only just escaped, it would seem thanks to his father's influence, from being thrown into the Tolbooth with the thieves and other criminals of the town.

In sharp contrast to her enemies, Elizabeth Hamilton behaved with the utmost dignity to conceal her disappointment. A few days later when the triumphant claimant, Archibald Steuart, was presented to the Queen, she met the baleful glare of Peggy, widow of the old Duke of Douglas, with one of equal disdain.

In May the Marques of Lorne took his two stepsons, George, Duke of Hamilton and his brother Douglas up to Scotland in advance of their mother. She arrived in Scotland a short time afterwards, to be met with the news that George was in Glasgow, ill with a mysterious fever, but that he seemed to be on the mend. Indeed, so much did he appear to be better that, within a few days, he was taken by coach over the ten miles to Hamilton Palace.

There he seemed to be recovering. A tall boy for his age he was thought to have overgrown his strength. Then suddenly came a relapse. The cause of his illness, undiagnosed at the time, may well have been tuberculosis, then such a common scourge, or even poliomyelitis, for Doctor John Moore, of Glasgow, said that all power left his limbs. In those days of primitive medicine nothing could be done to save him, and he died on 7th July, aged only fourteen.

Three days later a banquet was held at Bothwell Castle to celebrate the majority of Archibald Steuart, who, in honour of his inheritance from the Duke claimed to be his uncle, had taken the name of Douglas as his own. Cannons roared, and rockets lit the sky while only sixteen miles away as the crow flies, Hamilton Palace in all its magnificence, should dark and shuttered in the night.

Chapter 35
The Dream Completed

Despite the fact that the journey to Inveraray was now easier, thanks to the military road, Duke John still preferred to sail from the Clyde to Rosneath on the Gare Loch. Here, the castle, although old-fashioned, was still more of a home than the imposing but comfortless and still unfinished building of his cousin's creation, near the head of Loch Fyne.

'Colonel Jack' now Lord Lorne and his family, still frequent visitors, evidently shared his love of Rosneath, despite the tragedy of losing their eldest son, a boy named George, who died there when only eighteen months old.

By her second marriage to Lorne, Elizabeth had a daughter, Augusta, born in 1760. Happily, another son, also named George, survived to succeed his father as the 6th Duke of Argyll, while he in turn was followed by a younger brother named John. Thus, the penniless girl from Ireland, once the toast of London for her beauty having married two dukes, became the mother of four.

By 1767, Duke John, who had long suffered from rheumatism and bouts of fever resulting from his many campaigns, was becoming increasingly tired. Still mentally alert, although physically failing, he handed over almost complete control of the Argyll estates stretching from Mull and Ardnamurchan southwards to Kintyre to his eldest son.

Three years later, as the dark mists of November spread over the marshes of the coastal land of Kent, John Campbell, Duke of Argyll, lay ill in Combe Bank. What memories must have come back to him then of his life with his wife and their children in the Palladian house that he had built on his marriage nearly half a century ago? How too must his mind have wandered over the years at court when, risking imminent dismissal, he had rescued the lovely Mary Bellenden from the amorous advances of the king. So too must images have returned of the many battles he had fought, the noise, the stink of cordite, the screams of men and horses. Likewise, the smell of tar as the *Furnace* pitched her way through the Minch and crashed into the Atlantic swell on his wild chase through the islands searching for Prince Charles. Yet most clearly of all, perhaps like a ray of light through a cloud, came back the figure of the pale skinned, wide eyed girl from South Uist, who had faced him so bravely in the low cabin of the ship expecting a sentence of death.

Flora he had saved. But there were so many others. Men and women and whole families who, for what he knew to be mistaken loyalty, had lost all they possessed. He had done his best to make Cumberland see that they were not the uncouth savages he imagined them to be but fine people – the very salt of the earth – deluded into fighting for the man they thought their rightful king.

Lying there, as his mind wandered, he saw so many images becoming ever more confused…

On 9th November 1770, the nights were growing longer as John Campbell of Mamore, the soldier who had given so much of his life to his king and country, at the age of seventy-seven, died quietly without ostentation much in the way that he had lived.

ENVOI

Seven months after Duke John died, In June 1771, there was enormous excitement in Inveraray as his son of the same name, now the 5th Duke of Argyll, and his beautiful Duchess came to stay in the new castle. The house party of family and friends included the Conways, General the Honourable Henry Seymour Conway now an Under-Secretary-of-State, his wife Caroline (the Duke's sister) and their ten-year-old daughter.

Space in the castle was limited, some of the rooms being still undecorated. But such was the fame of Inveraray, that almost every house in the little town was crammed Even David Hume the philosopher, large as he was, had to be one of three in a bed.[290]

Two years later, in 1773, there was even greater excitement when no less a person than Doctor Samuel Johnson, in girth no smaller than Hume, and his companion, the advocate and author James Boswell, arrived at what Boswell described as 'an excellent inn' at Inveraray.

The next morning, however, when Johnson declared his intention of going up to the castle to pay his respects to the Duke and Duchess, Boswell was in a quandary. 'I told Doctor Johnson I was in some difficulty as to how to act at Inveraray. I had reason to think that the Duchess of Argyle [sic] disliked me, on account of my zeal in the Douglas cause'.

Despite his trepidation, Boswell was welcomed by the Duke. The Duchess, however, as he had every reason to expect, gave him an icy reception. 'I fancy you will be a *methodist'* being her only remark.

'I take it for granted, she thought it a good hint on my *credulity* in the Douglas cause', he wrote.

Nonetheless she was very attentive to Doctor Johnson who, when driven round the estate, although greatly struck by the grandeur and elegance of what Boswell termed 'this princely seat', thought the castle too low and wished it had been a story higher.[291]

After being entertained to dinner, while they were drinking tea, the Duchess made Doctor Johnson come and sit beside her.

"Why," she asked, "had he made the journey so late in the year?"

"Why, madam?" said he, "You know Mr Boswell must attend the Court of Session, and it does not rise till the twelfth of August."

"I know nothing of Mr Boswell."

The Duchess had the last word.

ENDNOTES

1 Willcock. J. *A Scots Earl*. P. 417.
2 Menary, G. The Life and Letters of Duncan Forbes of Culloden. P.1

Chapter 1

3 Following the death of his first wife, Mary, eldest daughter of the Earl of Moray, the 9th Earl of Argyll remarried in 1670 the widowed Countess of Balcarres, daughter of Colin MacKenzie, 1st Earl of Seaforth. See Willcock, J.A. A Scots earl. Appendix 1.p.431.
THE WAR OF THE SPANISH SUCCESSION
4 Campbell, Alastair of Airds. *History of Clan Campbell,* Vol.4. p.101

Chapter 2

5 Ibid. p.103.
6 Campbell, Robert. *Life of John Duke of Argyle and Greenwich*, p.70.
7 Ibid.
8 Ibid.
9 Ibid. p.72.
10 Ibid.
11 Ibid

Chapter 3

12 Memary. G. p.9.
13 Ibid. P.352.
14 Ibid. p.20.
15 Ibid.
16 Ibid. p.21.
17 Campbell, Robert, *The Life of John Duke of Argyle* etc. p.138.
18 Ferguson, W. *The Edinburgh History of Scotland*, Vol. 4.p.66.
19 Campbell, Alastair of Airds, *History of Clan Campbell*, Vol.3. p.108.

Chapter 4

20 Lenman, Bruce. The Jacobite Risings in Britain 1689-1746, p140

21 Halloran, the Right Revd. Brian M. The Scots College 1603-1792. p. 86.

22 From the 'Chartulary' quoted from an old pamphlet –Edinchip Papers.

23 History of the Rebellion raised against his Majesty King George I, By the Revd. Mr Peter Rae. 2nd Edition, London 1746.

24 Ibid.

25 Fergusson, Sir James of Kilkerran, *Argyll in the Forty–Five*. P. 35.

26 Campbell, Alastair of Airds, A History of Clan Campbell, Vo. 3. pp. 111-112.

27 Ibid. p.113.

28 MacGregor, A.G.M. *History of the Clan Gregor* p.286.

29 Campbell. R. *The Life of John Duke of Argyll & Greenwich*.pp.190-2

Chapter 5

30 Ibid. pp.266-7.
31 Ibid. p.269.
32 Menary, G. *Duncan Forbes of Culloden.*p.37.
33 Ibid.p.38.
34 Ibid.p.39.
35 Ibid pp.267-8.

Chapter 6

36 The Complete Peerage. Vol. 1. p. 209
37 *The Letters of Horace Walpole,* ed. Peter Cuningham, Vol.1. 1735-1748. p.69
38 Ibid.
39 Ibid. p. 59.
40 Ibid pp. 59-60.
41 Ibid. p.76.
42 Smith, Hannah, *Georgian Monarchy*, p.201.
43 Ibid. p.76.
44 Ibid. p.70.
45 Ibid. pp. 69-70.

Chapter 7

46 Culloden papers. 103.

47 Lenman Bruce. *The Jacobite Risings in Britain 1689-1746*. p.197.

48 The Revd. John Grant, Minister of Abernethy, contributor to *First Book of Statistics in Scotland 1791-99,*

49 Ibid.

Chapter 8

50 Culloden Papers. 109.
51 Menary. G. p.72.
52 More Culloden Papers., 11.p.309.
53 Menary G. p.73.

Chapter 9

54 *The Letters of Horace Walpole,* ed. Peter Cuningham, Vol.1. 1735-1748. p.70.
55 Ibid. p.71.
56 Smith Hannah, *Georgian Monarchy.* P.59.
57 Ibid p.67.
58 21 Ibid. p.70.
59 Smith Hannah, *Georgian Monarchy* pp.93-4.
60 Smith Hannah, *Georgian Monarchy*, p.100.
61 Ibid. p.101.
62 Ibid. p.107.

Chapter 10

63 Ferguson. W. *Scotland 1689 to the Present* pp.143-5.
64 Campbell. R. *The Life of John, Duke of Argyll.* pp. 304-8.
65 Menary. G. *Duncan Forbes of Culloden,* pp113-4.
66 Ibid. pp.114-5.

Chapter 11

67 Ibid. p.138.
68 Ibid. p.139.
69 Ibid.pp138-140.
70 Ibid. p.145.
71 Ibid.p.146.
72 Ibid.p.155
73 Ibid. p.166.
74 Ibid. p.171.
75 Ibid. p.186.

Chapter 12

76 Ibid pp.72-3.
77 Ibid. p.73.
78 Ibid. pp. 74-5.
79 Ibid. p.80.
80 Ibid. p.78.
81 Ibid.
82 Ibid p.79.

Chapter 13

83 *Lord Hervey's Memoirs*, p.247.
84 Walpole. H. pp.75-6.
85 Campbell, R. Life of John Duke of Argyll pp.312-17.
86 Ibid. pp.325-339.
87 Ferguson. *W. Scotland 1689 to the Present*, The Edinburgh History of Scotland Vol.4. p.146.
88 Walpole, H. Letters of Vol.1. p.229.
89 Ibid. p.230.
90 Menary G, p.191.
91 Ibid. p 192.
92 Campbell. R. The Life of John Duke of Argyll, p.341.
93 Ibid pp. 230-1.
94 Campbell R. *The Life of John Duke of Argyll*. p. 342.
95 Walpole, Horace. P.255.
96 Campbell, Alastair of Airds. *History of Clan Campbell*. Vol.3. p.290

Chapter 14

97 Anderson. M.S. *The War of the Austrian Succession* 1740-1748. p.117.
98 Menary G. p.335.
99 Walpole. H. Vol.1.p, 286.
100 Anderson, M.S. p.118.
101 Walpole. H. Vol.1. p.285.

Chapter 15

102 Menary G. 194.

103 Walpole H. Vol. I p.373.

104 ibid.p.378.

105 Mamore mss. 3.

106 Culloden Papers. 247

107 Ibid. 251.

108 See Dr James Taylor's *Historic Families of Scotland*

109 Menary G. p.202.

110 Culloden Papers. 404.

111 Ibid. 405.

112 Menary. G. p.207.

113 Wlpole. Vol. I. p.375.

114 MacLean, Sir Fitzroy, *Bonnie Prince Charlie.* P.60.

115 Walpole, H, Vol.1.p.384.

116 Ibid. p.377.

117 48 Ibid. pp 382-3.

118 Ibid.p382.

119 Fergusson, Sir James. *Argyll in the Forty-Five*. P.32.

Chapter 16

120 Campbell of Mamore Mss. 10.
121 Ibid.
122 Ibid.
123 Fergusson Sir J. p.43.
124 Culloden Papers. 280.
125 Culloden Papers. 285.
126 Menary. G. p230.
127 Culloden Papers.474.

Chapter 17

128 Fergusson. Sir J. p.56.
129 Ibid. p.57.
130 Ibid p 38.
131 Mamore Mss.22
132 Ibid.
133 Mamore Mss. 28.
134 Ibid. Mss.29.
135 Walpole, H. Vol.1. p.396.
136 Smith Hannah, *Georgian Monarchy*, p.106

Chapter 18

137 Walpole. Vol.1. p396
138 Ibid p.395.
139 Fergusson Sir J. p.48
140 Mamore Mss. 512.
141 Walpole. Vol.1 p.395.
142 Daiches. David. Charles Edward Stuart. Pp.168-9.
143 Lindsay, Ian. G. and Cosh Mary, *Inveraray & the Dukes of Argyll*.p.26
144 Ibid. pp.25-7.
145 Mamore Mss. 104.
146 Mamore Mss.59.
147 Fergusson, Sir J. pp.59-60.
148 Ibid. p.43.
149 Ibid. p.46.
150 Ibid.p.90.
151 Ibid.p.47.

Chapter 19

152 Fergusson, Sir J. p.61.
153 Mamore. 78.
154 R.C.A.H.M.S. Argyll. Vol. 2. pp. 238-40.
155 Mamore Mss. 104.
156 Ibid. 91.
157 Fergusson, Sir J. p.69.
158 Daiches, David. *Charles Edward Stuart*. P.187
159 Fergusson, Sir J. p, 59.
160 Ibid. p.75.
161 Maclean, Sir Fitzroy, pp.169-172. Also Daiches, David. pp. 190-192.
162 Fergusson, Sir J. p.84.
163 Ibid pp.84-5.

Chapter 20

164 Mamore Mss. 90.
165 Ibid. 135.
166 Ibid. 137.
167 Ibid.
168 Ibid. 140.
169 Ibid 145.
170 Ibid. 147
171 MacLean, Sir Fitzroy, p.174.
172 Fergusson, Sir J. p. 95.
173 Campbell of Stonefield Mss. 67.
174 Ibid 68
175 Fergusson, Sir J, p.100

Chapter 21

176 Culloden Papers.313.
177 Menary. G. p.267.
178 Mamore Mss. 204
179 Ibid.
180 Ibid 206.
181 Ibid. 204 and 205.
182 Menary G. p.278.
183 Ibid.

Chapter 22

184 Walpole, H. Vol 1. p.409.
185 Mamore Mss. 198.
186 Ibid 257.
187 Ibid 259.
188 Ibid.
189 Ibid 261.
190 Fergusson, Sir J.p.169.
191 Ibid. 514.
192 Fergusson, Sir J. p.172.
193 Mamore Mss. 278.

Chapter 23

194 Ibid. 320
195 Ibid. 314.
196 Ibid. 282.
197 Ibid 305.
198 Fergusson, Sir J. *Argyll in the Forty-Five*. P.185.
199 Ibid. 308.
200 Ibid. 312.
201 Ibid.

Chapter 24

202 Daiches, David. *Charles Edward Stuart.* p.226.
203 Daiches D. Charles Edward Stuart, p.p.228-9.
204 Forbes, Bishop. *The Lyon in Mourning* Vol.1. p.94.
205 *New Statistical Account of Scotland. Argyle.* p.141
206 Fergusson, Sir J. p.205.
207 Mamore mss. 320.
208 Mamore Mss. 321.
209 Ibid 337.
210 Ibid 364.
211 Ibid 343.
212 Fergusson, Sir J. pp.202-3.
213 Mamore Mss. 375.
214 Ibid. 359.
215 Ibid.391.
216 Ibid.394.
217 Ibid. 396.
218 Ibid.406.

Chapter 25

219 MacLean, Sir Fitzroy, *Bonnie Prince Charlie*, p.244
220 MacLean, A and Gibson, J.S. p.30.
221 MacLean, Sir Fitzroy, p.246.
222 MacLean and Gibson, p. 32.
223 Ibid, p.33.
224 Ibid. p.34-5.
225 Fergusson, Sir J, p.220.
226 Douglas Hugh, *Flora MacDonald – The Most Loyal Rebel*, p.31.

Chapter 26

227 Mamore Mss. 416.

228 Ibid 421

229 Ibid. 424.

230 Ibid, p.224,

231 Donald MacLeod's spectacles are on view in Dunvegan Castle.

232 Maclean, Sir F, *Bonnie Prince Charlie.* Pp.244-5.

233 Forbes, Bishop, *Lyon in Mourning.* Vol. 1. p.113.

234 Mamore Mss. 447.

235 Ibid, p.251.

236 Douglas, H. Flora Macdonald, *The Most Loyal Rebel*, p.79.

237 Ibid, p.256.

238 Fergusson, Sir J. p.224.

239 Douglas Hugh. Flora MacDonald, *The Most Loyal Rebel*. P. 85.

Chapter 27

240 Campbell of Stonefield Mss. 108.
241 Fergusson, Sir J, p.256.
242 Mamore Mss 470.
243 Ibid.474.
244 Ibid.
245 Fergusson, Sir J. p.240.
246 Mamore Mss. 475.
247 Ibid. 477.
248 Fergusson, Sir J, p.245.
249 Mamore Mss. 479
250 Lindsay I. G. and Cosh M. Inveraray and the Dukes of Argyll. P. 35.
251 Fergusson, Sir J, p. 248.
252 Lindsay, Ian. G. and Cosh Mary, *Inveraray and the Dukes of Argyll* p. 54.

Chapter 28

253 Menary. G. p.282.
254 Culloden Papers. 330.
255 Ibid. 336.
256 Culloden Papers. 171 and 172.
257 Menary p. 287.
258 Culloden Papers 332,
259 Ibid. 343.
260 Culloden Papers, 343.
261 Menary G. p. 340.
262 Ibid. p 389.

Chapter 29

263 *Inveraray & the Dukes of Argyll.* P377.n.18.

264 Nash Ford, David. *Royal Berkshire History.*

265 Walpole, Horace, *Letters of.* Vol.1.p. 465.

266 Ibid pp. 482-3.

267 Lindsay Ian. G. and Mary Cosh *Inveraray & the Dukes of Argyll.* p.101.

268 Fisher, H.A.L. *A History of Europe,* p. 843.

269 Walpole Horace, *Letters of* Vol.1 p.478.

270 Ibid.

271 Daiches, David. *Charles Edward Stuart* p. 268.

272 Ibid. p.479.

273 Daiches, David. *Charles Edward Stuart*, p. 298.

274 Walpole Horace, Vol.1.p. 479.

275 Lang, Andrew, *Pickle the Spy.* P. 88.

Chapter 30

276 Lindsay, 1an G & Cosh Mary, *Inveraray and the Dukes of Argyll*. pp. 122-125.

Chapter 31

277 Maclean, Sir Fitzroy, *Bonnie Prince Charlie*. P.330
278 Lang, Andrew, Pickle the Spy. Pp.106-7.
279 Daiches, David. *Charles Edward Stuart,* p.287
280 Horace Walpole, *Letters of.* Vol 2. p.174.
281 Lang Andrew, *Pickle the Spy. P.143.*
282 Lang, Andrew, *Pickle the Spy*, p.148.
283 Ibid. p.150.
284 Ibid p.151.

Chapter 32

285 Lindsay, Ian. G. and Mary Cosh. *Inveraray & the Dukes of Argyll*. P, 183.
286 See Burke's Peerage.

Chapter 33

287 Ibid. p. 181.
288 Ibid. p. 183.

Chapter 34

289 Bleakley, H, *The Story of a Beautiful Duchess,* pp 163-8.

Chapter 35

290 Lindsay I and Cosh M, Inveraray and the Dukes of Argyll. p.193.
291 Johnson, Samuel and Boswell James, *Journey to the Hebrides'* pp.425-433.